THE NEW YORK YANKEES

Series Editor's Note

In 1943, G. P. Putnam's Sons began a series of major league team histories with the publication of Frank Graham's history of the New York Yankees. From 1943 to 1954, Putnam published histories for fifteen of the sixteen major league teams. The Philadelphia Athletics ball club was the only one not included in the series, though Putnam did publish a biography of Connie Mack in 1945.

Thirteen of the fifteen team histories in the Putnam series were contributed by sportswriters who were eventually honored by the Hall of Fame with the J. G. Taylor Spink Award "for meritorious contributions to baseball writing." Three Spink recipients actually wrote eleven of the team histories for the series. The famed New York columnist Frank Graham, after launching the series with the Yankees history, added team histories for the Brooklyn Dodgers and the New York Giants. Chicago sports editor and journalist Warren Brown, once dubbed the Mencken of the sports page, wrote both the Chicago Cubs and the White Sox team histories. Legendary Fred Lieb, who, at the time of his death in 1980 at the age of ninety-two, held the lowest numbered membership card in the Baseball Writers Association, contributed six team histories to the Putnam series. He also wrote the Connie Mack biography for Putnam.

For our reprints of the Putnam series, we add a foreword for each team history by one of today's most renowned baseball writers. The bibliography committee of the Society for American Baseball Research has also provided an index for each team history. Other than these additions and a few minor alterations, we have preserved the original state of the books, including any possible historical inaccuracies.

The Putnam team histories have been described as the "Cadillacs" of the team history genre. With their colorful prose and their delightful narratives of baseball history as the game moved into its postwar golden age, the Putnam books have also become among the most prized collectibles for baseball historians.

Richard Peterson

THE NEW YORK
YANKEES

An Informal History

FRANK GRAHAM

With a New Foreword by Leonard Koppett

Southern Illinois University Press
Carbondale and Edwardsville

Library of Congress Cataloging-in-Publication Data
Graham, Frank, 1893–
    The New York Yankees : an informal history / Frank Graham ; with a
new foreword by Leonard Koppett.
        p. cm.— (Writing baseball)
    Originally published: New York : G. P. Putnam's Sons, 1943.
    Includes index.
        1. New York Yankees (Baseball team)—History. I. Title. II. Series
GV875.N4 G7 2002
796.357'64'097471—dc21

                                                            2001042823
    ISBN 0-8093-2414-8 (pbk. : alk. paper)

Reprinted from the original 1943 edition published by G. P. Putnam's Sons.

The paper used in this publication meets the minimum requirements of
American National Standard for Information Sciences—Permanence of Paper
for Printed Library Materials, ANSI Z39.48-1992. ∞

Contents

Illustrations

Foreword

When Frank Graham wrote this book in 1943, the name "Yankees" had unprecedented and unmatchable prestige in America's sports world. Since 1921, during the overlapping careers of Babe Ruth, Lou Gehrig, and Joe DiMaggio in a stretch of twenty-two seasons, the Yankees had won thirteen American League pennants and nine World Series. Because baseball was uniquely dominant as a "major league" sport at that time, no football, basketball, or hockey team could have similar impact.

In the period between the two world wars, only a handful of individuals attained long-range legendary status in sports. We had Bobby Jones in golf, Bill Tilden in tennis, and Jack Dempsey in boxing (to whom the new heavyweight champion, Joe Louis, was being compared). Knute Rockne had glamorized Notre Dame football on a national scale, but that was college when 90 percent of the population had no college affiliation. Jesse Owens, after his heroic victories in the Nazi Olympics of 1936, was being quickly forgotten.

So Graham was dealing with the cream of the cream in a culture that could go beyond daily journalism only through books. There was no television. Radio delivered play-by-play details but little comment or perspective. Magazines were unavoidably episodic.

What he produced was not only the first version of the full Yankee story but the most readable club history anyone had ever done.

He was a working sports columnist in a city that had twelve or more daily papers, and he had some exceptional qualities. His ear for dialogue was incomparable. His ability to earn the trust of the people he dealt with allowed him to know what was really going on. His grasp of the games, the people, and the lives he covered was wide and deep. And he could tell you about it in the most direct and plain-talk manner.

His *New York Sun* columns called "Overheard in the Dugout" delighted me as I was growing up; but what I learned later, when I got to work alongside him, was that they were as good and as reliable as court transcripts. He didn't take a lot of notes. He just absorbed what was being said—and what it meant in the right context—and reproduced it in graceful prose and natural speech. It is this style of narration through dialogue that makes his books come so alive. Obviously, the book records conversations he could not have heard; but knowing their substance and the way the people involved did talk, he could convey the situation vividly, dramatically, concisely, and (above all) as truthfully as he knew. He blended anecdote and information into a seamless story and a can't-put-it-down read.

The result is a treasure and the starting point for all subsequent Yankee histories. More important, this book offers priceless insight into the values and attitudes people brought to those events *then*. Later histories that turn up all sorts of controversial items invariably impose later judgments based on what has since become conventional wisdom (not to mention political correctness) but may not reflect the reality of the past.

Anyone who wants to know anything at all about the New York Yankees can't afford not to absorb what Graham put down amid his intimate contact with almost all those actually involved. And anyone who simply enjoys a good story well told should not miss this one.

Leonard Koppett
May 2001

THE NEW YORK YANKEES

THE BABE TAKES A SWING

I · The American League Enters New York

1

ON A JANUARY NIGHT IN 1903 Byron Bancroft Johnson was host to some twenty men in his suite in the Criterion Hotel, New York. His pince-nez riding precariously on the bridge of his nose, his round face beaming, Johnson stood up in his place at the head of the long table.

"Gentlemen!" he said, raising his glass, "the American League!"

The guests struggled to their feet.

"The American League!" they roared, draining their glasses.

"The American League is the greatest league in baseball," said Johnson, and sat down.

The glow that suffused him came not only from the wine he had drunk. It was the glow of victory. A bitter fight had ended that day with the announcement that the American League had put a club in New York.

Thus, in an atmosphere of conviviality began the story of the American League Baseball Club of New York. Hewn out of tumult, it emerged through quarrels and bickering and deep hatreds as the most powerful organization baseball ever has known.

2

Ban Johnson had been a baseball writer in Cincinnati. He was ambitious, tough-minded, and a tireless fighter for the things in which he believed; and most of all he believed in the American League. This was an outgrowth of the Western League, of which he also had been president; and, in 1902, after two years of ceaseless warfare with the deeply entrenched National League, he had clubs in Chicago, Boston, Philadelphia, Cleveland, Detroit, Washington, St. Louis, and Baltimore. He had the financial backing of Ben and Tom Shibe, Philadelphia sporting goods manufacturers, and of Charles W. Somers, a Cleveland contractor. On his side were such colorful and extremely practical baseball men as Charles A. Comiskey, the Old Roman; Clark Griffith; and Connie Mack. The playing strength of his new league was headed by a handful of heroes taken in raids by his commandos on the National League, which for many years had been the only major circuit.

But one move, he felt, was necessary to put the American League on an equal footing with the National. This was to take the franchise from Baltimore, which, he believed, was no longer a big league town, and put it in New York.

To that end he began a campaign against the most formidable opposition he had yet encountered. The Giants were owned by John T. Brush, whose enmity Johnson had aroused when he owned the Indianapolis club of the Western League. Brush subsequently owned the Cincinnati club in the National League, but sold it and moved to New York, where he bought the Giants from his friend, Andrew Freedman, for $100,000. Hating Johnson, he stoutly opposed the American League and fiercely resented Ban's plan to invade New York. His chief allies in defense of his territory were Freedman, arrogant, turbulent and closely identified with Richard Croker, the fat cat of Tammany Hall; and his manager, John McGraw, who had jumped from the National League club in St. Louis to the American League club in Baltimore, and then back to the National League when he received the offer to manage the Giants. It had been part of Johnson's plan to put McGraw at the head of his New York club. Now McGraw was in New York—but in Brush's camp.

Through December of 1902 Johnson's efforts to buy or lease property for a ball park were systematically thwarted. Brush beat him to options on most of the available spots; or, when Brush failed, Freedman threatened, through his influence with Croker, to have streets cut through any land that fell into the hands of the invaders. On January 10, 1903, committees representing the National and American leagues met in Cincinnati and agreed on a peace treaty; but their action was rejected by Brush, who insisted they had no authority to do more than consider proposals for such a treaty and report back to the leagues. At a National League meeting, also held in Cincinnati, ten days later, Brush's opposition seemingly was overcome and he gave reluctant lip service to a decision to end hostilities and admit the American League to New York. Lip service was all he gave, for he continued to combat Johnson and, through the Giants' secretary, Fred Knowles, to denounce the new league and scoff at its pretensions. Johnson, for his part, had yet to find a field for the club of which he talked so confidently—or a man to back it.

Both were found with a suddenness which amazed even Johnson. There was in New York a sports writer by the name of Joe Vila, whose friendship with Johnson dated back to the time when, as cub reporters, they had covered the Sullivan-Corbett fight at New Orleans. Vila, later to become Sports Editor of the *Sun*, already had won prominence as a writer and had a wide acquaintance among the leading figures in the sports world. Among them was Frank Farrell, one-time bartender and saloonkeeper, now a gambling-house proprietor, partner of Davy Johnson, the plunger, in the ownership of a racing stable that included the great Roseben, and pal of Big and Little Tim Sullivan and Tom Foley.

Within a few days after the Cincinnati meeting at which the peace pact had been ratified by the National League, Vila brought Johnson and Farrell together in New York, and Farrell offered to buy the Baltimore franchise. He seemed a little too eager, Johnson thought; but his skepticism vanished when Farrell laid a certified check for $25,000 before him.

"Take that as a guarantee of good faith, Mr. Johnson," he said. "If I don't put this ball club across, keep it."

Johnson was pleasantly surprised. He had been prepared, if necessary, to finance the club out of the war chest to which Somers and the Shibes were the heaviest contributors.

"That's a pretty big forfeit, Mr. Farrell," he said.

Joe Vila smiled. "He bets that much on a race, Ban," he said.

Farrell explained that, in the proposed purchase of the franchise, he would take into partnership with him his friend, William S. (Big Bill) Devery, who, like himself, had begun as a bartender and then, undecided whether to become a pugilist or a policeman, had chosen the latter course, eventually becoming chief of the department. He had recently retired, had plenty of money, and was in the real-estate business. They had, Farrell added, a desirable location for a ball park.

"Where?" Johnson asked.

"It runs from 165th Street to 168th Street on Broadway."

Johnson was dubious. "That's a long way uptown," he said.

"It won't seem so far uptown in a little while," Farrell said. "The neighborhood is growing; and the subway, which will start operating in the fall, will be extended up there sooner than most people believe."

And so the deal was made. Johnson agreed to sell the Baltimore franchise to Farrell and Devery for $18,000, transfer it to New York, and throw in a ready-made team to be managed by Griffith, who had managed the Chicago club the year before. Farrell and Devery agreed to buy the property and build the park for the opening of the season.

3

That was the night on which Johnson gave his party at the Criterion and announced his coup to his guests, most of them newspapermen. He was jubilant next morning as he boarded a train for Chicago. Under his arm were newspapers headlining the stories of the coming of the American League to New York. Ahead of him—and of Farrell and Devery— were years of stubborn fighting for the patronage on which the Giants had held a monopoly. He looked forward to that with zest; he throve on conflict.

Brush was taken by surprise. Freedman launched a swift threat to have streets cut through the property. Farrell and Devery laughed. Croker, no longer as powerful as he had been, was a good enough bogeyman against the lone and seemingly friendless Johnson; but Farrell and Devery had the backing of the Sullivans and Foley.

"I'd like to see Freedman try it," Farrell said.

Freedman did try it, but was quickly driven off. The American League was definitely in New York, with a team ready to put in a ball park. The partners had less than three months in which to build the park, and they threw themselves feverishly into the task. The rocky, uneven ground was torn and hammered into smoothness by a great force of workmen. Wooden grandstand and bleachers to accommodate 15,000 were built. A wooden fence sprang up about the park, and a wooden clubhouse was raised.

These were slender ramparts from which to engage the Giants, firmly established at the Polo Grounds. They had known lean days under the raffish direction of Freedman; but now they were rapidly recapturing their old popularity under the vigorous and aggressive control of Brush and Mc-Graw. But Farrell and Devery were prepared for a long war. They elected Joseph W. Gordon, a mild-mannered coal merchant, president of the club. This was the only distinction he ever achieved: he was the first president of the American League Baseball Club of New York. Actually, he was merely the suave front for a couple of rough-and-tumble fighters.

4

The team was christened the Highlanders because its park was on one of the highest points of Manhattan Island and the club president's name was Gordon. The Gordon Highlanders were perhaps the best-known regiment in the British Army at the time; and apparently had a special romantic appeal for Americans. They played their first game in Washington on April 22 and lost by a score of 3 to 1.

Griffith had George Davis in left field, Wee Willie Keeler in right, Dave Fultz in center, John Ganzel on first base, Jimmy Williams on second, Herman Long at short stop, Wid Conroy on third base, Jack O'Connor back of the bat, and Jack Chesbro in the box. Keeler, probably the greatest place hitter who ever lived, was famous also for his "I hit 'em where they ain't" description of his success at the plate. Ganzel had slowed down a little, but he was still rated among the game's leading first basemen. Long had been one of the great players of the time and one of Boston's Big Four in the National League—Tenney, Lowe, Long, and Collins. Chesbro had helped to pitch the Pirates to the National

BILL DEVERY

© *Brown Bros.*

FRANK FARRELL

© *Brown Bros.*

JOSEPH W. GORDON

CLARK GRIFFITH

League pennant in 1902. Griffith still was active as a pitcher and took an occasional turn in the box.

On May 1 came the opening in New York. Bright weather greeted the new club, and the park was gaily decorated. The crowd filled the grandstand and bleachers. The parade to the flagpole was led by Ban Johnson and Joe Gordon, Farrell and Devery modestly remaining in their seats in a box close to the Highlanders' bench. The band played "The Star Spangled Banner," "Yankee Doodle," and "Columbia, the Gem of the Ocean," and the crowd stood up and sang. Again the Washington club furnished the opposition, and this time the Highlanders won by a score of 6 to 2, with Chesbro again pitching. Keeler got two doubles and two walks, scored three runs, and was thrown out at the plate in a close play trying for a fourth. The crowd, which had gone to the game either out of sheer curiosity or to see old favorites such as Keeler, Chesbro, Long, and Ganzel in new surroundings, went home happy. New York had another good ball club and would have another good ball park when the ravine in right field had been filled in. That was the only defect in the rush job Farrell and Devery had done. On the first play of the game, the Highlanders almost lost the services of Keeler, who checked himself at the precipice as he sought to catch a smash by Robinson, the lead-off man for Washington.

The attendance figures, given as 20,000 in some of the newspapers of the day, probably were padded. Whatever the actual size of that crowd, there was a larger one a little while later. Rain fell one day when, through an oversight, the customers had not been provided with rain checks; and the club officials immediately announced that all those present could return the following day and see the game for nothing. The following day all those present—and thousands more—swamped the park, breaking down one of the fences and overrunning the field. The police had to herd them back before the game could get under way. At first Farrell and Devery contemplated ruefully the damage done to the park by the milling hordes; but soon they realized that the free show had been worth a lot to them in good will and publicity. Once was enough, however. They never were caught without rain checks again.

The Highlanders finished the season in fourth place, behind Boston, Philadelphia, and Cleveland. For the 1904 season, Griffith did some rebuilding. He brought in the scrappy Norman (Kid) Elberfeld to take Long's place at short stop; added Orth of Washington, Jack Powell of St. Louis, and Walter Clarkson of Harvard to his pitching staff; acquired Jack Kleinow as his first-string catcher; and bought John Anderson, an outfielder, who distinguished himself in his first year by trying to steal second with the bases filled. He failed in this but succeeded in gaining a sort of dubious immortality. To this day players call that kind of boner a "John Anderson," although they have no idea who Anderson was or where he played.

Griff almost won the pennant with his reconstructed team. He missed it by the slender margin of a wild pitch. With two games of the season remaining, his team was trailing the leading Red Sox by one—and those two games were to be played as a double-header in their own park. By taking both of them, they could win the championship. Excitement naturally ran high on the Hilltop, and the park was jammed long before noon. The first game was the setting for a thrilling pitchers' duel between Chesbro and Bill Dinneen and was decided when Chesbro let go with a wild pitch that sent the winning run across the plate. The Highlanders won the second game when Ambrose Putnam, a left-hander, hurled a shut-out; but the victory came too late and the pennant went to Boston.

The Giants won the pennant in the National League that

year, and Brush, still unrelenting toward the younger league, refused to permit his team to play the Red Sox in the World Series. This had the effect of slowing down the Highlanders' fight for the favor of New York fans. But in 1905 Hal Chase's presence on the Hilltop gave them new impetus. Chase, twenty-two years old and purchased from the Los Angeles club of the Pacific Coast League, was endowed with a catlike agility and a keen mind. Grinning, impudent, and, as it developed, unscrupulous, he was to become the greatest defensive first baseman who ever lived. Baseball men admit this grudgingly if at all, for in later years he was charged with having thrown ball games because he had bet on the other team. He was quietly dropped from the sport at the end of the 1919 season, and has been denied a place in the Hall of Fame at Cooperstown.

The attitude of baseball's brass hats toward Chase is, of course, beyond challenge. "Why," they ask, "should we honor a man who, left to his own devices, would have wrecked public confidence in the game?"

But he could play first base, and he became popular instantly. Fans partial to the Highlanders—and he increased their number rapidly—boasted that he made Dan McGann, the Giants' first baseman, seem slow and stodgy by comparison.

His range of operations on the field was fantastic. He startled ball players and fans alike one day when, with a man on second base and the hitter trying to advance him by bunting toward third, he cut across in front of the pitcher, scooped up the ball, and got it to the third baseman in time to retire the runner. Larry Lajoie, one of the great hitters of all time, was with Cleveland; and when he heard of this he said:

"I hope he tries that on me. If he does, I'll fix him so he won't try it again—on me or anybody else."

Shortly after that the Cleveland club went to New York; and in the first game Lajoie went to bat with a man on second base and none out. Nowadays, of course, a hitter of Lajoie's type would swing, trying to drive the runner in; but in the days of the dead ball it was accounted sound strategy for a man of even his power to sacrifice in a spot like that. As the first ball was pitched to him, he feinted a bunt to see what Chase would do. Sure enough, Chase, having started with the pitch, was almost in front of the plate as Lajoie let the ball go by. The big Frenchman grinned. That was what he wanted to know. Another pitch, and Chase on his way in. Lajoie swung savagely. He hit the ball solidly; but Chase, although only a few feet from him, caught it in his gloved hand, then calmly turned and tossed it to Williams at second base, doubling the runner off the bag.

Lajoie's ruse had failed; and so did the attempts of other enemy players to halt Chase or slow him up. The High-landers sagged that year, finishing sixth; but Chase kept the turnstiles clicking for them, not only at home but on the road. Surging back, they finished second to the White Sox in 1906, but they slid down to fifth place in 1907.

That year Farrell and Devery, coming out from behind the false front they had erected with the opening of their first season, dismissed Gordon as president. Farrell assumed the job and he and Devery, from their box near the dugout, took an increasing interest, not only in the business affairs of the club, but in the details of its games.

By 1908, friction between the owners and their manager became obvious. Griff, hotly resenting the attempts of Farrell and Devery to tell him how to run the team, fought them continuously. The team had got off to a good start, but reacted to the brawling in the front office by skidding rapidly. So did the fans. The attendance fell off so sharply that Mark Roth, now road secretary of the club but then a baseball writer on the *Globe,* remarked:

"If it gets any smaller, they'll have to put fractions on the turnstiles."

By midseason, Griff had had enough. Johnson, his sponsor, had tried vainly to restore peace. Griff walked out, and the partners appointed Elberfeld to manage the team for the balance of the season. Tough, hard-headed, and frequently embroiled with umpires and rival players, the Tabasco Kid was as harsh with his own players once he took command of the team. In September Chase quit, quietly leaving New York one night and bobbing up in California a few days later, where he joined the Stockton club of the outlaw California State League.

The season rolled to a dismal close with the Highlanders in last place. The Giants had made a great fight for the National League pennant. They wound up in a tie with the Chicago Cubs, and were beaten in a play-off game amid some of the wildest baseball scenes New York had ever known—or has known up to now. The crowd, swirling about the Giants, had almost completely forgotten there was another team in New York.

Farrell and Devery, seeking to repair the damage, first brought back Chase and then engaged George Stallings as their manager. Stallings, who became known as the Miracle Man when he piloted the Boston Braves from last place on July 4 to the pennant and the world championship in 1914, already had gained considerable reputation as a manager. He had managed the Detroit club as far back as 1901, then had returned to the minors and had just concluded a successful year in Newark when he agreed to take over the Highlanders.

He finished fifth in 1909 and had refurbished and relighted the team to such an extent in 1910 that it wound up in second place and, with the crowds storming back, made money for the first time in its history. But George missed the last game, and the final check-up in the counting room, which showed the profits to be $80,000. He had been a consistent winner everywhere except in the box where Farrell and Devery sat every afternoon. Very nervous, with a hair-trigger temper, he had been driven almost frantic by their suggestions before a game and, if the game was lost, their second guesses. In a final burst of rage he had resigned.

One episode from the Stallings regime caused considerable indignation at the time, but baseball veterans chuckle over it in retrospect. It seems that, over one stretch, the Highlanders, feeble enough at bat on the road, slugged every pitcher who faced them when they were at home. The pitchers couldn't understand it. The Highlanders explained it by saying that, on the Hilltop, the background was perfect for hitters. One man refused to accept the explanation and began to look about him carefully, on the theory that something was loose somewhere. This was Harry Tuthill, trainer of the Tigers, whose pitchers had been moaning loudly over the batterings they were taking in New York. One day, either because he had found the answer himself or had been tipped off, he made a lone raid during the ball game on a spot close to the scoreboard on the center-field fence. At his approach, someone scrambled away among the caverns and recesses of the board; but on a small platform he found a half-eaten sandwich and a freshly opened bottle of beer. Inspecting the fence at that point, he discovered a handle that operated a shutter over a letter O in a sign on the other side of the fence, and so was visible to the players on the field.

His deduction was that someone, peering through field glasses, got the opposing team's signals as they were flashed from the catcher to the pitcher and, having decoded them,

WEE WILLIE KEELER

© *Brown Bros.*

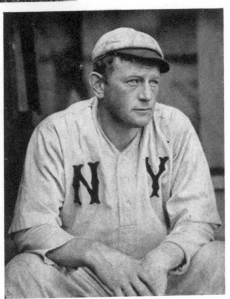

JACK CHESBRO

THE OLD PARK ON THE HILLTOP

relayed them to the New York hitters. He assumed that, roughly, when the center of the O was open, it meant that a fast ball was about to be pitched; when it was closed, a curve ball; when it was half open, a slow ball.

He reported his discovery and his conclusions to Hughie Jennings, manager of the Tigers, who promptly charged the Highlanders with trickery. The reply was that if anything like that had been going on, they had been ignorant of it. The half-eaten sandwich and the bottle of beer? Oh, they undoubtedly had been left there by a painter at work on the fences in the early spring.

When Tuthill heard that he snorted.

"Some bread and some beer!" he said. "The bread was as fresh as if it had come out of the oven the day before, and the foam was still on the beer. Boy, if I could make bread and beer like that I'd be richer than Rockefeller in no time."

Long afterward it was tacitly admitted that the signal-tipping scheme was operated very much as the Tigers suspected. It was even hinted that a man then employed as a scout by the club was the one who had fled at Tuthill's approach, leaving his sandwich and beer behind him. But he never confessed, and nobody could prove it. The story, a three-day wonder, soon was forgotten by all but those to whom it became a source of sly laughter.

The answer of Farrell and Devery to the departure of Stallings was the appointment of Chase as his successor. At the time, the Highlanders still had a chance to win the pennant, and the partners were sure that under the urging of the brilliant first baseman the players would sweep on to the triumph they had visioned ever since they became club owners. But Chase was no manager. Gifted as he was as a player, he was without the gift of leadership. Nor was he as popular with his team mates as he was with the fans.

The Highlanders, who might have won had Stallings remained, were good enough to finish second under their own momentum and to keep the fans excited about them; but in 1911 the full force of the error of the partners' choice of manager was felt. That year the team, steadily becoming disorganized, ended in sixth place.

Blind to their own part in the mounting troubles by which they were beset, Farrell and Devery sought a remedy in another change of managers. They kept Chase as their first baseman, and brought in as manager Harry Wolverton, who had earned considerable fame as the manager of the Williamsport club of the Tri-State League. Wolverton was one of baseball's more colorful figures. With the sombrero and the long cigar, which were the hallmarks of the character he had evolved for himself, he arrived in New York and announced, with gestures, that he would put the Highlanders where they belonged—at the top of the league. He made a brave try, but he wasn't equipped to manage a major league club. The team hit, not the top of the league, but the bottom.

With 1913 coming up, there was an almost complete new deal. Jim Price, Sports Editor of the *New York Press,* had been calling the team the Yankees because he found the name Highlanders too long to fit his headlines; and by 1913 the new name had been generally adopted. The old park on the hilltop was outmoded, too; and, amity between the clubs having been achieved two years before when the Giants, burned out of their own park, had taken shelter with their rivals, it was decided to move the team to the rebuilt Polo Grounds as tenants of the Giants. And then Farrell and Devery, having brushed Wolverton off, made an abrupt switch, turning from a minor leaguer to one of the most famous managers in the game. Frank Chance, the Peerless Leader of the Chicago Cubs, had resigned at the end of the

1912 season and declared his intention of going into retirement in California. But the owners of the Yankees, possibly at the suggestion of Joe Vila, long Chance's friend and admirer, dragged him from his retreat and installed him as manager. Chance, at a loss in a new league and inheriting a crumbling ball club, could do little better than Wolverton, and tottered home a sorry seventh.

In 1914 the Farrell-Devery dynasty crashed. Most of the ball players were misfits. Some of them didn't even look like ball players, and such spectators as they attracted got their money's worth by deriding them. The owners, their tempers raked by years of failure, were constantly quarreling with Chance or with each other. Chance had quit pleading for competent players, and was now angrily demanding them. A raging, towering figure, he kept most of his athletes in a state of terror, thus greatly impairing whatever slight skill they may have had.

Chase, still a great ball player, took a perverse delight in Chance's rages. He mimicked him behind his back, deliberately misinterpreted his orders, and, taking advantage of the fact that Chance was deaf in one ear as a result of having been hit in the head so often by pitched balls in his playing days, sat on his deaf side in the dugout and slyly mocked him for the amusement of the other players. Ed Sweeney, the big catcher, loyal to Chance and sympathizing with him in his troubles, told him one day what Chase was doing.

"I'm no stool pigeon," he said, glaring at Chase, "but you're not going to make fun of the big guy in front of me any more."

The wonder is that Chance didn't strangle Chase or that Sweeney didn't do it for him. But Chance, who always had liked the first baseman, now shook in the grip of a cold, quiet hatred of him.

"Get out," he said. "Go to the clubhouse and take off that uniform."

That night he made a deal for Chase with the White Sox, taking Rollie Zeider, a third baseman, and Babe Borton, a first baseman, in exchange for him. Zeider had a bunion so big it crippled him, and Borton was a dreadful failure at first base.

The town chuckled when Mark Roth wrote: "Chance traded Chase for a bunion and an onion."

But it was no laughing matter to Farrell and Devery. Sensible as they were of the fact that Chase had destroyed his usefulness to the club, they felt that Chance, in his angry haste to get rid of him, had been bilked and that the club had been further weakened by the deal. The tension between manager and owners grew, with Chance accusing them of trying to run the club over his head. The climax was a terrific row after a game one day, with Chance, undaunted by the presence of a group of strong-armed cops about their former chief, trying to slug Devery.

That night Chance left for California without speaking to the owners again. Roger Peckinpaugh, the shortstop and one of the few good ball players on the team, was appointed manager. On the last day of the season the team rested in sixth place.

Meanwhile, two very good friends of John McGraw's, who had wanted to buy the Giants and been informed by McGraw that the club definitely was not for sale, were becoming interested in the Yankees. One was Colonel Jacob Ruppert, multi-millionaire brewer and sportsman; the other, Captain Tillinghast L'Hommedieu Huston, soldier-engineer, reported to have at least one million dollars in the bank.

II · Ruppert and Huston

⊖

R

1

UPPERT AND HUSTON had two things in common: money and a love of baseball. In background and manner they were utterly different. Ruppert, although he had added to his fortune by his own skill and industry, had been born to millions. Huston had made his money the hard way, starting from scratch. Ruppert had built about him a protective wall of reserve which few were permitted to pass. Huston roamed wide and was on friendly terms with almost everyone. Ruppert was a dilettante; Huston was lusty and earthy. Even in the matter of dress they differed sharply. Each day Ruppert—or his valet—selected his clothes carefully from an extensive wardrobe. Huston, who wouldn't have had a valet on a bet, would wear the same suit for days on end; and no matter which suit he wore, it always was rumpled. The only distinctive detail of his attire was his derby. To W. O. McGeehan, a great newspaperman and his favorite companion, he was always "the Man in the Iron Hat."

Ruppert was born on August 5, 1867, at Lexington Avenue and Ninety-third Street in New York City and attended Columbia Grammar School. The first baseball team he ever controlled was composed of neighborhood boys of his own age. He later admitted that his enthusiasm for the sport far exceeded his ability to play it, and he was elected captain of the team because he bought all the uniforms and equipment. His career as a player was short-lived. Called in from short stop to pitch one day when the regular pitcher was being batted freely, he managed to save the game, but the strain on his arm was so great that it never was any good again and he regretfully retired.

He passed the entrance examinations to the School of Mines at Columbia University, then suddenly decided he didn't want to be a mining engineer. He would enter his father's brewery. This greatly pleased his father, who was determined the boy should have a thorough knowledge of the business. He put him to work at the very lowliest job in the plant, washing kegs. Within a few years, however, he was running the business.

His was the typical life of the wealthy young man of the period. He danced well, went to parties and the opera, and was considered one of the most eligible bachelors in the town—a role, incidentally, he never relinquished. He was a private in Company B of the Seventh Regiment, the silk-stockinged, kid-gloved, socially dominant outfit of the New York National Guard. In 1889, at the age of twenty-two, he was appointed a colonel on the staff of Governor Hill, an honor also conferred upon him by Governor Flower, who followed Hill.

He had a town house on Fifth Avenue and an estate at Garrison on the Hudson. He collected jades, porcelains, Indian relics, first editions, race horses, yachts, dogs, and monkeys. His Counter Tenor won the Metropolitan Handicap in 1906. He was a member of the Coney Island Jockey Club, the Brooklyn Jockey Club, and was rewarded with that final badge of honor of the turf, membership in The Jockey Club. He bred and sometimes raced harness horses, and Gus Axworthy was in his stud. He had show horses that took blue ribbons at Madison Square Garden. His St. Bernards were famous. It was his own opinion that one of them, Oh Boy, which he bred, was the finest the world ever had seen. His yacht, the *Albatross*, was known in every port along the Sound. He belonged to the New York, Larchmont, and Atlantic yacht clubs. His other clubs were the Manhattan, the New York Athletic, the Catholic, the Lambs, and the Liederkranz and Arion societies.

For a long time he was interested in politics and was a member of Tammany Hall. He was defeated when he ran for the office of Vice Mayor, since abolished; but he served four consecutive terms in Congress.

At the time he turned to the Yankees, however, he had few interests in any sport other than baseball. Although he occasionally attended the races, he had sold his stable when Governor Charles E. Hughes had closed the tracks in 1910. Piqued over a judge's decision at a National Horse Show, he had withdrawn from that phase of the sport; and his enthusiasm for the trotters had waned. Yachting, too, had palled on him, and the war in Europe had so disrupted his importation of St. Bernards for breeding that he gave that up as well.

He was a Giant rooter, was seen at the Polo Grounds frequently, now and then in McGraw's company. He had had two opportunities to get into baseball, one of them to buy the Giants. About the turn of the century other National League club owners, eager to force Andrew Freedman out, had tried to persuade the then youthful Ruppert to take the club, but at that time he wasn't interested. Some years later he could have bought the Cubs, but his ties were in New York and his civic pride was great. He had no desire whatever to own a ball club in Chicago.

Huston, born to moderate circumstances in a small town in Ohio in 1869, grew up in Cincinnati. There he studied engineering, and his first job was city engineer. He had no money then but was ambitious and far-seeing. Later he was to say:

"The way to make money is to put others to work for you. Never do anything you can hire someone to do for you. It's the one who tells the other fellow what to do who reaps the profits."

At the outbreak of the Spanish-American War, he helped to organize the Second Volunteer Engineers and went to Cuba with his regiment as a captain. Once peace was declared, Cuba seemed to most of the men a place to leave as quickly as possible. But Huston saw opportunities there for a young man, especially an engineer. He stayed and, with little or no capital, set himself up in business. He was capable and tireless, and he knew how to deal with the politicians in the struggling republic, so that lucrative contracts fell to him. Among the larger jobs he had were harbor improvements in Havana, Santiago, Cienfuegos, and Matanzas.

He remained in Cuba for more than ten years, and during that time McGraw was a regular winter visitor, either taking the Giants down there to play or, with Mrs. McGraw, spending a couple of months at the Havana Country Club. Huston and McGraw met, liked each other from the start, had many good times together; and when Huston left Cuba and went to New York to live, the friendship between the men grew.

It was McGraw who introduced Huston to Ruppert. They began to meet at the Polo Grounds, to sit together, rooting for the Giants. It never has been quite clear whose idea it was in the beginning that they should buy a ball club, but at any rate they both liked it. They approached McGraw on the subject of buying the Giants. McGraw shook his head.

"No," he said. "No chance."

Brush had died, but his widow and daughters were of no mind to sell. They, too, were fans. Harry Hempstead, who had married one of the daughters, was president of the club. McGraw was the biggest figure and the Giants the most popular club in baseball. Owning the Giants was fun, and profitable, too.

"But if you really want to buy a ball club," McGraw said, "I think I can get one for you. How about the Yankees?"

Ruppert and Huston weren't interested. So far as they were concerned, there was only one New York club. But McGraw's vision was broader than theirs. He set about convincing them that, under proper direction and with fresh money—in the amount they had, for instance—much might be done with the Yankees. At last they weakened.

"See Farrell," they said. "Ask him if they want to sell."

Both Farrell and Devery were receptive. Farrell, in temporary financial straits, had considered pledging his stock as security for a loan and so his hand was forced. Besides, he and Devery, having fought for years with their managers, were now fighting with each other. The years they had spent in baseball had yielded only bitterness; and their friendship, begun in the old rough-and-tumble days when Farrell was a saloonkeeper and Devery a cop, had been badly shaken.

The negotiations were brief and ended in the purchase of the club by Ruppert and Huston for $460,000.

Farrell and Devery split the money and went their way, still quarreling. Within a short time there was a sharp and lasting break between them. Efforts by Joe Vila and other friends—Tom Foley, Al Smith, Johnny Walters—to reconcile them were futile. They died, Devery in 1919 and Farrell in 1926, without ever having spoken to each other again.

Ill luck had attended both. Farrell had prospered for a time in the execution of contracts for the extension of the subway, but had gambled heavily, especially on the horses. His will was designed to dispose of $100,000. Actually, he left $1,072. Devery had continued his real-estate operations, but property and money had slipped away from him. He left only one asset—the sum of $2,500, which represented his share of the original payment made by Harry M. Stevens for the catering privileges at the hilltop park and which, curiously, had lain untouched in his strongbox. This reduced his debts—his only legacy—to $1,023.

2

The dark, or Farrell-Devery, era of the Yankees was behind them, the bright years ahead. It would take money and patience to bring about the things for which Ruppert and Huston hoped—it developed that they had more of the one than of the other—and Huston passed from the scene before all the things for which they hoped had been achieved. But on the morning of January 11, 1915, they were the proud possessors of a ball club, dedicating themselves to seeing that the Yankees equaled or surpassed the Giants in the affections of the New York fans.

Their entrance into baseball was generously applauded in the game's councils and in the press. Ban Johnson had been aware of Farrell's financial difficulties and feared that the club might be sold to someone he didn't like. Now he was happy that such a catastrophe had been averted. The other club owners looked with relish on the prospect of richer gleanings at the gate when the Colonel and the Captain had strengthened their team. The New York newspapers, weary of supporting a second-division team in the American League and weary, too, of the constant undertone of friction in office and clubhouse, hailed the advent of two such solid citizens.

The first thing to be done was to select a manager, Peckinpaugh having slipped back, almost unnoticed, to the rank of a mere player as the 1914 season ended. There were some who thought that he rated a chance to lead the team again, but they met with no encouragement from the new owners. Candidates for the post were numerous. Ruppert and Huston turned to their friends among the baseball writers for advice. Their choice was Bill Donovan, and in it they had the backing of many baseball men. And so, after some deliberation, Bill got the job.

Donovan, big, smiling, popular with fans and players, had been a great pitcher with the Tigers. When his pitching days were over, he had been engaged by Joe Lannin, owner of the Red Sox, to manage the Providence club of the International League, which he also owned. Donovan had been immediately successful there and had won the 1914 pennant.

Ruppert automatically had become president of the club and Huston vice president, but a business manager was needed. Here again McGraw was helpful, presenting his friend, Harry Sparrow, who was quickly accepted.

Although he had had no official connection with professional baseball, Sparrow was well known to many of those in the game and those who wrote about it. Born in Orange, N. J., in 1875 and known in his youth as a baseball and football player with the famous Orange Field Club, he had been close to McGraw for a number of years, had made southern training trips with the Giants and, in the winter of 1913-1914, had accompanied the Giants and the White Sox on their tour of the world.

He had set out on the world tour purely for pleasure; but before it was more than a few days old, he was managing it. Neither McGraw nor Charles A. Comiskey had thought to take a business manager with them; but, with Sparrow handling all the details of the transportation and hotel accommodations, everyone was made comfortable and happy. McGraw was sure that his likable friend could do an equally good job for the Yankees—and he did.

To assist him, not one road secretary, but two were hired.

One was Mark Roth, who, as a baseball writer on the *Globe*, had covered every game the Yankees had played from the day they opened in Washington. The other was Charles McManus, little known then but soon to prove himself an extremely capable member of the organization.

Now the great need was for ball players. Other American League club owners had said, possibly with an eye to the Yankees' new bank roll, that they would be glad to help with the bolstering of the team. However, the only one to come through was Frank Navin, in Detroit, who delivered Wally Pipp, a young first baseman who, on option from the Tigers, had played with Rochester the year before, and Hugie High, an outfielder. This was a gesture of genuine good will on Navin's part, for he sold them for the waiver price of $7,500 and they—especially Pipp—were extremely useful players.

For the rest, Donovan had to do the best he could with the survivors from the year before. He had Pipp on first base; Paddy Baumann and Lute Boone sharing second; Peckinpaugh at short stop; Fritz Maisel on third base; and High, Roy Hartzell, and Birdie Cree in the outfield. Sweeney remained as the first-string catcher, and Leslie Nunamaker was acquired from the Red Sox in midseason to help him. Ray Fisher, Ray Keating, Slim Caldwell, and Cy Pieh did most of the pitching. Keating was effective when he could take his turn, but he was out part of the time with a lame arm.

On paper, there was scant improvement over 1914 in the performance of the team. It won one game less—and lost one less—and finished in fifth place, or one notch higher. Nevertheless, it was a livelier club somehow; and everybody was saying that with Donovan at the helm and Ruppert and Huston willing to spend money freely for new material, it wouldn't be long before it would be on its way to a pennant.

3

As the 1916 season approached, it was plain that something would have to be done about getting a new third baseman. Maisel was not yet through as a major-league ball player—Donovan was planning to shunt him to the outfield —but he had lost some of the spryness a third baseman needed, especially in those days, when more hitters were trying to beat out bunts or rolling sacrifices down the third-base line and there was more base stealing than there is today. Donovan attempted to make a deal with one or two clubs but got no encouragement. Then the idea struck him that he might be able to lure J. Franklin Baker back to the big leagues.

Baker, for six years a standout with the Athletics, had refused to report at the opening of the 1915 season. His reason was simple: he was tired of knocking about the country all summer long. He had a farm near Trappe, Maryland, and that was where he wanted to be. Connie Mack's efforts to induce him to change his mind were futile. And so his name was placed on the voluntary retired list, and Connie looked about for a new third baseman.

With the coming of late spring, however, Baker decided that he might as well play ball if it wouldn't take him too far from home, so he joined up with the town team at Upland, near by. He had played in fifty games or so, had kept himself in shape and his eye on the ball—and now Donovan gazed at him longingly.

Since Baker still was the property of the Athletics under baseball rules, Bill had to get permission from Mack to talk to him. This Connie freely gave, being convinced that Baker either would not return at all or, if he did, would prefer New York to Philadelphia. It took some talking on Bill's part to win Baker over, but he finally managed it. Baker said he would sign with the Yankees if they could buy his release from the Athletics. That was managed, too, for $25,000.

Baker's arrival in New York was greeted with enthusiasm. The blows he had dealt to earn the name of "Home Run" Baker had fallen upon the Giants in critical moments of the 1911 and 1913 World Series. The New York fans wanted a fellow like that on their side. Overnight he became the biggest drawing card the club had had since Chase. He was the first of the long line of glamour boys introduced to New York fans by Ruppert and Huston.

Pipp remained at first base and Peckinpaugh at short stop. Baker was on third. Second base had been taken over by Joe Gedeon. Frank Gilhooley had been added to the outfield. The pitching staff presumably had been strengthened by Donovan's corralling of Nick Cullop, George Mogridge, Urban Shocker, and Bob Shawkey. Maybe this was the year, the fans began to think. Not the year for a pennant, with the Red Sox riding high, but the year in which, for the first time since 1910, the Yankees would be in the thick of the pennant fight. But it was another year of disappointment.

Misfortune first hit the team when Baker, chasing a foul fly, crashed into the grandstand, suffering injuries that kept him out of more than fifty games. The outfield was a scramble—Rube Oldring finally was bought from the Athletics to help out—and the pitching didn't meet expectations.

The team commanded admiration because of the way it hustled, and Donovan was praised for his resourcefulness. There were days when it looked as though he wouldn't be able to muster nine able-bodied athletes to start a game, but somehow he always came through with the required number. But the Yankees were only briefly in the pennant fight, and the end of the season found them in fourth place.

COLONEL JACOB RUPPERT

BILL DONOVAN AND CAP HUSTON

4

Ruppert had been a fairly regular attendant at the ball games during 1915 and 1916, but the ball players had seen little of him. Huston was the one they knew. He was at the training camp in the spring, he was in and out of the clubhouse at the Polo Grounds, he took frequent trips during the season. If there was even a promise of excitement on a trip, Cap was on the train when it pulled out of New York.

The newspapermen were his usual companions. Bozeman Bulger, Sid Mercer, Harry Schumacher, Bill Hanna, Jimmy Sinnott, Bill Slocum, Bill Farnsworth, Fred Lieb, Damon Runyon, Grantland Rice occasionally, Bill McBeth—above all, Bill McGeehan. No one ever got a greater kick out of being around with the ball players than Huston did. But he couldn't keep the ball players up all night. So he spent his afternoons watching the ball games and his evenings—and most of his nights—with the newspapermen, and in general was very happy.

He was unhappy, of course, when the team lost. He was disappointed when, after a bright beginning, it had skidded in 1916. He looked forward eagerly to the spring of 1917 and another whirl at the pennant; but in the spring of 1917 the nation plunged into the World War—and Cap lost interest in the pennant race.

Other baseball men, bewildered by the declaration of war, wondered what they were going to do about it and what part baseball could play in it. Huston had no doubts on either score. He knew that he was going into the Army, and he saw no reason why all other able-bodied men in the game shouldn't follow him. He was instrumental in having drill sergeants assigned to all the American League teams to put the players through their daily paces with bats instead of guns. Before the summer set in, he was in uniform—and before it waned he was in France with the Eighteenth Engineers.

On the home front, Ruppert and Donovan kept the Yankees going as best they could. Setting out with about the same team they had had in 1916 but hoping for better luck, the Yanks moved briskly at first. Then, as Ruppert looked on impatiently and Donovan toiled and fretted, their stride shortened. For the first time under Donovan's command they were losing ground. The crowds they had attracted fell away rapidly. To make matters worse, the Giants were winning the pennant in the National League. The Yanks were rapidly becoming once more, as they had been a few years before on the hilltop, New York's forgotten team.

At the end of the season it was written of them in *Reach's Guide:*

They not only failed to perform up to expectation all season but finished in the ruck. The team was in the lead only one day, May 19, and second for two days. Then it made a battle, running to June for third place. In July the fight was for fourth place. By August, it was altogether out of the running for anything higher than fifth place. Accidents, which put the team out of it in 1916, also got in more deadly work this season, outfielders Gilhooley and Marsans suffering broken bones. But this was not the cause of defeat, as the team had available good substitutes. The team played a very good defensive game but was hopelessly weak in batting and pitching. Not a batsman performed up to form and most of them were far below. A pitcher led in batting and the actual leader, Frank Baker, hit but .280 and not one outfielder hit as high as .265. In pitching also the team was deficient, Fisher, Russell, Shawkey, Caldwell, Mogridge and Cullop all pitching far below their regular form.

That brief review doesn't say so, but they finished in sixth place. Ruppert was in very low spirits over his ball club. With Huston in France and Sparrow ailing—the business

manager had an attack of acute indigestion at Albany, Ga.,
on the way north from the training camp in the spring which
very nearly had cost him his life and his recovery was slow—
the Colonel did most of his suffering in silent loneliness.
He was seldom seen at the Polo Grounds and as seldom conferred with Donovan.

By the end of the season he had decided that he needed
not only a new group of ball players but a new manager as
well.

"I like you, Donovan," he said at their last meeting in his
office in the brewery, "but we have to make some changes
around here."

"I know it, Colonel," Bill said.

Bill had known it for a long time. So, it seems, had the
players. That was almost the only thing they did know. They
didn't know whether there would be any baseball in 1918
or, if there was, whether they would have a part in it. And
so, through the last month of the season, they were simply
playing out the string.

III · The Engagement of Huggins

⊖

U¹P TO THIS TIME, relations between Ruppert and Huston
had been very amiable. Now, in 1918, a rift developed that
ultimately brought about a sharp and lasting break between
them. It began in the discussions, by cable, of a successor to
Donovan.

Huston's choice was Wilbert Robinson, then manager of
the Brooklyn club. There was a great affection between Cap
and Uncle Robbie, and they were very much alike. They
hunted and drank together at Dover Hall in Georgia in the
fall and winter months and saw as much of each other as
possible during the baseball season. Indeed, Uncle Robbie
was closer to Cap than Ruppert ever could be. Moreover,
Robbie had been successful as manager in Brooklyn, and was
very popular. The name of the Brooklyn team had been
changed from Dodgers to Robins because of him, and he
seemed to Huston the ideal man to lead the Yankees. He
cabled Ruppert, virtually dictating the engagement of Robbie.

In spite of the close companionship between Robbie and
Huston, Ruppert knew Robbie only slightly. He called him
to the brewery for an interview, which was very short and
not a happy experience for Robbie. Questioning him
brusquely on his qualifications for the post, Ruppert concluded by shaking his head.

"No," he said, "you will not do. For one thing, you are too old."

Robbie, at fifty, had never had thought of himself as an old man. Old! Why, he was as robust, as full of vigor, as ever! Hadn't he won the pennant in Brooklyn the year before? And couldn't he, if the occasion demanded, still lick any man on his team? Ruppert, eyeing him coldly across the desk, might as well have hit him in the face. Robbie picked up his coat and hat, growled a good-by, and strode heavily from the office. His cable to Huston infuriated Cap, who hurled a blistering message across the sea to Ruppert. Ruppert, on receiving it, shrugged—and pursued his quest for a manager.

He turned to Ban Johnson for advice.

"Get Miller Huggins," Ban said.

Huggins was a scrawny little man, touched by baseball genius. Born in Cincinnati on March 27, 1880, he had learned the game on the sandlots of that city, and at nineteen was playing with Mansfield in the Interstate League. Two years later he was the regular short stop of the St. Paul club of the Western League, which was shifted to the American Association the following year. In 1904 he had come up to the major leagues with the Cincinnati club. Meanwhile, during the off seasons, he had studied law and been admitted to the bar.

In 1910 he was traded to the St. Louis Cardinals, and in 1913 was appointed manager. He continued to play until 1916, when he retired to the dugout after eighteen games.

"I just got tired," he explained.

At the time when Johnson urged Ruppert to hire him, he was in New York as the representative of the St. Louis club to attend the National League meeting, held annually in December. When he heard that Ruppert wanted to see him and for what purpose, he wasn't interested. He was nicely settled in St. Louis and doing well. The Cardinals had finished third that year. He had a heavy financial investment in the club, and his stock was beginning to pay dividends. He was regarded by everyone in St. Louis, himself included, as a fixture. He had no wish to change.

It is probable, indeed, that he would have left New York without seeing Ruppert but for his friend, J. G. Taylor Spink, publisher of the *Sporting News*, the baseball bible. Spink urged him to go to the brewery; and when he continued to refuse, the publisher said:

"If you won't go willingly, I'll hit you over the head and drag you up there."

"All right," Huggins said at last. "To please you, I'll go."

Ruppert and Huggins liked each other immediately. Ruppert, ready to be impressed by the strong recommendations with which Johnson had supplemented his original suggestion, quickly offered the job to Hug—and Hug, somewhat to his own amazement, accepted it.

The reverberations from overseas were terrific. It is unlikely that Huston had anything against Huggins; but, incensed at Ruppert's rejection of Robinson, he railed at the selection of Huggins as he would undoubtedly have done at the selection of anyone else. Nor was Huggins unaware of the attitude of one of his employers. Huston never was one to keep his feelings to himself, and in letters to his friends among the newspapermen in New York he made it clear that Ruppert's choice was not his and bluntly accused his partner of perfidy, made worse by the circumstance that it was practiced on one who was fighting for his country.

Thus Huggins had an unhappy beginning as manager of the Yankees. He hadn't wanted the job in the first place, had accepted it in what he now must have felt was a moment of weakness—and the first result of his signing was a breach between the owners.

He was not to feel the full force of Huston's displeasure, however, until Cap's return from the war in the spring of 1919.

Through 1918, with the season ending on Labor Day with the stiff application of the work-or-fight order to the ball players, he had done well. He had brought in new players, but had held some of them only briefly until they enlisted in the Navy or were claimed by the Army. Eleven Yankees, some veterans, some rookies who had but scant fame then, entered the armed forces. Aaron Ward spent the entire season of 1918 in the Army. The others, who started the season but didn't linger long, were Bob Shawkey, Wally Pipp, Alex Ferguson, George Halas, Bob McGraw, Frank (Lefty) O'Doul, Muddy Ruel, Pete Schneider, Ernie Shore, Sam Vick, and Frank Kane.

Working with such material as he could hold, learning a lot about American League ball players and the strategy of American League managers, Huggins revived interest in the Yankees both at home and elsewhere on the circuit. He finished fourth and looked ahead confidently to a time when, the war over, he could proceed with plans for the further improvement of the team.

Now it was the spring of 1919, the pennant races were on again, and enthusiasm for baseball was one of the marked impulses of the nation's reaction to peace. But Huston, out of uniform (he had won the rank of colonel in this war) and at his desk in the club's offices in Forty-second Street, was glowering at Huggins. He wasn't swayed by the progress Huggins had made and the obvious fact that, slowly but surely, he was putting together a team which might yield a pennant within a year or two. He was cool to Ruppert, even cooler to Huggins. At a later date Huggins said:

"I wouldn't go through again, for all the money in the world, the years from 1919 to 1923."

This was only the first of those years, and not the worst of them; for, strangely, Ruppert and Huston were temporarily reunited in spirit, bound together by a common resentment of an act by Ban Johnson. During this period Huston was too much occupied with Johnson to pay attention to Huggins.

2

The row in which Ruppert and Huston stood shoulder to shoulder against Johnson had its beginning, curiously enough, in a game in Detroit late in July between the Tigers and the Red Sox, and the cause of it was a pitcher by the name of Carl Mays.

Mays, combining a blazing fast ball with a sweeping underhand delivery in which his knuckles actually scraped the ground sometimes as he let the ball go, was one of the best pitchers in either league. He was also sharp-tempered, truculent, and, when crossed, abusive. This day in Detroit the Tigers hammered him hard; and when Ed Barrow, the manager, removed him from the box, he·hurled the ball against the screen and stormed into the clubhouse, declaring he never would pitch for the Red Sox again.

At the hotel that night, Barrow learned that Mays had left for Boston and promptly suspended him. Little attention was paid to the story except in Boston, and even there it was accepted as just another explosion on the part of a chronically rebellious player. When the Red Sox got back to Boston, Mays, seemingly contrite, assured Barrow that he was ready to resume his place on the pitching staff. His attitude, however, had no softening effect on Barrow. The manager could not brook the player's insubordination, had no faith in his promises to behave himself in the future, and set about disposing of him. His first thought was the Yankees. Their pitching staff needed strengthening, and if Ruppert and Huston were interested in Mays, they would pay more for him than any of the other club owners. The Yankees were interested. A deal was quickly arranged by which Mays went to New York in exchange for two other pitchers, Alan Russell and Bob McGraw, and a check for $40,000.

Announcement of the deal in New York drew a rumbling noise from Chicago as ominous as it was unexpected. At first no one could make out what it was that made Johnson object. But Ban quickly made himself clear: The Red Sox had sold a player who was under suspension for flouting the authority of his manager and deserting his team. Ban suspected that Mays had deliberately brought about the incident in order to force the Red Sox to sell him. In other words, he had looked greedily on the new bonanza for ball players in New York and had made up his mind to share in it.

This was denied with great heat by all concerned—by Frazee, who owned the Red Sox and had pocketed the $40,000; by Barrow, whose main thought in making the deal was to rid himself of a vexatious player; by Ruppert and Huston, who wanted another winning pitcher; by Mays, who roundly denounced Johnson for intimating that his methods were as underhanded as his pitching delivery.

But Johnson had only jabbed lightly with his left. Now he threw his Sunday punch: As president of the American League, he would not approve the deal. The New York club must forthwith return Mays to Boston. Frazee must, also forthwith, return the Colonels' check.

Complete understanding of Johnson's position is necessary to appreciate what followed. He was not merely the president of the league. He had created it; and, with few exceptions, the men whom he permitted to own or manage the clubs were his creatures. He had taken them from here and there, put them where they were, looked after them, coddled them and abused them by turns. When he spoke, they listened—and never talked back. When there was anger in his voice, they quailed. They knew that if he was really displeased with them, he would first cut their legs from under them and then pitch them into the outer darkness. He was the most powerful and, at times, the most ruthless figure in baseball. Theoretically, the baseball business was ruled by the National Commission, composed of August Herrmann, president of the Cincinnati club, chairman, and the presidents of the two leagues—Johnson and, at this time, John Arnold Heydler. Actually, Johnson dominated the commission as completely as he dominated his own league. Thus, when he declared the Mays deal invalid, it was taken for granted by Ban and his subjects that the pitcher would go back to Boston and Ruppert and Huston could put their check, returned by Frazee, among their souvenirs.

But Ban and the others little knew Ruppert and Huston. Ruppert had been born to wealth; Huston had acquired it. Both knew the power of it. Furthermore, neither owed the slightest fealty to Johnson. They were not in baseball because of his interest or indulgence in them. They had bought their way in and had paid their way ever since. They had taken a bedraggled ball club and, by pouring money into it, were making it one of the league's greatest assets. Now Johnson was attempting to block a move intended to increase its strength and prestige, and they were determined to thwart him.

Their declaration of independence was widely and, in some quarters, jubilantly hailed. Not all the newspapermen covering baseball—and this was especially true in New York—were overfond of Johnson. Those who were not leaped to the issue and urged Ruppert and Huston on with eager cries. Johnson, calm in the knowledge of his seemingly limitless powers, politely wanted to know what Ruppert and

Huston were going to do about it. They answered quickly: "If necessary, we will go to the courts."

To the courts! Club owners, even in the minor leagues, reeled in consternation. Johnson was stunned, unbelieving. As if baseball couldn't govern itself without the courts! The last time baseball had been in the courts was to defend itself against an action brought by the Baltimore club of the Federal League, which had charged the major leagues with operating in restraint of trade. That case—still dragging through endless appeals—had turned out rather well so far. Still, baseball didn't trust the courts. There was no telling what might happen to you when you got in there with a hostile lawyer examining you and a judge staring down at you from the bench.

There was only one thing Johnson could do in the face of this fearful threat. That was to defy Ruppert and Huston to go ahead with it. The defiance was accepted. The battle was on. Before it was over, old friendships had been smashed, old loyalties breached, threats of a new league had been hurled. the National Commission had been scrapped, and Kenesaw Mountain Landis was the Commissioner of Baseball.

The battling Colonels engaged the firm of Davies, Auerbach, and Cornell; and, with Charles Tuttle appearing for them, petitioned Justice Robert F. Wagner for an injunction against Johnson. This was on August 3, and that day in Detroit, Frank Navin intimated that, regardless of the court's decision, the other clubs might refuse to play the Yankees until Mays had been surrendered. This brought Johnson's quondam pal, Charles A. Comiskey, into the tussle on the side of the Colonels and, of course, Frazee. The Old Roman had helped to found the league and had been one of Ban's stanchest supporters for years, but of late he had been annoyed by some of Ban's rulings and was eager to impose some restrictions on him. Now a good fight loomed and, to Johnson's dismay, he moved into it.

Justice Wagner issued a temporary injunction on August 6 and called for additional briefs. Ruppert and Huston immediately furnished these and ordered Huggins to pitch Mays, which, of course, he did. Four days later the row within the league was going full blast, with Johnson fighting to use the league's sinking fund to finance his defense; and the Colonels, Frazee, and Comiskey screaming that this was illegal. Justice Wagner agreed with them on that score, too, and Ban's wrath mounted.

Ruppert, Huston, and their allies among the club owners and the newspapermen thundered:

"Johnson must go!"

Heydler had maintained a discreet silence; but Herrmann, plainly on Johnson's side all along, got himself so deeply involved that Huston roared:

"Herrmann must go, too!"

The league's board of directors started an investigation, Mays went on pitching, the season rolled along. The first time the Yankees went to Detroit following the outbreak of the row, their lawyers, remembering Navin's implied threat, got out an injunction against him, too. Not until October 25, with the season and the World Series over, did Justice Wagner grant a permanent injunction. Ban had one more shot left in his locker. It was a blank cartridge, but he fired it anyway: The National Commission met on October 29 and, somehow managing to keep a straight face, refused to recognize the fact that the Yankees had finished in third place and withheld their share of the World Series money. On November 5 Ruppert and Huston paid the players out of their own pockets.

At the December meeting of the leagues everything was patched up. The patch was to blow off the next year, but for the present there was peace. Herrmann, too old and tired to fight any more, resigned as chairman of the Commission. The Commission admitted the Yankees had finished third and reimbursed the Colonels for the money they had paid to the players. Johnson, although badly shaken by the beating he had taken, still held on. He thought that, presently, things would get better. Instead, they got worse. It took the exposure in 1920 of the perfidy of the White Sox in 1919 to demolish the Commission and bring in Landis, but the drive against Johnson really began the day he tried to send Mays back to Boston. The fierce fighting which broke out in 1920 was virtually the end. He remained as president of the American League until 1927 when, shorn of power and embittered, he resigned. He died in 1931.

3

The team which finished third in 1919 was by all odds the best the Yankees had ever had. Ruppert and Huston were spending their money freely; and, although many of the players they bought weren't worth a tenth of their cost, others proved to be sound investments. Huggins, scorned by Huston and almost unnoticed by the crowds, was slowly building.

He had Pipp on first base, Peckinbaugh at short stop, and Baker on third. The second baseman, new to the Yankees, was Derril Pratt, obtained from the Browns for Shocker and Cullop. Duffy Lewis, Ping Bodie, and Sammy Vick patroled the outfield, with Chick Fewster as utility outfielder. Truck Hannah and Muddy Ruel divided the catching. The pitching was done mainly by Shawkey, Shore, Mogridge, Thormahlen, Quinn, and, through August and September, Mays.

It was a good enough team to arouse interest and make a stab at winning the pennant; but it was not good enough to finish higher than third. The pitching was uncertain—Mays was the leader and ranked third in the league, but the others had difficulty keeping up with him. The defense was pretty good, but the big punch was missing on the attack, Peck, with an average of .305, being the leading hitter. The team got off in fourth place, moved up to second and back, hit the top in June, and stayed there until late in July, fell back as far as fifth, then fought its way to third and hung there to the finish.

The fans and the newspapermen liked the players, and the club was getting a better press than ever before. The old favorites were Pipp, Peck, Shawkey, and Hannah; the new, Lewis, Bodie, and Ruel. Lewis had been one of the Lewis, Speaker, and Hooper trio which had shone so brightly in Boston. He had been in the Navy through 1918, and had been sold to the Yankees as soon as he was discharged. Bodie, a San Francisco Italian, was by no means a great ball player, but he was a hard-swinging hitter. McGeehan called him the Rock Roller of Telegraph Hill. Ruel, a little fellow, had been with the club for two years but had been in the Army most of 1918 and, all told, had caught only nine games for the Yanks since his purchase from Memphis. But he was a big-league catcher now, and the crowd liked to see him work.

IV · The Arrival of Babe Ruth

⊖

1

THE BOSTON TEAM of 1919 had another player destined to affect the fortunes of the Colonels and their Yankees far more than Mays. He was already famous then, and later his fame was greater than any other ball player had ever known. Later, many people considered him the greatest ball player who ever lived, greater than Ty Cobb, or Hans Wagner, or any of the others.

Let us go back for a moment beyond the summer of 1919, when a young pitcher turned outfielder, back to the spring of 1914 in the city of Baltimore. Let us listen for a moment to Brother Gilbert, who discovered the young player:

"I was coaching Mt. St. Joseph's College team, and we had a great kid pitcher named Ford Meadows, and scouts from five major-league clubs were on his trail that spring. Then Jack Dunn sent Fritz Maisel down to look him over for the Baltimore club and I was so afraid Dunnie would sign the boy—because I knew Fritz would recommend him—that I said to Dunn:

"'Jack, if you let this fellow alone, I'll give you the best young left-hander I ever saw.'

"Now, the truth is that I never had seen this young left-hander pitch. But I had seen him play ball and, while I do not profess to be one of those who can look down the years and see greatness in line for any individual, I had reason to believe that, with proper handling, this boy would become a

43

great pitcher some day. His name was George Herman Ruth.

"I was at St. Mary's Industrial School one day, and I had seen this boy who, so far as I was concerned, was just a big kid in blue overalls in the beginning. He was catching for one of the teams in a league they had at St. Mary's, and if you ever wanted to see a bone out of joint or one of nature's misfits, you should have seen him, a left-handed catcher, squatting behind the plate. All he had was a mask and a glove, which he wore on his left hand. When he had to make a throw to second base he would take off the glove and tuck it under his right arm before he made the throw. And how he could throw! The ball was three feet off the ground going through the box and three feet off the ground when it got to second base.

"I knew that with an arm like that he could be made into a pitcher. And then I saw him go to bat. The pitcher for the other side was a tall, lean boy by the name of Tom Paget. As he wound up he turned his back to the hitter before he let the ball go. I looked at him winding up and then I looked at Ruth. There he stood, just as you saw him standing at the plate when he was at the very peak of his career. There was determination in his attitude—he had the will to do. Paget pitched the ball and Babe hit it against the right-field fence. The next time up, he hit it over the center-field fence. The third time he hit it over the left-field fence. Ah, but the fourth time he delightfully, deliciously, delectably— struck out. And he looked better striking out than he did hitting home runs."

Dunn, president and manager of the Baltimore Orioles and a power in the International League, looked at the Babe, liked him, signed him and became, in spirit if not in a strictly legal sense, the guardian of this fatherless boy and baseball prodigy. To the other ball players, he was Jack's baby, this big, powerfully built boy of nineteen, and it was at the Orioles' training camp that he was first called Babe.

That same year he was sold to the Red Sox, then owned by Lannin. With him went two other players, Ernie Shore, a pitcher who was to become reasonably famous, and an infielder named Egan, who shortly went back to the minors. The price for the three was $22,500—$19,000 in cash and the cancellation of a debt of $3,000 that Dunn owed Lannin, who had loaned him the money to help carry on his fight against the Federal League invasion of Baltimore.

The Babe was not quite ready for major-league company when Lannin bought him. Bill Carrigan, the Red Sox manager, soon discovered that and farmed him out to the Providence club of the International League, where, incidentally, his manager was Bill Donovan, and he pitched and played the outfield. Recalled before the end of the season, he pitched in four games, was credited with winning two and losing one. In 1915 he won eighteen games and lost six. In 1916 he won twenty-three games and lost twelve and, in the World Series with Brooklyn, beat Sherrod Smith, 2 to 1. He won twenty-three games again in 1917 and lost thirteen. In 1918, with the Red Sox capturing the pennant again, he won thirteen games and lost seven and, in the World Series with the Cubs, won two games, one of them a shutout in which he triumphed over Jim Vaughn.

Fine as it was, it was not his pitching in 1918 that captured the attention of the public and of baseball men all over the country. It was his home-run hitting. Between pitching engagements, he played the outfield and hit eleven home runs. Enemy pitchers learned to fear him. In all the dugouts the ball players were talking about him.

In the spring of 1919, at the Red Sox training camp at Tampa, Fla., Barrow converted him into an outfielder. He reasoned that, in spite of the fact that Babe was the best left-handed pitcher in the American League at the time, by his great power at the plate he could help the team even more by being in the ball game every day. The move was a tremendous success. Ruth, batting .322, hit twenty-nine home runs.

No major-league player had ever hit that many home runs in the course of a single season. In the National League Frank (Wildfire) Schulte of the Cubs had hit twenty-one in 1911, and in 1915 Clifford (Gavvy) Cravath of the Phillies had hit twenty-four. Away back in 1902, Socks Seybold of the Athletics had hit sixteen, which still was the American League mark.

Ruth's name was roared across the country. Wherever the Red Sox played, crowds swarmed to see him. In New York, Ruppert and Huston, looking on, wanted him. They were ambitious to make their club the greatest club in baseball. Here, people were saying, was the greatest player—and certainly the most spectacular, the most awe-inspiring—in baseball. He belonged, they felt, in a Yankee uniform.

2

The season of 1919 had ended, and the winter lull had set in. Ruppert and Huston were discussing the amount of money they should offer for Ruth when, to their joyful amazement, an opportunity to get him virtually at their own figure was dropped into their laps. Frazee, a colorful figure who had started as a bill poster in Peoria, Ill., had made and lost several fortunes in the theater. No catch-penny promoter, when he had a hit he cleaned up; and when he had a failure, he was wiped out. With Ruth making the turnstiles hum in 1919 and a couple of his shows flopping about the country, he was putting money in one pocket and taking it out of another. Not even Ruth could square the deficit created by the shows. Frazee was broke again.

Now, Harry never was one to want money just to look at and count. He wanted money for operating purposes and, broke as he was, he had great faith in some shows he was about to produce. But they would be costly productions. So he went to New York and asked Ruppert to lend him $500,000.

Ruppert immediately countered with an offer for Ruth, vaguely mentioning cash and players. Frazee dashed back to Boston to consult Barrow.

"You want cash, don't you?" Barrow asked.

"Yes."

"Well, get it. Never mind the players. There aren't any players on that ball club I'd want on mine."

Frazee was in New York the next morning. He and Ruppert and Huston came to an agreement shortly: Ruth was to go to the Yankees for $100,000, to be paid out of the Yankee coffers. As a sort of bonus, Frazee got a personal loan of $350,000 from Ruppert, who took a mortgage on Fenway Park as collateral.

Rumors that Ruth was going to New York had got about. Now they were confirmed by an announcement from Ruppert's office in the brewery. The news thrilled New York fans—and dumbfounded the fans in Boston. They had looked upon the Babe as their own. The Babe himself apparently had given no thought to leaving the town. He had founded a cigar factory there (the Babe Ruth cigar, made from Connecticut tobacco and selling, with a picture of the Babe on every wrapper, for a nickel) and a farm near Sudbury.

Word that he had been sold to the Yankees he received with regret.

"I am not stuck on the idea of going to New York," he told reporters. "My heart is in Boston."

"He means," wrote the cynical Neal O Hara, "that's where his cigar factory is."

But whether he liked it or not—and within a short time he liked it very much—the Babe was in New York. There his fame was to grow and widen. There he was to give the Yankees a terrific impetus and to read, one day, when the great Yankee Stadium had been constructed, that this was "the House that Ruth Built." Boston had claimed him once; now New York claimed him. Soon the whole nation was to claim him, so it could be written of him that, while he wore the uniform of the Yankees and drew his pay from the Yankees' till, he belonged to everyone who had a love of baseball in his heart.

3

Never before had the transfer of one ball player created such a stir. Ruth not only had smashed existing home run records in 1919 but plainly was at the very beginning of a career as a hitter that would revolutionize baseball. There were other great hitters in the game—Cobb, Speaker, Jackson, Sisler, Hornsby. But in one year the Babe had swept past all of them. If the fans in Boston were in despair at losing him, those in New York were overjoyed at the prospect of seeing him in seventy-seven games a year at the Polo Grounds.

Innocent bystanders hit by this deal were the Giants. Up to this time they had kept the edge in the patronage fight, but they had no one (who had?) to match Ruth, and it was certain the Yankees soon would be the top team in the town. Nor did the Giants have to wait until the season opened to realize what, from their standpoint, the Babe meant in a Yankee uniform. Sensible of his drawing power in the provinces, as far back as November they had arranged a spring tour with the Red Sox and had planned to bill the Babe like a circus all through the South. Now it was spring, and they were touring with the Red Sox—but a few days ahead of them the Yankees were cleaning up with Ruth.

Bob Meusel had been added to the roster, coming up from Vernon in the Coast League to play third base or the outfield, Ward or Baker also being available for use at third. Freddy Hofmann had joined Hannah and Ruel back of the bat, and "Two Gun" Rip Collins from Texas was retained as a pitcher.

But, at home or abroad, Ruth was the one. As early as May he was pulling crowds through the Polo Grounds turnstiles that far outnumbered any the Yankees had seen. And he was giving them something to rave about as he hammered the ball into the stands or, on one occasion, over the stand. He played right field at the Polo Grounds, left field in most of the other parks. He said he didn't like to play the sunfield, and Huggins had no mind to press the point. After all, the big guy was in a spot where he could have things his way.

Ruppert went to the games more often now. Huston was there practically every day. Cap—he never could get used to being called Colonel, so nobody ever called him that any more—was the greatest Ruth fan in a town rapidly going wild over the Babe. The presence of Ruth almost—but not quite—made Cap forget the presence of Huggins. There was no chance Cap would ever warm up to Hug, but the sight of the Babe walking up to the plate and slugging the ball out of sight made him forget who was running the team on the field. It made virtually everybody else forget, too, including most of the baseball writers. The only time Hug got his name in the papers was when the Yankees lost. When they won the headlines went to Ruth—or Pipp or Shawkey, or someone else.

On May 7 Harry Sparrow died. His health had not been good since his almost fatal attack three years before, but he had been as smiling, as willing, as hard-working as ever.

On the evening of May 7 he left the ball park after the game in apparent good health, but that night, at his home, his heart just stopped.

Ruth went swinging from town to town—on and off the field. Technically, he was Ping Bodie's roommate, but the only time Ping ever saw him was on a train or in the ball park.

"Who are you rooming with, Ping?" one of the other players asked him one day.

"With a suitcase," Ping said.

The crack went around the league. It was Ping's major contribution to the history of baseball.

One day Joe Judge, first baseman of the Senators, met the Babe coming out of the Willard in Washington.

"Your ball club stop here?" he asked.

"No," the Babe said. "They're over at the—the what's-it, down the street."

He gestured vaguely.

"But I'm staying here," he said.

Judge shook his head. "It must be nice to be rich," he said. "How much do they soak you, Babe?"

"A hundred bucks a day for a suite."

"A hundred bucks a day!"

"Well," the Babe growled, "a fellow's got to entertain, don't he?"

He tied his home-run record against Bill Burwell of the Browns at the Polo Grounds on July 15. On July 19, also at the Polo Grounds, he broke it by hitting two off Dick Kerr of the White Sox. By this time everybody on the club was swinging with him. Meusel, Bodie, Pipp, Peckinpaugh. The craze for home runs spread—and fattened on a lively ball introduced surreptitiously into the American League. (The National League got it the next year.) Somebody apparently had figured that if one Babe Ruth was so popular, ten Babe

Ruths would be ten times as popular and, accordingly, hopped up the ball. Home-run totals mounted, of course. But there was only one Ruth, and nobody could keep within a million miles of him.

With the Babe showing the way, the Yankees moved into a three-cornered fight for the pennant with the Indians and the White Sox. Later it was believed that the Sox, who admitted having chucked the 1919 World Series, had chucked this pennant race, too, winning or losing games according to the bets they had made. But the Yankees and Indians were on the level, at any rate, and were hammering away at each other in midseason when tragedy struck. In a game at the Polo Grounds on August 16, Mays, pitching for the Yankees, hit Ray Chapman, Cleveland short stop, in the head. Chapman was carried unconscious from the field and removed to a hospital where, early the following morning, he died.

In the wide-spread grief over Chapman's death there was an undertone of anger. There was no evidence or reason to believe that Mays had intended to hit Chapman, but the bean ball or duster was very much in use at that time, and some of the players either intimated or charged outright that, while Mays had not meant to injure the batsman, he had sought to drive him back from the plate. Cobb was quoted by a press association as saying that he believed the pitcher had thrown at the hitter. Appearing in New York a day or two later, he was booed from the time he left the clubhouse in center field until he reached the dugout. Then he said he had been misquoted.

The Yankees hotly defended Mays, although few of them liked him personally—Huggins, who had no use for him, being one of his most loyal supporters. Mays, for his part, said the ball had sailed. Public opinion was on his side, naturally, and the bitterness engendered by the tragedy subsided as Chapman was buried in Cleveland on August

20. Two days later Mays returned to the box, beating Chicago.

The White Sox scandal broke late in September. It looked as though the honest survivors of the blast still might win the pennant, but the Indians got the nod in a photo finish, winding up two games in front of Chicago and three games in front of the Yanks.

There was, however, rejoicing in New York. Although the Yanks had finished third, they had won ninety-five games. Ruth had hit .376, fourth in the league behind Sisler, Speaker, and Jackson, and had made the astonishing, almost unbelievable total of fifty-four home runs. Because of him a new type of fan was appearing at the Polo Grounds. This was the fan who didn't know where first base was but had heard of Babe Ruth and wanted to see him hit a home run. When the Babe hit one, the fan went back the next day to see him hit another. Pretty soon he was a regular, and knew not only where first base was but second base as well.

V · The First Pennant

1.

THE YANKEES were on the high road at last. They had the Babe, they had the crowds, and they had come within striking distance of a pennant. But there still was much to be done, on the field and off.

The death of Harry Sparrow had knocked out such business organization as the club had. Ruppert had other interests that took up his time. Huston was more concerned with rooting for the team than he was with its books; its scouting system, which was negligible; its minor league connections, which were few; and the numerous other details that go into the operation of a ball club. Sparrow, a tireless worker, had looked after these things almost alone. Now that he was gone, there were loose ends all over the office and no one to pick them up. Huggins, his mind filled with plans for the next season, didn't know which way to turn.

Ruppert was the first to realize where they were drifting and how much money it was costing them. His brewery, his real-estate companies, his factories were run efficiently and economically. And his ball club, in which his pride was so great, was bumbling along without any directing force. Obviously, it needed—and quickly—a thoroughly experienced, thoroughly competent executive.

The events of the last year or so, growing out of the Mays case, had put Ruppert and Huston in close touch with such a man. They had known Ed Barrow before, of course, but not well. Now, having had an opportunity to study him, they knew him for the robust character he was and wanted him in New York.

They broached the subject to Frazee. Whatever Harry might have thought about parting with Barrow, his relations with the Yankee owners were such that he was unlikely to oppose their wishes. Besides, his welcome in Boston was beginning to wear very thin indeed, and this may have looked to him like a good opportunity to get Barrow safely and profitably placed while the going was good. At all events, Barrow resigned as manager of the Red Sox shortly after the end of the season, and on October 28 arrived in New York to become business manager of the Yankees.

Barrow was fifty-two years old and could look back on thirty-four years of association with baseball in one capacity or another. There were few places he hadn't been, few baseball men he hadn't known, few angles he hadn't learned. He had played baseball, written it, managed teams, headed clubs and leagues. He had been through the minor leagues, up to the majors, back to the minors, up once more to the majors, this time to stay. Big, broad-shouldered, deep-chested, dark-haired, and bushy browed, he had been through the rough-and-tumble days of baseball. Forceful, outspoken, afraid of nobody, he had been called upon many times to fight, and the record is that nobody ever licked him. The last time he had been challenged was in Boston in 1919 when one of his pitchers threatened to punch him in the nose.

"Nobody has punched me in the nose in a long time," he said quietly. "Don't you try it. If you do, you won't pitch again for a week."

The player decided he probably was right. No punches were thrown.

Barrow wasn't actually born in a covered wagon, but he might have been if, a short time before, his father hadn't thought he had found the sort of place for which he had been looking. In the early spring of 1868 his father, who had fought in the Civil War, and his mother were driving across the Illinois plains in a wagon, seeking a site for a homestead. He pulled up in the farm country near Springfield, built a house, and began to till the land. There the boy was born and christened Edward Grant Barrow—Edward for his father, Grant for Ulysses S., his father's hero.

The elder Barrow, however, soon changed his mind. Abandoning his house and his fields, he loaded his wife, the baby, and the household effects into the wagon, hitched up the horses, and set out again. The little family rolled on, through Illinois, Missouri, Nebraska, and then turned·back to Iowa, finally settling near Des Moines.

Ed went to school in Des Moines and at sixteen was the star player on the baseball team. Following his graduation from high school at eighteen, he went to work as a reporter on the Des Moines *Leader,* his beat taking in the police station, the courthouse, the theater, and the ball park. On Sundays he managed a team in the city league. One of his players was Fred Clarke, who became a big-league outfielder and reaped his greatest fame as playing manager of the Pittsburgh Pirates.

Before he was twenty, Barrow had put Des Moines and the newspaper business behind him and was headed east. He sold oil pumps and soap in Chicago and then moved on to Pittsburgh, where for a time he was associated with Harry M. Stevens, the caterer. Leaving Stevens, he helped to form the Interstate League, and, getting a franchise for Wheeling, W. Va., managed the team and won the pennant. One year in Wheeling was enough for him. In 1896 he went to Paterson, N. J., as manager of the club representing that town in the Atlantic League.

While he was with Paterson he discovered a young man who, he still believes, was the greatest ball player that ever lived. He had heard that, near Carnegie, Pa., there was a kid of great promise and went there to look at him.

"I'll never forget the first time I saw him," he said. "They told me, when I asked for him at his house, that I would find him down along the railroad track. When I came upon him, I had to smile. He was broad-shouldered, bow-legged, and ungainly. He wore an old rumpled blue suit and a derby hat with a feather stuck in the band. He seemed suspicious of me at first but, when I told him what I wanted to talk to him about, he was interested and then a little nervous. To cover his nervousness, he began to pick up lumps of coal and throw them at some tin cans along the right of way. I never had seen him play ball, but now I didn't have to. As he threw that coal, I knew I was looking at a ball player. I signed him right there."

The young man was John Henry Wagner.

In one brief year, Barrow had made an impression on the club owners of the Atlantic League, and at the end of the year they offered him the presidency of the league. He accepted and remained in that position until, with some of the clubs too hard hit financially, the league folded in 1899. Now came an opportunity to go to Toronto, buy an interest in the Eastern League club in that city, and manage the team. He won the pennant there in 1902, and then shifted to Detroit to manage the Tigers in the American League.

No matter where he had been he had done well. But the urge to move constantly was upon him. He left Detroit and went to Indianapolis, left Indianapolis and went back to Toronto. There he had a chance to go into the hotel business and he took it, quitting baseball. One year in the hotel was all he could stand. It was fun, in a way, and it was profitable. But it lacked the excitement, the contacts, the changing scenes of baseball. He sold out, went to Montreal, and took over the Eastern League club.

That was in 1910. At the end of the season he was elected president of the league. At the same meeting, the name of the league was changed to the International. It had been a Class A league. Barrow gained Class AA rating for it and performed one of his greatest achievements when he guided it safely through the Federal League war. The outlaws, as the National and American League club owners referred to those who sought to establish a third major league, put clubs in Newark, Baltimore, and Buffalo, three of the International League cities, raided the league's playing ranks, and gave it a severe battering in the struggle for patronage. Barrow called on the major leagues for help; but they, too, rocked sometimes under the blows hurled upon them by the Feds and were in no position to help him.

Federal League emissaries made him tempting offers, but he refused them. The focal point of the Feds' attack on so-called Organized Baseball was his old friend Ban Johnson, and he was loyal to Ban and hated the Feds as bitterly as Ban did. Disaster frequently threatened, but the end of the war in the winter of 1915-1916 found him still fighting, still holding his ground, his league shaken but intact.

For two more years he remained at the head of the league. Then, with the 1918 season coming on, he resigned to become manager of the Red Sox. There, in his first year, he won the pennant and then pushed on to beat the Cubs in the World Series.

This, then, was the man who, on October 29, 1920, signed a contract in New York to become business manager of the Yankees. On that day the future greatness of the club was sealed.

2

After his first conference with Barrow, Huggins was immensely cheered.

"I know what you have been up against," Barrow said. "That's one of the things I'm going to take care of right off. Ruppert and Huston may own the ball club—but you tell me what you want and I'll make the deals. And I'll be responsible for any deal I make."

Huggins hadn't heard that kind of talk since he had been in New York.

"What do you want right now?" Barrow asked.

"Well," Hug said, loading his pipe, "I could use about eight players. But I'll take what I can get."

Barrow checked over with him the Yankee players he was willing to use in trade and got from him an idea of precisely what he wanted. Between them, it didn't take long to cook up a deal—nor did it take long for Barrow to put it over. Ed simply made a brazen raid on the dwindling stock of good ball players he had left behind him in Boston, taking Waite Hoyt, Wally Schang, Harry Harper, and Mike McNally in exchange for Muddy Ruel, Herb Thormahlen, Derril Pratt, and Sam Vick.

The reaction in Boston was unpleasant, of course. At Barrow's direction, Frazee tried to stem it by alleging that the Red Sox had obtained four Yankee regulars for the price of one—meaning Schang. But that fooled nobody, and the trade panned out exactly as the Boston critics feared. Ruel became a great catcher in a Red Sox uniform, but Pratt was passed on to Detroit, Vick ate his way out of the league, and Thormahlen simply wasn't a true major-league pitcher. In New York, Schang averaged more than a hundred games a year for five years, Hoyt was a first-rate pitcher for eight years, Harper was a very useful one, and McNally was a handy fellow around the infield for a long time.

Seven years later, however, Huggins made an interesting comment on one phase of that deal. With the passing of those years, he had become recognized as one of the soundest judges of talent in baseball, and one day a baseball writer said to him:

"Hug, did you ever make a mistake on a young ball player?"

"Certainly," Hug said. "Many a one."

"No," the baseball writer said.

Hug nodded.

"All right," the writer said, "name one."

"Muddy Ruel. I was—and still am, of course—very fond of Muddy personally. I thought he was one of the nicest young men I had ever known. But I thought he never would be a real major-league catcher. I was wrong, of course. I have never had a catcher since who was his equal."

"Not even Schang?"

"Not even Schang," he said.

One young fellow on whom Huggins didn't make a mistake was Hoyt. He hadn't seen very much of him. Waite, although only twenty-one at the time he joined the Yankees, had moved too fast for any one person to see very much of him. Signed out of Erasmus Hall High School in Brooklyn in 1916 by John McGraw, he had pitched for minor-league teams until the summer of 1918, when he had enrolled as a student officer and been ordered to Middlebury College for training. The war over, he reported back to McGraw, reminding the Giant manager of an assurance, given before he went away, that his minor-league wanderings were over and that he would be kept by the Giants. McGraw said he remembered it, all right, but unforeseen circumstances, etc., etc.

"I don't know where you're sending me," Hoyt said, "but I'm not going."

"You're going to Rochester," McGraw said. "I'm sending you as part payment for Earl Smith."

Hoyt reached for his hat.

"Not me, Mr. McGraw," he said.

He meant it. That was in the early spring of 1919. When he refused to report to Rochester, that club sold him to New Orleans, but he refused to report there, either. Meanwhile, he had got a job pitching once or twice a week for the strong independent team maintained by a shipyard in Baltimore and soon attracted attention by beating all the major-league clubs that, unable at that time to play Sunday baseball in Philadelphia, dropped down to Baltimore of a Sabbath to pick up a little easy money playing his team. When he shut out the Reds, who were about to clinch the National League pennant, a number of major-league clubs bid for him. Since he could make his own choice, he accepted that from Boston where, he figured, a young pitcher would have a better chance than on one of the other clubs that wanted him. So the Red Sox got him by paying him a bonus for signing —and the New Orleans club the sum of $2,500.

He had done little with the Red Sox in 1920. He had been in twenty games but won only six of them while losing as many, and his earned-run average of 4.39 was nothing to rave about, even with the new rabbit ball in use. But he was a big, strong kid with a smooth pitching motion, a good fast ball, and an air of confidence. Hug liked him. They had never met until the league meeting in New York a few days after Hoyt had become the property of the Yankees. A newspaperman was talking to Huggins in the lobby of the old Belmont Hotel, where the meeting was held, and Hoyt, who knew him, walked up and greeted him. Then Hoyt looked at Huggins.

WAITE HOYT

MILLER HUGGINS

BOB SHAWKEY

© *Brown Bros.*

HOME RUN BAKER

© *Brown Bros.*

"Don't you fellows know each other?" the newspaperman asked. "Or are you kidding me?"

"No," Hug said. "I never met the young man."

"Then," the newspaperman said, "permit me: Mr. Huggins, Mr. Hoyt. Mr. Hoyt, Mr. Huggins."

They grinned and shook hands. The frail Huggins almost went to his knees. Hoyt, unaware of his own strength, had almost crushed Hug's hand.

"That's a fine way to treat your new manager," Hug said ruefully as Hoyt stammered his apologies.

In the years to come, the relationship between them came to be almost that of a father and son. But not right away. Hoyt, young, thoughtless, strong-willed, sometimes flouted Huggins, roused his wrath—and brought it down on his own head. That was their first meeting. Hoyt will never forget their last.

3

A curious air of confidence hung over the Yankee camp at Shreveport, La., when the players assembled in the spring of 1921. The reason for it wasn't easily discernible. The squabbling in the front office continued, despite the presence of Barrow. All the assurances of support he had received from Barrow left Huggins still unconvinced that he had the measure of authority he needed. Moreover, the make-up of the team was undecided. Huggins had Ruth in right field, Pipp at first base, Peckinpaugh at short stop, and Schang behind the bat. Center field, left field, second base, third base, and the pitching staff posed problems that would take considerable thought and experimentation. Yet no one seemed to be at all worried. No one, that is, except Huggins.

Hug set to work grimly putting his team together. Bob Meusel was posted in left field. Aaron Ward, who had played both short and third, was tried out with Chick Fewster at second. Baker was slowing down at third, and McNally was schooled as his replacement. "Chicken" Hawks, a speed demon from the coast, was stationed in center. The pitching staff had possibilities, but the only members of it on whom Huggins felt he could depend were Mays, Bob Shawkey, and Hoyt. Their support had to be molded from a group that included Harper, Jack Quinn, Lefty O'Doul, Rip Collins, Bill Piercey, Tom Sheehan, and a number of rookies.

The team worked out twice a day. The pitchers, left to their own devices, took part in pepper games, chased fungoes, limbered up their arms. The infielders cracked away at the jobs they were trying to make. The outfielders were forever hitting. Huggins had little to say on the field, and the players took to coaching each other. It was a haphazard training, but they seemed to thrive on it. At least they were getting into shape, even if no one but Ruth, Pipp, Peck, and Schang and three of the pitchers was sure of his job.

When the day's work was over, the young men took advantage of the opportunities that Shreveport offered in the way of social life and contacts. An enterprising automobile agent had loaned Ruth a car—a snappy green roadster bearing a sign, "Babe Ruth's Essex"—with which the Babe frightened the inhabitants by roaring through the streets at a terrific speed. Shawkey, Mays, Hofmann, and Hoyt played golf. The girls in the town got a big play from the romantically inclined athletes. Fewster, excused from morning practice because his health had been impaired by a beaning in an exhibition game with the Dodgers the previous spring, was supposedly spending his mornings in bed. Huggins discovered that he was putting in his free time training a race horse he had bought, and the discovery put a definite check on Chick's career as a horseman. Huggins ordered him to report at the ball park every morning and sit in the stands while his team mates worked out.

With the opening of the season, the Yankees were listed as possible pennant winners, yet few of the experts thought they were strong enough to overcome the Indians, who had won the pennant the year before and flattened the Dodgers in the World Series. The sports writers closest to the team—Sid Mercer, George Daley, Bill Hanna, Bill McGeehan, Buck O'Neill, and one or two others—knew that a lot of welding would have to be done to tighten it up for the long race to the wire. The players themselves, however, seemed to have few misgivings.

As a group, their deportment left much to be desired. As he had feared, Huggins lacked sufficient authority to crack down on his men. He had the support of Ruppert and Barrow, but there still was Huston who, broadminded, affable, even expansive in most things, remained adamant in his attitude toward the manager he had never wanted and could not bring himself to accept. When Hug admonished the players for some of their pranks off the field, they simply laughed at him and went on their way to more pranks. Threats of suspensions and fines meant nothing to them. They had reason to believe that any shackles placed on them by Huggins would be struck off by Cap.

This year the Yankees unwittingly established a reputation as carefree spirits which was to prove an asset to them. The recklessness with which they frequently played and the freedom of movement they enjoyed off the field stamped them among their adversaries as supermen. How, the rest of the league began to wonder after a while, were you going to stop a lot of fellows who went so blithely about when night had fallen, yet showed up on the field the next day full of zing and power?

In the East, the players were allowed to travel in their own cars from town to town. The Babe, finding that travel by train was not as invigorating as a whiz under the summer sky, made all the jumps between New York and Washington, Philadelphia, or Boston in a twelve-cylinder car with a cruising speed of ninety miles an hour which could be pushed up to 110. One midsummer evening, after a game in Washington in which the Babe had hit two homers over the right-field wall and was in unusually high spirits, he set out for Philadelphia with Mrs. Ruth in the front seat and in the rear Hofmann, O'Doul, and Charlie O'Leary, the coach. The night winds whispered of World Series money, and all was right with the world. O'Leary sang his famous South Side ballad, "Tonight's the Night I'm Going to Slug Your Father." Ruth boomed a solid bass as they harmonized.

Thirty miles out of Philadelphia they whirled through a town that nestled pleasantly in the moonlight.

"Kennett Square," O'Leary said, clutching his straw hat. "This is where Herb Pennock lives."

A half-mile farther on was a sharp curve, faced with a stone embankment. Ruth, booming through "The Trail of the Lonesome Pine," cursed horribly and jammed on the brakes. The car swerved, its tires screeching against the roadway. It spun, skidded, and turned over twice, coming to rest with the wheels still spinning.

O'Leary had been flung clear of the car. The others were pinned under it; but, miraculously unhurt except for minor bruises, they crawled free. Ruth rushed to O'Leary, lying face down and unconscious on the road. He turned Charlie over, and then, kneeling beside him and cradling the coach's head in his arms, he wailed:

"Oh, God! Bring him back! Don't let him die! God! Take me instead!"

O'Leary stirred and the Babe pleaded: "Charlie! Speak to me, Charlie!"

Charlie suddenly sat up. "Hey!" he yelled. "What the hell happened to my straw hat?"

The Babe let his head thump back on the pavement.

Having called Huggins on the nearest telephone and informed him of what had happened, Babe and the others saw the battered car hauled away to a repair shop and completed the journey to Philadelphia by taxi-cab. The news of the crack-up spread, was enlarged upon, and finally appeared in the headlines of a morning newspaper:

BABE RUTH KILLED IN AUTO ACCIDENT!

The Babe laughingly denied he was dead and clinched the denial that afternoon by hitting a home run off Scott Perry, pitching for the Athletics.

Huggins, alarmed by the Babe's narrow escape, sought to put a stop to travel by automobile on the part of his players but was overruled by Huston. The Yankees were winning, and Cap said he had no intention of disturbing the players by cramping their style.

Speeding through the countryside at night between games, taking their fun where they found it, baiting Huggins in the clubhouse and the dugout—but winning ball games the while—the Yankees were in front when they reached September. Mays had won twenty games and still was racking up victories. Ruth was hitting home runs at an unbelievable pace. Murderers' Row—Pipp, Ruth, Meusel, Baker, and Schang—had come into being. Huggins had brought Elmer Miller up from the American Association to play center field and lead-off, and Miller had been caught up in the surge of the team.

With the coming of September and the knowledge that they could win, most of the players changed their attitude. Now that the stake toward which they had romped all summer was within reaching distance, they were sobered, especially as the stake loomed larger than they had thought. In the National League the Giants, coming from behind in a great drive late in August, had passed the Pirates and were certain to win. This meant that if the Yankees won, New York would have its first World Series on the subway—a series that in all likelihood would crack existing records for gate receipts. This, indeed, could be the richest prize for which ball players ever had striven.

They hammered and smashed along and then, as the month waned, came to the most critical point in their progress, a four-game series with the Indians, who trailed them by only a game. The Indians had been through all this before. They had been seasoned and hardened and toughened under fire in 1920. They had the poise of champions. They were determined to rip the Yankees right down to the roots.

Indicative of the sobering influence that the tightness of the race and the richness of the reward for the victors had on the Yankees was a strange scene that took place in the kitchen of an apartment on Riverside Drive in the very early hours of the day on which the opening game of this series with the Indians was to be played. The apartment was shared by Shawkey, Hofmann, and Hoyt. They had laughed and capered and tripped through the season as lightly as any of the others, but this—well, this was different. Now the checks were down.

Hoyt, who was to pitch the first game, went to bed about eleven o'clock. But not to sleep. Over and over, in his mind, he was pitching to the Cleveland hitters. Pitching high to this one, low to that one. Inside, outside, fast ball, curve ball. ...At two-thirty he got up, went into the kitchen, fixed a bowl of cereal, and sat down to eat. To his surprise, Hofmann came in and then Shawkey. They helped themselves to cereal, sat down, and began to talk about the impending games. They went over the Cleveland batting order. They speculated on the order of Yankee pitching, wondering if

Huggins would follow Hoyt with Mays. It was after four o'clock when Shawkey said:

"Well, if we're going to play this afternoon, it might be a good idea for us to get some sleep."

They were up at nine and at the Polo Grounds by ten, two hours ahead of the usual time for reporting. Nor were they the only ones. Most of the players were in the club-house when Huggins arrived at eleven o'clock, which must have surprised the little manager.

With Hoyt pitching, the Yankees won the first game. They won the second behind Mays. In the third game their pitching was bad; they cracked wide open and the Indians won. Then came the fourth game, and with it a surprising confession of indecision on the part of Huggins.

The loss of the third game had terrified Ruppert and Huston. They had rushed to him, demanding to know who was going to pitch on the final day—and he didn't know what to tell them. Nor had he made up his mind when, early in the afternoon, the players gathered in the clubhouse. Badgered by the timorous Ruppert and the openly hostile Huston, his nerves were taut as he faced his players. They watched him in silence as he walked up and down, up and down, before them. Then suddenly he stopped walking and said:

"I want to talk to the pitchers. The rest of you go out on the field."

The other players walked slowly from the room, their spikes scraping on the floor. Huggins shut the door behind them and turned to the pitchers.

"Fellows," he said, "I'm up against it. I don't know who to pitch. Hoyt pitched the first game, Mays the second—and we used up everybody else yesterday but Jack Quinn, here. Jack hasn't pitched for three weeks. But he shut them out in Cleveland. I can use Quinn, who hasn't had much work, or I can use Hoyt with two days' rest. What do you fellows think I should do? I'll leave it up to you."

The pitchers didn't know what to say. None of them ever had heard a manager talk like that. It was the manager's place, not theirs, to make decisions. Bewildered, they looked at each other. No one wanted to be the first to speak.

Huggins took a few short paces away from them, turned and came back.

"Well?"

They all began to talk at once. The discussion lengthened, grew heated. It ended in a decision to pitch Quinn, an old man as ball players go—no one ever did get from him the secret of his true age—but crafty and stout-hearted and one of the last of the spitball pitchers.

It was an unhappy choice. His three weeks' absence from the box had affected his control, so that while he wasn't terribly wild, he was just enough off the beam to make him easy to hit. The Indians hammered him out, scoring three runs before Hoyt could be rushed to the rescue. The Yankees lashed back and scored four runs in their half of the first inning. Now the teams slugged away at each other, and the Yankees increased their lead with both sides scoring. Twice, as the Indians threatened to tie the score, Ruth drove them back with home runs. In the eighth inning Hoyt tired and was slammed hard, and Mays stalked in from the bull pen. The Indians, going to bat in the ninth inning trailing by a score of 8 to 7, filled the bases with two out. The next hitter was the catcher, Steve O'Neill, a good hitter in any circumstances and a better one in a pinch.

Hoyt had gone down to the bull pen, where, in the gathering haze of the late September afternoon, he stood with Harry Harper, Rip Collins, and Hofmann to watch the final scenes of the struggle. A door in the old wooden bleachers opened, and a man came through it, then slid it closed behind him. Colonel Ruppert, unable to stand the strain of watching the game from his box near the dugout, had been pacing up and down under the stand since the sixth inning, getting word of the progress ᴼf the game from an usher as excited as himself. Now, scarcely able to bring himself to look, yet afraid not to, he joined the players in the bull pen.

"Hofmann," he whispered hoarsely, "you think we'll win? Say 'Yes,' Hofmann. Don't tell me no. You think Mays can get this man O'Neill, Hofmann? Is O'Neill good?"

Hofmann leaped from the turf as he saw O'Neill miss his first swing.

"What is it?" Ruppert asked. "Is it a strike, Hofmann?"

"Yes," Hofmann said. "One strike. Two to go."

"Two more," Ruppert said. "Oh, fellows, win this game for me! Please win this game! If you win it, I'll give you anything."

He hesitated, but only for a moment. Then he went the whole way:

"I'll give you the brewery!" he said.

Mays got another strike on O'Neill. Then two balls. Another pitch was wide of the plate. Now it was three and two. The crowd was on its feet. It was hard to see the plate from deepest right field. Mays hunched his strong shoulders. His arm fell, swooped low. None of those in the bull pen saw the ball on its flight to the plate. They saw O'Neill swing, saw the runners on the bases suddenly stop in their tracks and turn toward the clubhouse. O'Neill had struck out.

The game was over and the Yankees had won. The crisis had been passed. They rushed on to win the pennant and move into the World Series with the Giants. But Ruppert kept the brewery.

4

Owing to the power of Murderers' Row and the pitching of Mays and Hoyt, the Yankees were favored to win the World Series, played that year for the first time under the direction of Commissioner Landis. As in the two previous years, the decision was reached in five victories out of a possible nine games. New York, which since then has come to accept its World Series as a matter of course, was wildly excited. The Yankees had developed a tremendous following. The Giants had hit a new peak, and John McGraw was at the very top of his career.

At the end of the first two games, the series had taken on the aspect of a pushover for the Yankees. Mays, starting against Phil Douglas, shut the Giants out with five hits, winning by a score of 3 to 0. The following day Hoyt and Art Nehf engaged in a pitching duel, in which Hoyt yielded only two hits and Nehf held the Yankees to three. But the Yankees, aided by three Giant errors, won the game, again by a score of 3 to 0.

Yankee fans were jubilant. Giant fans, depressed by this sorry beginning, did not abandon hope of at least a man-sized struggle on the part of their heroes. The Yankees might win, they conceded—no team in the history of the World Series had won the first two games and then failed to win the series. But the Yankee pitchers couldn't go on shutting the Giants out like that. Sooner or later Kelly, Bancroft, Groh, Irish Meusel, Snyder, Young, and the rest of the Giants were going to start hitting the ball.

They were right. In the third game the Yankees made four runs in the third inning and for a moment seemed to have the game firmly in their grasp. But in their half of the third, the Giants fell upon Shawkey, drove him from the box, and scored four runs. In the seventh, they mauled

Quinn, Collins, and Rogers for eight runs. Each side scored a run in the eighth. Fred Toney had been hammered out in the Yankees' third-inning attack, but Jess Barnes had held the Yanks off except for that one run in the eighth. The final score was 13 to 5.

The Giants won the fourth game, 4 to 2, as Douglas took a decision over Mays, and now the series was even. The Yankees went to the front again in the fifth game, Hoyt beating Nehf again, this time by a score of 3 to 1; but in that game Ruth was injured and had to withdraw, making his only subsequent appearance as a pinch hitter in the final game. But by that time the Babe was too late, for the Giants swept through the sixth, seventh, and eighth games, beating Harper in the sixth game and Mays again in the seventh. The last game found Hoyt and Nehf tangling on the mound again, and Nehf won, 1 to 0.

"The long series beat us," Huggins said. "The strain was too much for our fellows in the last three games."

The Yankees had lost the series, but they had taken a tremendous step forward. They had won the pennant and established themselves as a major power in the American League. Moreover, the players' expectations concerning the crowds had been fulfilled. Old records had been shattered, as 269,977 persons had paid $900,233 to see the games. Each Giant player got a winner's share of $5,265. Each Yankee's gloom was lightened by a check for $3,510.

The disposition to accept the defeat philosophically, marked in most of the fans and some of the players, was not in evidence in the Yankee office. There it was regarded by Ruppert, Huston, Barrow, and Huggins as a sorry and humiliating blow. It had emphasized, for one thing, weaknesses at third base, in center field, and in the pitcher's box. These weaknesses must be corrected.

Peckinpaugh, still rather generally looked upon as one

of the game's ablest short stops, had lost caste completely with Huggins, who was determined that, in making changes in his team, he would make one at short stop, too. So Peck went to Boston in a deal by which the Yankees obtained Everett Scott, Joe Bush, and Sam Jones. Scott was rated as the best short stop in the American League, rivaled only by Dave Bancroft and Rabbit Maranville in the National. Bush and Jones were capable right-handed pitchers. The problems at third base, where no adequate substitute for Baker had been found, and in center field, where Miller had faded after a robust beginning, remained. A solution for them was to elude Huggins until another season was under way.

There were two other developments of that winter affecting the Yankees. One was a ruling by Commissioner Landis that Ruth, Meusel, and Hofmann, having defied him by making a barn-storming tour at the end of the World Series, would be ineligible until May 1 of 1922, although they were to be permitted to train with the team. Another—and happier—one was an agreement on the part of Ruppert and Huston, diplomatically engineered by Barrow, not to visit the clubhouse after lost games to ask Huggins about his moves.

VI · 1922: A Turbulent Year

⊗

F

1

OR THE 1922 season the training site had been shifted from Shreveport to New Orleans where the Yankees could draw on a larger and more baseball-minded population in their exhibition games.

The Yankee players were ready to spread themselves properly now. They had missed the championship of the world, but at least they were champions of the American League and they had very definite ideas as to how champions should live and enjoy themselves. And where, in all the land, could they have given freer rein to these ideas than in the hospitable atmosphere of "the City That Care Forgot?"

Huggins cut the training routine from two workouts a day to one. This new program fit snugly into the one which the players had outlined for themselves, because it gave them more time for enjoyment. There was much to be done in the late afternoons, they discovered, and more in the evenings. They were to be seen at cocktail parties, in Antoine's and the other famous restaurants, in the late night spots. Their favorite rendezvous was the Little Club, happily situated just across the street from the Roosevelt Hotel, where they made their headquarters.

In writing their stories, the newspapermen accompanying the team ignored the nocturnal adventures of the athletes as long as they could; but, since everybody in New Orleans knew about them, it was inevitable that, sooner or later, one

73

of the writers would break into print with them in self-defense. When the story broke, under the heading: YANKEES TRAINING ON SCOTCH, it might have made amusing reading in some quarters, but it touched off a resounding blast in the clubhouse.

Huggins saw it before any of his players. When he had recovered from seeing in print what he had known for a long time, he called the players together and read it to them. Then he gave them a lecture on the impropriety—not to mention the perils—of their course and wound up by threatening to fine any player seen in the Little Club again. The players, reckoning that while they still could take some liberties with their manager, it might not be safe to disobey him too flagrantly, took him seriously. The chief sufferer was, of course, the proprietor of the Little Club.

2

That rollicking training trip was a fitting prelude to the most turbulent year the club ever had known. It was a year marked by quarrels, fist fights, mob scenes, a tilt with Ban Johnson, a brush with Commissioner Landis, another pennant, and, most important of all, the virtual eviction of the Yankees from the Polo Grounds and the beginning of the construction of the Stadium.

With Ruth and Meusel missing from the outfield through the first six weeks of the season, the Yankees lacked much of their accustomed power; but the purchase of Whitey Witt from the Athletics on April 17 tightened the outer defenses, and the addition of Sam Jones and Joe Bush to the pitching staff was a tremendous help, so that the team got off to a good start and was in first place when the culprits returned to the line-up on May 20.

That was a great day at the Polo Grounds, a sort of second

opening day. But the Browns, opposing the Yankees, spoiled the show. Neither Ruth nor Meusel got a base hit; and the Browns, trailing 2 to 1 going into the ninth inning, suddenly fell on Jones and, with the aid of some loose fielding by the Yankees, made seven runs.

However, all that mattered was that Ruth and Meusel were back. Now the Yankees were themselves again. So, very definitely, was the Babe. Five days later he climbed into the stand back of the dugout to take a punch at a fan who had been hurling insults at him. The fan immediately took out for the rear of the stand, and the Babe had to be restrained by ushers, special policemen, and players from chasing him. Ejected from the game by Umpire Tommy Connolly, he was fined $200 by Johnson, who also directed the club to relieve him of his duties as team captain. Since no one, including the Babe, ever had discovered what those duties were, the big guy wasn't at all disturbed about being reduced to the ranks.

Before the month was out, Charles A. Stoneham, owner of the Giants, notified Ruppert and Huston that he wanted the Polo Grounds for his team alone, and that he would be pleased if they would make plans to build a ball park of their own as quickly as possible. Although Stoneham was at pains to point out that, in separate parks, the clubs would be in a position to accept more Sunday dates, to the greater profit of each, the move generally was accepted as a sign that relations between the clubs, for so long very cordial indeed, had been strained by the growing strength and popularity of the Yankees.

The peremptory wording of Stoneham's letter, copies of which were released to the newspapers as soon as the original had been received at the office of the Yankees, roused the Colonels' tempers. For a long time, as a matter of fact, they had considered having a park of their own and had been urged toward that end by Johnson and some of the other club owners. As far back as 1920 they had taken an option on property at 161st Street and River Avenue in the Bronx, just across the Harlem River from the Polo Grounds.

Now, determined to have a bigger and better park than any other club in either league, they acted swiftly. They closed for the property, drew their plans and let their contracts. Within a short time construction gangs were at work with snorting steam shovels and rolling trucks. The Yankees would be in their own park with the coming of another season. This gave the Colonels an added incentive for the 1922 pennant race. They were eager to hoist on opening day in 1923 not only a pennant but the flag of the world championship in the park that already had taken shape if not in actuality at least in their vision.

Meanwhile, the Yankees continued to win—and to enjoy themselves between ball games. Stories of some of their escapades drifted back, inevitably, to the office on Forty-second Street. Ruppert, Huston, and Barrow went into a huddle; and out of that huddle came an episode as bizarre as the Yankees themselves.

On the first western trip a smiling young stranger introduced himself to Wally Schang in the lobby of the hotel in St. Louis. He had met Wally before, he said.

"Oh, sure," Wally said. "I remember you now."

It was easy, later, for the other ball players to forgive Wally. After all, ball players meet a lot of people. And when a stranger approaches one of them and says, "Remember me? I met you last year in Chicago?" the player, unless he is a clod, is likely to say, "Oh, sure. I remember you."

So that was the way it was this time. Kelly, the young fellow said his name was. He was a companionable young fellow. Schang liked him and introduced him to some of the other players. They liked him, too. They liked him even better when—it was an unseasonably hot night, even for St. Louis at that time of the year—he had a couple of cases of beer sent up to his room and packed in ice in his bathtub.

Over the beer they fell to talking of many things. Finally, with Kelly steering the conversation, they got around to horse racing.

"Like to play the horses?" he asked.

A couple of them said they did.

"See me tomorrow," he said. "I have some friends that own horses. Maybe I'll hear something."

They saw him the next day. He had heard something. They wanted to bet, and he said he would place their bets for them and took their money. Their horses won. That night they were looking for him. There was more beer, some Scotch—or rye, or whatever the boys wanted. He had the number of the best bootlegger in town. He also had money—and more tips on the horses.

By the time the series was over, he was the little pal of— well, not all the Yankees. But all the Yankees who liked to knock over a few at night and have a bet on the horses the next day.

"Why don't you come on to Chicago with us?" one of them asked.

Kelley pondered the invitation for a moment.

"All right," he said. "I haven't got anything to do for the next few days, and I don't know a nicer bunch of fellows to be with."

And so, when the Yankees boarded a train for Chicago, Kelly was with them. There also was a new baseball writer on the trip, Marshall Hunt of the *Daily News*.

"Who's that?" Kelly asked.

"A new writer," one of the players said. "Hunt, I think his name is."

Kelly arched his eyebrows.

"A writer, eh? You know what I think? I think he's a detective. Take it easy when he's around. Don't let him see you taking a drink—and don't have anything to do with him."

It was some time before Marshall discovered why the players shunned him or, when he went to one of them with a question bearing on a ball game, spoke to him gruffly or not at all.

At the ball park in Chicago, Kelly, from his seat in a box near the dugout, extended an invitation to the ball players.

"A friend of mine is throwing a party at his brewery in Joliet tonight. He wants you all to come out there. We'll have a swell time. Big steaks—and all the beer we can drink."

The invitation was accepted with alacrity. It was a great night. Big steaks, as Kelly had promised, and foaming brew in copper mugs. "Sweet Adeline" and "Old Black Joe" and "For He's a Jolly Good Fellow." When the party was at its height, a photographer appeared, one of those photographers who take pictures at banquets and produce a print in a few minutes.

"Just a minute, fellows!" Kelly cried, above the harmony. "I just want a picture of this party as a souvenir. Everybody sit down for a moment, please!"

The picture was taken. The photographer was back in a short time with the print. The players examined it with interest. There they were. Some sitting, some standing, coats and ties off, mugs held aloft, batting eyes looking four ways at once.

"Now, then," Kelly asked, "will you all autograph it for me? Each one sign his name under his picture."

They signed, naturally.

Kelly put the print away carefully.

"All right!" he yelled. "Let's get on with the party! 'Sweet Adeline, My Adeline....'"

Chicago... Detroit... Cleveland... then Washington.

One night in Washington, after another of Kelly's parties, Ruth said to Mays:

"I got a hunch there's something wrong"

"Wrong? What's wrong?"

"I think that guy Kelly is a detective," the Babe said.

Mays hooted. "You're nuts," he said.

The Babe shook his head. "Maybe. But I'll bet you a hundred bucks he's a detective."

"You're on," Mays said.

From Washington the Yankees went to Boston. Kelly had dropped out. He had to go to New York on business, he said. He'd see them when they got back to the Polo Grounds—and then, one day in Boston, Judge Landis appeared in the clubhouse. He asked Huggins to call a meeting of the players. When they had gathered, he looked at them sternly.

"I'm going to read something to you," he said.

He began to read. It was all there. A party in Kelly's room in St. Louis. Who was there and how much beer was drunk. A party here, a party there. Who drank Scotch and who drank rye. Who bet on the horses and how much he had won—or lost. The party in the brewery in Joliet. And then the picture.

Landis looked at the crimson faces of the players.

"Is there any of you who wishes to deny that this is his signature under his picture?" he asked.

There was no reply. Landis resumed reading. Detroit... Cleveland... Washington... It was all there. Every word of it. Dates, places, names, drinks, horses.

A lecture from the Judge that blistered their ears. In the course of it, the players learned that Kelly had been hired by the ball club. That when he had made his report, Ruppert and Huston had sent it on to Landis, deeming that action by the Judge would have a more salutary effect than any they might take.

When, at length, the meeting broke up, Ruth turned to Mays.

"All right, sucker," he said. "I'll take cash or a check."

Beyond a quick reformation on the part of the players, especially in regard to betting on the horses, there was only one aftermath. The late Bob Boyd, one of the baseball writers covering the Yankees at the time and closer to most of the players than any other writer, met Kelly on the street in New York one day.

"You had a lot of nerve, at that," Bob said. "If those fellows had got wise to you, you might have got a fine trimming."

Kelly laughed. "That was one of the softest touches I ever had," he said. "I'm used to working with hoodlums and gangsters. You don't think I was afraid of a lot of country boys, do you?"

On July 23 the Yankees, needing help badly at third base, with Baker now truly slowed down to a walk, reached into Boston again. This time they traded Fewster, Miller, and Johnny Mitchell, a utility infielder, for Joe Dugan, third baseman, and Elmer Smith, an outfielder.

At the time, they were engaged with the Browns in a struggle for the lead and had fallen back to second place. The deal with Boston brought about angry reverberations in St. Louis and Chicago. In St. Louis the fans howled and the Chamber of Commerce adopted a resolution bitterly denouncing the Yankees for their lack of sportsmanship in taking an unfair advantage over the Browns. In Chicago, Ban Johnson let out a terrific roar. Deals of that nature, made so late in the season, were injurious to baseball, he said. Admitting that there were no irregularities in the transfer of the players, he loudly abhorred the Yankees' attempt to buy a pennant and declared that something should be done about it. Something was done about it, but not then. The major leagues subsequently adopted a rule prohibiting the trading or purchasing of major-league players except on waivers after June 1. The Yankees, deaf to the indignation in St. Louis and the reproof by Johnson, went serenely on their way.

Serenely? Well, not quite. They now had the best third baseman in the American League and were more certain than ever that they were going to win the pennant. But serenity was not one of their virtues that year.

In St. Louis again, Wally Pipp, at first base, was having a bad time of it, and Ruth was riding him hard. There had been some angry words between them when Wally mussed up an easy play in the first inning and then, in the seventh inning, the first baseman was slow fielding a bunt and, although he got the ball, could make no play on it. When the inning was over, he still was fuming.

"If the big guy says anything to me this time, I'll let him have it," he said.

Ruth, who played left field in most of the ball parks save the Polo Grounds, was last in.

"What's the matter with you, Pipp?" he began.

He didn't get any further. Pipp punched him right on the nose. They fought and wrestled all over the dugout until the other players pried them apart.

"I'll get you in the clubhouse!" the Babe roared.

"Don't worry," Pipp said. "I'll be waiting for you."

"Shut up," Huggins said. "Both of you. Wally, it's your turn to hit."

Wally, still burning, walked up to the plate—and hit one into the right-field bleachers. Ruth, following him, hit one to the same spot. When the Yankees finally had been retired, Jimmy Austin, the Browns' veteran third-base coach, chuckled.

"You birds ought to fight every day," he said.

There was no return engagement in the clubhouse. By the time the game was over, Wally and the Babe had cooled out. The fact that the Yankees had won had something to do with it, no doubt. Anyway, they shook hands and each said he was sorry.

The following day there was another fight, this one between Aaron Ward and Braggo Bobby Roth. They threw a lot of punches, hit almost everybody in the dugout but each other, and were separated before a decision was reached. From St. Louis the team went to Detroit. There were two fights in two days. The opening day, Mays and Al Devormer traded slams. The next day, Devormer was in action again, this time with Freddy Hofmann. The chief damage in this fight was to Hofmann's shirt, which was ripped off as the players wrestled on the dugout floor.

Huggins finally put a stop to the fisticuffs.

"I'm running a ball club, not a fight club," he said. "Hereafter, if there is any fighting, you'll pay for it in fines and suspensions."

The Little Miller was slowly tightening his grip on his players. They heeded what he had to say.

It had been a long, hard race, with the lead shuttling back and forth between the Yankees and the Browns. The Browns were very strong that year, with players such as Tobin, McManus, Ellerbe, Gerber, Ken Williams, Baby Doll Jacobson, Hank Severeid, Urban Shocker, and, best of all, the great George Sisler, hitting over .400 and playing first base as no one had played it since Chase.

In mid-September the Yankees entered St. Louis for the last time. They were in front, but only by a half game; and their coming turned the town upside down. On the train out of Chicago, the players had talked the series over and, realizing the importance of it, vowed to bury their personal differences until it was over. They were a determined crew as they climbed into the cabs that were to take them to their hotel in the West End.

"What are those for?" one of the players asked a cab driver, pointing to some small brown barrels on the street corners.

"Money," the driver said. "A committee of fans is taking up a city-wide collection to buy presents for the Browns when they knock you off and clinch the pennant."

The players looked at each other grimly.

With Shawkey pitching against Shocker, the Yankees won the opening game, 2 to 1. The park was jammed, and feeling against the Yankees ran high. Witt, chasing a fly ball in deepest center field, was struck in the head and knocked unconscious by a bottle hurled out of the crowd. He was carried from the field, bleeding profusely from a two-inch cut on his forehead. With rare presence of mind, Charlie O'Leary smeared the blood across his face, making the wound—which was bad enough—seem even worse. The sight of the blood frightened, then sobered, the hysterical crowd. No more missiles were thrown.

In Chicago, Ban Johnson, fired by righteous wrath, offered a reward of a hundred dollars for anyone who could tell who threw the bottle. The reward was paid, a few days later to—believe it or not—a fan who reported that the bottle, having been tossed out of the stand, was lying on the field and that Witt stepped on it as he charged for the ball, so that it flew up and hit him.

The Browns won the second game and again were within a half game of the lead, but the Yankees hammered back to win the third and final game. The season still had nearly three weeks to run, but when the Yankees moved out of

St. Louis that night they knew the pennant was theirs. So did the Browns and the St. Louis fans. The street-corner barrels into which coins had been tossed for presents for the Browns were kicked into the gutter and the money turned over to charity.

3

In the National League the Giants, out of the lead only briefly away back in July, had won the pennant again. The Yankees swept into the second World Series on the subway, bound to take vengeance for the defeat they had suffered the year before. They were repulsed in a manner at once savage and humiliating. The series lasted only five games, and one of them was a tie, with the Giants taking the others.

Later, the Yankees were inclined to blame the catastrophe on a four-day lay-off in Boston just before the end of the season. They might have been right about that. Whatever the cause, they were helpless at the plate—and none more so than the Babe who, in seventeen times at bat, came off with only a double and a single for an average of .118.

Arthur Nehf and Bill Ryan combined to beat Bush and Hoyt in the first game. The second game, with Jess Barnes pitching against Shawkey, was tied at 3-3 at the end of the ninth inning when, to everybody's amazement, Umpire Hildebrand, working back of the plate, called a halt because of darkness.

The sun wasn't still high in the heavens, as later was alleged, but twilight had not yet descended. As the players, as bewildered as the spectators, left the field, the crowd hooted, then turned to Landis, seated in a box back of the Giants' dugout. So did reporters, who rushed from the press box, which then was on a level with the field. The Judge, plainly upset, was loyal to the traditions of the game.

"I stand behind the umpire," he said. "His judgment is final with me."

As he left the park, crossing the field to Eighth Avenue, the crowd was at his heels, yelling abuse at him, calling him a fraud, demanding its money back. That night the Judge summoned the club owners of both leagues to his hotel suite.

"There is only one thing for us to do," he said. "Every cent of the gate receipts, beyond the players' share, which is out of our control, must go to the charities of this city."

So it was. His quick action mollified the public.

After the third game, which the Giants won 3 to 0, as Jack Scott, veteran pitcher cast off by the Cincinnati Reds because he had a lame arm and picked up by John McGraw as a gamble, hurled a four-hit shutout, there was a lively scene in the Giants' clubhouse.

The players were getting out of their uniforms and taking their showers when the door opened and Ruth and Bob Meusel walked in.

"Where's Rawlings?" Ruth demanded.

"Right here," Rawlings said.

Rawlings, one of the heroes of the 1921 series but now a utility infielder, was sitting in front of his locker putting on his socks. He was a little fellow. The Babe strode over to him.

"If you ever say again what you said to me out there today," he said, "I'll beat your brains out. I don't care how small you are."

Rawlings grinned up at him. "What's the matter," he asked quietly, "can't you take it?"

"I can't take that," the Babe said.

Earl Smith, hard-boiled Giant catcher, walked over while the other players looked on in silence.

"What did he say to you, Babe?" he asked.

The Babe told him. Repeated here, it would burn a hole in the paper.

Smith shook his head. "That's nothing," he said, and walked away.

"You're not so tough," Hughie McQuillan said. "Pipp punched you in the nose and made you like it."

"Never mind that," Babe said. "I'm not talking about Pipp."

"And I hear Meusel rolled you in the dirt, too," McQuillan said.

Meusel looked uncomfortable.

"You can leave Meusel out of it," Ruth said. "And mind your own business. I'm talking to Rawlings."

Jess Barnes, fully dressed, was at his elbow.

"What are you squawking about?" he asked. "You called me plenty when I was pitching yesterday."

"That's a lie," the Babe said. "I never called you any-thing."

Barnes ripped off his coat.

"I'll show you who's lying," he said.

Ruth was out of his coat in an instant and they squared off. Just at that moment, Hughie Jennings, McGraw's first lieutenant, came in.

"Here! Here!" he said. "What's going on here?"

"Ruth is trying to get his name in the papers," Frank Frisch said. "He can't hit the size of his hat so he comes in here and puts a blast on Rawlings because he knows the reporters are in here and they'll write a story about him."

The Babe looked about him and saw a half-dozen base-ball writers among the players. He was genuinely dismayed.

"Gee, fellows," he said. "I didn't know you were here. Please don't write anything about this. Please! I'm sorry I came in."

"You should be," Jennings said sternly. "You have no

business in here. You either, Meusel. Now get out. Both of you."

The Babe put his coat on and started for the door. Meusel, obviously relieved at the turn of affairs, trailed him. At the door the Babe turned.

"I'm sorry about this," he said. "But"—he looked at Rawlings—"lay off that stuff. I don't mind being called a —— or a ——, but none of that personal stuff."

The Giants howled.

Heinie Groh, the little third baseman whom the Babe had bowled over in a desperate slide that day, was standing on a stool, watching the rumpus over the heads of the other players.

"All right, you big bum!" he said. "And remember tomorrow that we're playing baseball, not football."

So ended in a laugh a situation that might have wound up in a brawl. The newspapermen kept their promise to the Babe. Not until years later was the story ever printed.

McQuillan, off to a rocky start the next day, recovered quickly and beat Mays and Jones. In the final game, Bush was outpitched by Nehf. The series was over. Over, too, was the Colonels' dream of seeing the world championship flag flying over the Stadium in the spring of 1923.

Ruppert was fuming and Huston was bellowing. Ruppert, with the Stadium under construction, feared that the mauling suffered by the Yankees in the series and the added prestige gained by the Giants would be reflected in great patches of empty seats the following season in the Stadium. Huston hammered at a single theme: that Huggins could not control Ruth and the other players and the club never would get anywhere unless Hug was fired and a new manager engaged.

They wrangled through November about that. Finally Barrow could stand it no longer.

"I'm through," he told the partners. "You brought me in here to run this club on a businesslike basis. How can I do that with you two quarreling all the time? I've got to know who's boss around here, and I can't find out, listening to you. Get somebody else to try to straighten things out after you get through snarling them."

Huston simply glared. Ruppert obviously was shocked. He knew how much Barrow meant to the club and what a sorry blow it would be if he actually did quit.

"I'll call you tomorrow," he said.

The following day he asked Ed to meet him at his office in the brewery.

"Look, Ed," he said, when Barrow arrived, "I'm going to make a declaration to Huston. I'll buy him out—or he can take over my share. I'd like to own the club. If I get it, will you stay?"

"I will," Barrow said, without hesitation.

There is no record of the conversation when Ruppert and Huston met to discuss the matter. But apparently Huston gave a promise, for on December 12 Ruppert announced that he had agreed to purchase Huston's stock and soon would be the sole owner of the Yankees.

Barrow, in the office on Forty-second Street, heaved a sigh of relief. Huggins, at his home in Cincinnati, grinned happily as he stuffed tobacco into the bowl of the short-stemmed pipe he smoked almost continuously.

Their relief was premature. Whatever he had told Ruppert, it soon developed that Huston wasn't quite ready to quit.

VII · The Departure of Huston

1

N INETEEN TWENTY-THREE was a fateful year in Yankee history. It began quietly enough. On January 3 Barrow and Huggins negotiated still another trade with Boston, giving up Devormer for George Pipgras, a young pitcher, and Harvey Hendrick, an outfielder. Devormer and Hendrick were—and remain—negligible figures. Pipgras, young and with scant experience, needed careful training to fit him for a starting post with the Yankees, but a time came when he helped to win pennants.

The following day Huston made an announcement which disturbed Ruppert, Barrow, and Huggins. No word had been heard from him since Ruppert's statement on December 12; but now, on January 4, he declared that, after careful deliberation, he had decided not to sell his stock.

A little jittery, not knowing what to expect but inclined to be hopeful because Huston made infrequent visits to the office and seemed to have little interest in what was going on, Barrow and Huggins went ahead with their plans. On January 30 they made still another deal with Boston, giving up George Murray, a pitcher, and Camp Skinner and Norman McMillan, outfielders, for Herb Pennock.

The deal for Pennock caused no resentment in Boston and no elation in New York. Herb had shown little in Boston or, for that matter, in Philadelphia, where he had pitched before going to the Red Sox. His record in 1922 had been ten victories and seventeen defeats. His earned-run average of 4.32 was one of the poorest achieved by any of the regular pitchers.

Looking back from this distance, it is easy to see that this was one of the most profitable transactions ever engineered by the Yankees or, for that matter, any other club. Murray, Skinner, and McMillan barely were major-league ball players, and their careers on the big time were brief and undistinguished. Pennock became one of the great pitchers of all time.

On February 3 Frank Baker retired. He could be spared easily because of Dugan on third base; but his passing was a matter of regret to New York fans. The rugged farmer from Trappe, Md., had been for many years a favorite at the Polo Grounds.

The Babe, eager to get in shape quickly after a winter of ease, left for Hot Springs, there to take the baths and run over the hills before reporting at the training camp in New Orleans. On March 1 came the alarming report that he was ill, and that his temperature was climbing rapidly. Fortunately, his recovery was a matter of only a few days. Little more than a week later he checked in at the Roosevelt, looking surprisingly fit after his bout with the fever.

The training began with practically the same line-up which had stumbled through the World Series of the previous fall. The most important addition was Pennock. Now the Yankees had what the sports writers called the "Six Star Final" pitching staff—Pennock, Bush, Jones, Hoyt, Shawkey, and Mays. Ruppert was very proud of that staff. But one day, as the season wore on, he thought he detected a flaw in it.

"What's the matter with you, Hoyt?" he asked. "You win all your games by scores of 1 to 0 and 2 to 1 and 3 to 2. Pennock, Shawkey, Bush, those fellows—they win their games by

9 and 10 to 1. Why don't you win some of your games like that?"

The team rounded into shape, swung north for the opening of the season and, on April 18, the Stadium was opened with the Yankees playing the Red Sox. This was the greatest, the most magnificent ball park ever seen. The huge triple-decked grandstand towered, it seemed, almost to the sky. Wooden bleachers ranged from foul line to foul line. The exact seating capacity was not divulged, but when all who could be admitted had jammed the stands and thousands of latecomers had been turned back by the police, the attendance was announced as 74,200. Later it developed that the figures had been padded considerably, but the newspapers were correct when they said that this was the largest crowd that ever had seen a ball game. It probably numbered close to 60,000, and before that 40,000 had been tops.

It was a perfect game, from the Yankees' point of view. The pitching assignment, for sentimental reasons—backed up by the fact that he was a good pitcher and in great early-season form—went to Shawkey, the oldest member of the staff in point of service. He was opposed by Howard Ehmke. The Yankees began to hit Ehmke in the third inning. Shawkey already had scored, Witt was on third base, and Dugan on first when Ruth loomed at the plate. Ehmke, trying to work on the Babe as the Giant pitchers had in their World Series encounters with him, pitched him a slow curve ball— and the Babe hammered it into the right-field bleachers. Shawkey, who yielded only three hits, was rapped for a run in the seventh inning. The final score was 4 to 1—and Ruth had won it with his homer.

April 24 was another great day at the Stadium. Warren Harding, President of the United States, and the most enthusiastic fan ever to occupy the White House, was Ruppert's guest that day. Before the game, the players were introduced to him.

On May 2, in Washington, Everett Scott, the short stop, received a gold medal for having played in 1,000 consecutive games. The presentation was made at the home plate before the game by Secretary Denby of the Navy. A thousand consecutive games! Even the graybeards of baseball wagged their heads over that. None of the old-time players, of whose ruggedness the graybeards boasted, had ever done anything like that. It was freely predicted that, with the ball players softening up, Scott's record never would be equaled.

Three weeks later—on May 21, to be precise—another announcement came from Huston: He had sold his stock to Ruppert. The reported price was $1,500,000. From the Yankee office came a confirmation of the sale, plus the information that Huston, although no longer a stockholder, would remain as a director of the club. However, it is doubtful if he ever attended a meeting of the directors. Certainly, he never again wielded any influence, directly or otherwise, in the affairs of the club.

The Yankees were in Chicago. Ruppert sent a wire to Huggins which, he ordered, was to be read to the players.

"I now am the sole owner of the Yankees," it said. "Miller Huggins is my manager."

For the first time in their history the Yankees were owned by one man. For the first time Huggins had vested in him the authority he needed to control his players. In that direction, the Little Miller's troubles were over.

The following day, Ruth performed another of his amazing feats at bat. The Yankees and the White Sox were tied at 1-1 when they reached the end of the ninth inning. The game went into the tenth inning, the eleventh, the twelfth. Mark Roth had made arrangements to have them leave the park immediately after the game and catch a train for New

York at Englewood. Now, with the game in extra innings, he was in a sweat, fearing they would miss the train. He called the railroad, explained the situation, and received the assurance that the train would be held for him—but not for too long.

On the field, the teams had moved into the thirteenth. Mark watched feverishly from a box next to the dugout. Then the fourteenth inning came, and no score. The Yankees went to bat in the fifteenth. Dugan singled. Ruth, on his way to the plate, saw Roth.

"What's the matter with you?" he boomed. "Sick?"

"Yes," Mark said. "If you bums don't wind up this ball game in a hurry, we'll blow the train."

"Take it easy," Ruth said. "I'll get us out of here."

Mike Cvengros, a little left-hander with a tantalizing curve ball, was pitching for the Sox. Ruth hit the first ball pitched to him into the right-field stand, jogged around the bases behind Dugan, and as he returned to the dugout said to Roth:

"See you in the taxicab."

Meusel was retired, the Yankees quickly put the Sox out in their half of the inning, showered and dressed hurriedly, and raced for the train. As he was climbing aboard, the Babe said to Mark:

"Why the hell didn't you tell me about that before?"

On May 31 there was a reorganization of the club executives. Ruppert remained as president. His brother George, who before that had had no connection with the club and hadn't seemed to be especially interested in baseball, was elected vice president. Barrow, in addition to being general manager, was made secretary.

Ruppert was supremely happy in his ownership. Nothing he ever had done before had pleased him so much as the purchase of Huston's stock. One of the first things he did was to outfit the team with two additional sets of uniforms, so that the players could always have one fresh from the cleaners.

"I want the boys to look neat," he said.

Some of the boys privately scoffed at this; it was part of the tradition of the game that a ball player's uniform should look as though it had seen service. But they soon took pride in their appearance and the comments they evoked as the best-dressed team in baseball.

About that time two additions were made to the playing ranks. Both were infielders. Ernie Johnson was obtained from the White Sox, and Mike Gazella was signed right out of Lafayette College.

The Yankees rolled on, smashing enemy teams, riddling enemy pitchers, piling up big scores. Huggins, quiet, thoughtful, unobtrusive, trailed behind his players as they went from town to town, or crouched, watchful, on the dugout steps as they mauled their opponents. This was his team now, too. His grip on the players was tightening, slowly but surely. One day, when a Yankee pitcher was being shelled, he looked along the line of players in the dugout for a relief pitcher. His gaze rested on Mays for a flickering moment, then passed on. Mays, with whom he had had numerous clashes in the past, hadn't pitched for weeks.

"What's the matter with me, Hug?" Mays asked. "Why don't you send me down to warm up?"

Hug looked back at him.

"Carl," he said, "I'd forgotten you were on the ball club."

Mays was silent. He knew that he couldn't talk back to Hug with impunity, as he had before. He felt, too, that his days as a Yankee were numbered—and they were. He never pitched for them again and was sold, on waivers, to the Cincinnati Reds the following winter.

The Yankees won the pennant by seventeen games, clinching it in a game with the Browns on September 20. Eight days later the Giants also clinched the pennant for the third time in a row.

And now, in the World Series, the Yankees proceeded to take revenge for the two setbacks they had suffered at the hands of McGraw's team. The Giants won the first game, 5 to 4, with John Watson and Bill Ryan pitching against Hoyt and Bush. The decisive run was a homer by Casey Stengel in the ninth inning. The Yankees won the second, 4 to 2, behind Pennock. In the third game, Nehf pitched a shutout for the Giants, and Stengel again hit a home run, this time off Jones in the seventh inning, to win the game 1 to 0.

After that game, a press-box wag said: "Stengel has won two games, and the Yankees have won one. When are the Giants going to win one?"

They weren't going to win any—or, to be serious about it, any more. Shawkey and Pennock combined to hold the Giants in check the following day as the Yankees hammered Jack Scott out in the second inning, making six runs and then going on to win, 8 to 4. Now they really were hitting, and they ripped off an 8-to-1 triumph for Bush in the fifth game. In the sixth game, Nehf had yielded only one run and the Giants were leading, 4 to 1, going into the eighth inning; but there Nehf weakened and, suddenly growing wild, was removed. Ryan, who replaced him, gave up the hit that decided the game, a smash through the box by Meusel. The Yankees made five runs in that inning and won the game, 6 to 4.

Ruth made three home runs in the series, two in succession in the second game. He also had a triple, a double, and two singles and walked eight times for an average of .368. As usual, he had been out in front as the Yankees pounded their way to victory.

After the final game, Ruppert must have felt as though he were sitting on top of the world. His team—and his alone —playing in his ball park, were the champions! That night, beaming, he entered the press headquarters at the Commodore. Somebody thrust a drink in his hand as the newspapermen milled about him.

"Say something, Colonel!" one of them shouted.

"Well..."

The group was silent. He looked about him nervously for a moment, and then said:

"Well, in 1921 we won the pennant but we couldn't win the World Series. In 1922 we won the pennant but we couldn't win the World Series. But this year we won the pennant and the World Series. Miller Huggins is a great manager. Witt, he's a great player. Meusel, he's a great player. Dugan..."

"How about Ruth?" somebody yelled.

The Colonel beamed even more brightly than before. "Ruth is a great player, too," he said.

2

Still another event of great importance befell the Yankees in 1923. At the time no one understood its significance. In June of that year, Lou Gehrig made his first appearance at the Stadium.

Paul Krichell had seen him for the first time playing in the outfield for Columbia University in a game with Rutgers at New Brunswick and had been struck by the power of his hitting.

"I think," he told Barrow that night, "I saw another Ruth today."

Barrow laughed.

"All right," Paul said, "laugh. But unless I am seeing

things out here today, I saw another Ruth. Andy Coakley
tells me he's a pitcher, too, and I'm going to see him pitch
against Pennsylvania in a couple of days. And then I will
see if he really can hit the ball like he hit it against Rutgers."

The day Paul saw Gehrig against Pennsylvania, Lou hit a
ball out of South Field with such force that it cleared 116th
Street, the northern boundary of the field, and struck on the
steps of the library across the street. He never had seen
anyone but Ruth hit a ball like that.

"I was right!" he yelled exultantly over the telephone to
Barrow after the game. "He's another Ruth!"

He told Barrow what Lou had done.

Now Barrow was impressed. "Can you get him?" he asked.

"He and Coakley are going to be at the office in the
morning to see you," Paul said.

The next day Gehrig had a brief talk with Barrow. He
had, he admitted, played briefly as a professional with the
Hartford club of the Eastern League under the name of
Lewis while he was a freshman at Columbia, but had not
signed a contract and so was not on the reserve list of the
Hartford club. Just previous to that, he had worked out on
the Polo Grounds; but McGraw, busy with his regular players, had taken no notice of him, and the Giants had no tie
on him. Barrow offered him a Yankee contract and he
signed it, stipulating that no announcement should be made
of the signing at the time, since he wished to finish out the
college season with Columbia.

Thus it was not until the day after Columbia ended its
season and Lou reported at the Stadium that it became
known he had signed with the Yankees. It made a story in
the newspapers, of course, for Gehrig was well known locally.
He had attained a degree of fame as the Schoolboy Babe
Ruth when he was hitting home runs for the High School
of Commerce, where he prepared for Columbia. But it

wasn't much of a story. The Yankees were on their way to their third consecutive pennant. There were the Babe and Meusel and Dugan and Pennock and all the rest to write about.

But if Lou made only a slight impression on the newspapermen, he made a big one on the players. The Yankees were at batting practice when Huggins brought him out on the field. The players looked at the boy, towering above the manager.

"Who is it?" Ward asked. "Zbyszko?"

The other players laughed.

Witt had just finished a turn at the plate, and Dugan was moving up to take a swing when Huggins said:

"Wait a minute, Joe. Let this boy hit."

The boy picked up a bat—one of Ruth's, by some curious chance—and advanced to the plate. He was obviously nervous, missed the first two pitches, then bounced one weakly over second base. Then he hit one that soared into the right-field bleachers, high up, where only Ruth ever had hit the ball. The players were amazed. He hit another ball in there —another—still another. His nervousness had slipped from him now. The balls that flew from his bat crashed into the bleachers or struck the rim.

"That's enough," Huggins cried. He turned to the players. "His name's Gehrig," he said, and walked slowly behind the hulking figure of the youngster toward the dugout. The players looked after them in silence. They sensed that they had seen a great hitter in the making.

Gehrig, relieving Pipp at first base occasionally, finished up thirteen games, went to bat twenty-six times, hit .423, and then was sent out on option to Hartford for seasoning.

"Gehrig farmed out," the reporters said the next day. They added that he would return in the spring. But none of them, not being clairvoyant, could look ahead and see the brilliant career the boy was to have—nor the tragedy that would cut him down.

3

Only once before—when the Tigers had triumphed from 1907 through 1909—had an American League team won three pennants in a row. No team in either major league ever had won four in a row. But the Yankees, assembling at their training camp at New Orleans in the spring of 1924, were favored heavily to win again. Hadn't they won by seventeen games the year before? Hadn't they come from behind to beat the Giants in the World Series? They had, indeed. And wasn't this team, led by the incomparable Ruth and cleverly managed by Huggins, the best team the league had known in a very long time—barring, of course, the blackened White Sox of 1919-1920 that no one liked to mention or even remember? It was, certainly. The opposition, while not precisely feeble, scarcely seemed strong enough to haul the Yankees down. The Tigers, who had finished second in 1923, had not been strengthened, nor had the Indians, who had finished third. The Senators had finished fourth; but Donie Bush, their manager, had been fired and Clark Griffith had appointed Stanley Harris, his boyish second baseman, to succeed Bush, so Washington hardly loomed as a threat. The other clubs didn't matter.

The Yankees felt that way about it themselves. It is possible that even Huggins was a bit complacent that spring. He had won a hard fight, not only for supremacy in the league but for command of his players and recognition as a first-rate manager. Now all these things were his, and he had grouped about him that spring all the players with whose help he had achieved them, plus Earle Combs, who had hit .380 in Louisville the year before and had been the most talked-of player in the minor leagues. Of all his regulars, only Witt had shown definite signs of slowing up, but Huggins didn't have to worry about Whitey now. He had Combs, a good hitter, fast on the bases and a ball hawk on defense, for center field.

The training season was uneventful. The ball players stepped out of an evening now and then in New Orleans—as ball players always have and undoubtedly always will. But there were none of the shenanigans of past springs to plague Huggins. They knew who was boss now. Huggins watched the regulars move through their paces and was satisfied with their condition when the training season ended. He cut the squad, releasing some of the rookies outright, farming out the others. Gehrig, although marked for another season in Hartford, was brought north with the team. He had done well in Hartford the year before, hitting .304 and making twenty-four home runs. He wasn't quite ready for the big show yet, but Hug wanted him to have a little time around the Stadium before going out again.

Later, much later, Huggins said:

"The first pennant is the easiest to win, no matter how hard the struggle may seem at the time. Then it is all new to your players. Once they have been through it, some of the shine has gone off it."

That was the way it was with the Yankees in 1924. They had won the pennant three times in a row and believed so implicitly that they could do it again that they were in no great hurry to get started. They lagged through the first couple of weeks as the despised White Sox and Red Sox fought for the lead—and even as they lagged, a blow fell upon them: Combs, after playing only ten games, broke a leg. He had been hitting at a terrific clip, and he and Ruth and Meusel formed an almost perfect outfield. Now they could count on him no longer, and Witt was back in center field.

Rallying quickly from this shock, the Yankees hammered their way into the lead. Perhaps they went to the front too quickly, thus strengthening their belief that they could take command of the league almost any time they wished. At any rate, there they were—and there they stayed through eight weeks. Then Aaron Ward, at second base, was hurt. Mike McNally and Ernie Johnson, tried one after the other, were inadequate substitutes for him. The Yankees began to skid.

Behind them, the Senators were climbing fast. By the last week in June, with the Yankees still skidding, the Senators moved into first place. Harris, although totally lacking in managerial experience until that spring, was driving his players hard—and driving himself hardest of all. The Tigers leaped in to make it a three-cornered fight. By the end of July they were in first place. The Yankees, having regained the lead and lost it again, were second, and the Senators had been shoved back to third.

As August came on, so did the Yankees. Once more they were in front. They met the Senators in Washington and beat them five times in a row. That seemed to clinch it. The Tigers, dropping back to third place, had reached their true level, and held it for the balance of the year. The Yankees now had only to keep the Senators in subjection and, with the Giants winning again, there would be a fourth World Series on the subway. So certain were the Yankees that this could be managed, after the beatings they had dealt out to the Senators in their own park, that they were beginning to count their October gold.

But the Senators, with Walter Johnson hurling victory after victory and Firpo Marberry doing an amazing job as a relief pitcher when the other pitchers faltered, came on again. Storming into the Stadium in the last week of August, they took two games out of three from the Yankees and went to the front. The Yankees roared along behind them, winning eighteen out of twenty-two games in the run through the September stretch; but the Senators held to a dizzy pace, won the pennant, and then toppled the Giants in the World Series.

Ruth was a mighty figure in defeat that year. He led the league in batting, with an average of .378, and made forty-six home runs. There were times when he seemed almost to be carrying the other players on his back. But hard as he fought and valiantly as he struggled, he couldn't win the pennant single-handed. The injuries to Combs and Ward, a let-down in the pitching at times, and the recurrent feeling of false security on the part of most of the players—these were combined with the fury of the Senators to send the Yankees reeling from the peak.

VIII · With a Resounding Crash

⊖

HUGGINS WAS SO keenly aware of the part played by overconfidence in the defeat of his team in 1924 that he overlooked something even more important. Some of his key players had aged almost overnight. Neither did Barrow realize it, nor Ruppert. All three had been blinded by the rush of the Yankees through September, so well sustained that it would have overcome a less resolute crew than the Senators.

The time had come to tear the team apart and rebuild it, but no one realized it. Huggins made only two moves during the off season. He acquired Howard Shanks, an infielder, from the Red Sox and brought Urban Shocker back from St. Louis.

"Changed your mind about Shocker as a pitcher, eh?" one of the newspapermen asked him the day the deal was announced.

Huggins shook his head. "No," he said. "I didn't have to. I knew all along he was a good pitcher."

"Then why did you get rid of him in 1918?"

"Because I was foolish. I asked advice of too many people, took most of it, and learned later that some of it was bad. Remember, I was a stranger in this league. There were a lot of things I had to find out, even about my own players. So I poked around and found out as much as I could about them before the training season started. One of the things

I was told was that I would do well to get rid of Shocker as quickly as possible because he was a trouble-maker. Naturally, I had reason to believe that the fellow who told me that knew what he was talking about; and to protect myself I did as he had suggested. I later discovered that my informant had done Shocker a very grave injustice. Urban never has made trouble for anybody."

"Who told you he was a trouble-maker?"

Huggins shook his head. "I can't tell you that," he said. "It seems he simply heard it from somebody else. He still feels badly about it."

Whoever it was should have felt badly. He cost Shocker, who had his best years in St. Louis, thousands of dollars. In the first place, the pitcher would have been paid a better salary in New York than he drew in St. Louis. And, in the second place, there were those World Series checks he missed.

At any rate, those were the only notable additions made to the roster before the team went south to train for the first time at St. Petersburg, Fla. Among the younger men in the camp were three whom Huggins kept. Gehrig, back from another successful season in Hartford, where he had hit .369 and made thirty-seven home runs, was held; but Pipp still was the regular first baseman. Peewee Wanninger, up from St. Paul, was retained; but Scott remained as short stop. Benny Bengough, who had sat on the bench for two years, got more attention than usual.

There were, of course, the usual number of rookies in on trial; but most of them didn't count, then or later.

There was a feeling that, once the season began, the Yankees would deal harshly with the upstart Senators and regain their rightful place at the top of the league. This feeling was not confined to Huggins and his players. Baseball experts around the league generally believed that they would win the pennant.

Once the crash had come, it was easy to see that signs of its coming had not been lacking. The first intimation that all was not well came when the Babe was stricken with acute indigestion when the team reached Asheville, N. C., in the course of its annual exhibition tour with the Dodgers.

"The world's most important stomach ache," W. O. Mc-Geehan called it.

It was. The Babe's moans figuratively were heard around the world. He had collapsed on the platform of the railroad station and, as it was obvious that he was seriously ill, he was placed on a litter and put aboard the next train for New York. Half the correspondents accompanying the team climbed on the train after him and put off bulletins reporting his condition at every stop.

On his arrival in New York, an ambulance waited to rush him to St. Vincent's Hospital.

"RUTH GRAVELY ILL!" the headlines said.

There was the almost inevitable rumor, quickly coursing through the city, that the Babe had died shortly after reaching the hospital. Newspapers, news agencies, radio stations, and the hospital staff spent hours denying it.

There was no doubt, however, that he was a sick man. The possessor of a prodigious appetite, he had given it full swing. The immediate cause of the attack was an outlandish early-morning indulgence in hot dogs and soda pop, but behind it were weeks, even months, of free-style eating and drinking. He had absorbed enough punishment off plates and out of bottles to have killed an ordinary man. Only his tremendous vitality enabled him to survive it.

Starting the season without him, the Yankees started badly. They won the opening game, but immediately after it went into a tail spin. On the face of it, there was no cause for alarm that they were in fourth place at the end of the first week. But, unbelievable as it would have sounded if anyone had said so at the time, they were never that high again for the rest of the season.

When the Babe returned to the line-up after a couple of weeks in the hospital, he was pale, unsteady on his legs, and had so little reserve strength that several times he almost fell down. That night he returned to the hospital. He was back the next day, however, gamely trying to play, seeking, if he could, to pull the team out of the slump by hitting a few into the bleachers. But he was not himself and, even if he had been, he alone could not have done much with the team.

Huggins, watching anxiously, saw that the supposed slump went deeper than a mere temporary lapse, that some changes would have to be made. On May 6 he benched Scott and sent Wanninger in to play short stop. He didn't make the move lightly. Scott had played in 1,307 consecutive games, and the veteran's removal from the line-up meant the snapping of the longest record of its kind that baseball ever had known. But Scott had slipped so badly that, as even he realized, the change was imperative.

Curiously enough, as Scott, for the first time since June 20, 1916, sat in the dugout while a game was being played, he could have reached out and touched the man who would shatter his record. Just a few feet from him sat Gehrig.

Less than a month later, on June 1, Lou started his streak, going to bat as a pinch hitter for Wanninger. He failed to hit safely, and there was no mention of it in the stories in the papers that day or the next, except, of course, in the box score.

The following day, Pipp, who suffered recurrent headaches as a result of having been hit in the head with a pitched ball some time before, asked Huggins if he might remain out of the game. Huggins readily gave assent. As a matter of fact, Pipp hadn't been doing very well and Huggins had contemplated benching him for a week or so.

"You're playing first base today," he told Gehrig in the clubhouse a few minutes later.

Years would elapse and pennants and World Series be won, and Gehrig would become one of the great ball players of all time before he left the post he took up that afternoon. But no one could know that then. He was just another rookie going in to take the place of a faded regular as the Yankees stumbled on their uncertain way.

Huggins had to make another change. Schang had slowed down woefully back of the bat, and he wasn't hitting. Bengough was moved up to first-string catcher. And still the team stumbled, and there was trouble brewing. Huggins coaxed, threatened, cajoled. Barrow sent his scouts through the sticks looking for help. Huggins began to get rid of some of the older players. He asked for waivers on Scott, and Washington claimed him. Witt was released unconditionally. Walter Beall, a pitcher with a lot of stuff but no control, over whom Hug had worked patiently, was farmed out to Hartford. Barrow, on the advice of his scouts, bought two young infielders—Leo Durocher from Hartford and Tony Lazzeri from Salt Lake—for spring delivery.

Ruth, having started as robustly as his health would permit, had slipped. His health was better. Indeed, he was as well, or almost as well, as ever. But he had become affected by his environment. He wasn't used to playing with a team that bobbed up and down in the second division without ever seeing daylight. In his time in Boston the Red Sox had been pennant winners or stout contenders. Since his coming to New York the Yankees had won three pennants and never had been worse than third. This was something new for him. Some of his old pals had departed and others were marked, and he knew it as well as they did. There were strangers in Yankee uniforms, and the team was bewildered. His batting average dropped to .246, a new low for him.

The Babe, probably reasoning that a fellow must have fun somewhere if he couldn't have it on the ball field, extended his operations by candlelight. He never had been very careful of the training rules, but as long as he was hitting and the Yanks were rolling, Hug wisely had given him plenty of elbow room. Now the situation was different. He wasn't hitting, the team had tumbled into seventh place, and Huggins lost patience with him.

Quarrels between them became daily occurrences. They usually began with Huggins wanting to know, out loud, how anybody expected the team to get anywhere when the players didn't bother to keep in shape. Ruth, of course, knew whom he was talking about and would counter with criticisms of Huggins's changes in the line-up, choice of pitchers, and strategy in general. After a while the exchanges fitted into a regular pattern, which went something like this:

"Never mind me. How about some of these other fellows?"

"I'm talking about them, too."

"No, you ain't. You're talking about me. I could talk about you, too, if I wanted to. I been around a long time, but I never saw a club run as lousy as this one."

"If you don't like the way I'm running the club, you can pack up and go home."

"Why don't you send me home?"

"Why don't you send me home, you big stiff?"

"Why don't you send me, you shrimp?"

"Go home, if that's what you want."

"Send me. You haven't got guts enough."

It would end with Hug stalking from the room, muttering, and the Babe saying:

"Can you imagine that guy! Talking to me like that!"

It got so the other players didn't take it seriously. They heard it so often and didn't have a true understanding of the clash. Ruth felt that, as the biggest figure in baseball's playing ranks, he had a position to maintain. In a heavy-handed way, he was trying to do just that. Huggins felt that he had his position to maintain and that if the team ever were to get out of the doldrums, discipline must be restored and that the most certain way to restore it was to put pressure on the chief offender.

One day, as the argument waxed fiercer than ever, the Babe advanced, glowering, on the little manager.

"I wish you weighed fifty pounds more!" he roared.

Huggins glared up at him.

"It's a good thing for you I don't," he said.

The showdown came in St. Louis. The Babe had been out very late the night before, had slept late, and was late reaching the clubhouse. The team was at batting practice when he arrived, and the only ones in the clubhouse were Huggins and Hoyt, who was to pitch that afternoon. His coat was on his arm, and he was unbuttoning his shirt as he came in.

"Sorry, Hug," he said blithely. "I had some business to attend to."

He tossed his coat and cap into the locker and ripped off his shirt.

"Don't bother to uniform today," Huggins said. His voice was cold, his face expressionless.

The Babe wheeled on him. "What did you say?" he demanded.

"I said for you not to bother," Hug said.

The Babe looked as though he couldn't believe what he had heard. "Now what's the matter?"

"You know very well what's the matter," Hug said. "And I'll tell you something else."

He was speaking with difficulty now. His voice shook and he gripped his belt tightly.

"I'm sorry," he went on, "but this is the finish. You're fined $5,000 and suspended indefinitely."

Ruth raged at him. "You'll never get away with this! I'll never play another game of ball for you, you little ——! I'll go to New York and see Jake! You don't think he'll stand for this do you? Why . . ."

Huggins shrugged.

"Do as you please," he said, and walked from the room.

Within an hour the Babe was on his way to New York. Across the country typewriters pounded, telegraph wires hummed, presses rolled, radio stations seethed. Miller Huggins had fined Ruth $5,000 and suspended him indefinitely! It was the biggest news of the day.

Ruth, still raging in his drawing room on the train, didn't know that before Huggins had delivered the sentence he had told Barrow, over the telephone, what he was going to do and that Barrow had said:

"You're right. Something has to be done, and you'll have the support of the Colonel and myself. But on one condition."

"What's that?" Huggins had asked.

"That you don't weaken. You've got to make it stick," Barrow had said.

And Huggins had replied: "Don't worry. I won't weaken."

A crowd of reporters and cameramen met the Babe at the Grand Central. He paused long enough to pose for the cameramen as he got off the train. To the reporters he said:

"Come up to my hotel. I'll talk to you there."

A cab whisked him away. The reporters climbed into other cabs in the line and followed him. At the hotel he held court.

"I'll never play for the Yankees again as long as Huggins is the manager," he said. "He's trying to alibi himself at my expense, and I'm not going to let him get away with it. It's either me or him. If Jake still wants him to run his club, he can get somebody else to play right field."

A telephone at his elbow rang.

"Hello!" he said. "Who? Oh, yes. Tell him I'll be right down."

He reached for his cap.

"That was Jake's office," he said. "He wants to see me right away. There isn't anything else I have to say, fellows. From now on, Jake will do the talking."

He seemed pleased at the prospect.

With the reporters trailing him, he sped to the brewery. There he was ushered at once into Ruppert's dark paneled office where the Colonel and Barrow waited. The door closed behind him and the reporters made themselves comfortable in an outer room while they discussed the case and spec-ulated on the outcome of the conversation going on within. Five minutes passed . . . ten . . . fifteen. No sound came from behind the closed door. And then suddenly the door was opened by Barrow.

"Come in, gentlemen," he said.

The Colonel and the Babe sat at a desk. The Colonel's expression was grim. The Babe looked defeated.

"Ruth has changed his mind," Ruppert said. "He will continue to play for Mr. Huggins. Is that right, Ruth?"

"Yes," the Babe said.

"Ruth is sorry about the whole thing," Ruppert said. "We are all sorry. But it had to be."

"When will the Babe be allowed to play again?" one of the reporters asked.

"That's up to Huggins," Ruppert said. "Ruth will report to him at the Stadium when the team returns."

"How about the fine?"

"The fine goes. I think that is all, gentlemen."

The one-man rebellion was over. The rebel was, in a manner of speaking, in chains. Huggins's authority was stronger than ever before, and never again was it to be questioned.

The Babe accepted defeat gracefully. His attitude had been that of a spoiled boy. Now it was that of a man. With the return of the team to New York, he apologized to Huggins and promised that, in future, the little manager would not have the slightest trouble with him. Huggins immediately lifted his suspension, although he did not remit the fine. Ruth, as though trying to work it off, went on a hitting rampage so that in the remaining month of the season he raised his average from .246 to .290.

But try as hard as he would, he couldn't improve the position of the Yankees. Nor, try as hard as he would, could Huggins. He brought Mark Koenig up from St. Paul to play short stop, and Koenig was an improvement over Wanninger and the others who had sought to fill that spot; but the team tottered on, winding up in seventh place. Almost the only one who could look back with pleasure on the season was Gehrig, who had established himself as the regular first baseman, had hit .295, and made twenty-one home runs.

That winter Christy Walsh, who syndicated the Babe's ghost-written baseball articles and generally managed his affairs for him, gave a dinner for him at which James J. Walker, then the Mayor of New York, made his famous speech about the Babe's duties to the fans, including the dirty-faced little boy in the bleachers or on the sidewalk. With tears in his eyes, the contrite Babe reiterated the promise he had made to Huggins in early September, assuring those present and all those to whom he knew his words would be relayed, including the dirty-faced little boy, that he was a completely reformed character.

IX · The Upswing to Greatness

⊖

T
OO MANY who remember the 1926 season at all remember only that the Yankees barely staggered into the pennant and then lost the World Series to the St. Louis Cardinals. In their minds the revival of the Yankees' greatness, dimmed in 1924 and all but obliterated in 1925, dates not from 1926 but from 1927. Yet 1926 was a tremendously important year. Although the team missed the world championship, it did so by the narrowest of margins. Meanwhile, it had been rebuilt, had taken on a new character, and plainly was headed for the triumphs that fell to it through 1927 and 1928.

At the St. Petersburg training camp in the spring, there was at least a suggestion, so far as the onlookers were concerned, of the mild confusion that had marked the first days of Huggins's command. There were so many things to be done before a complete recovery from the débacle of 1925 could be effected, and Hug was going about them so quietly and making so many seemingly strange moves that especially the traveling correspondents, bobbing in and out of the camp, got a distorted view of what actually was going on and concluded that the Yankees were hopeless.

"The Yankees," one commentator wrote, "are a collection of individuals who are convinced that their manager is a sap."

That wasn't true, of course. The players knew what was going on, if no one else did. They realized that Huggins was compelled by circumstances to take some long chances. But they believed in him. If they hadn't, they might have cracked all around him before the season was well under way.

Hug had no worries about his outfield. He had the chastened Ruth in right field, Combs in center, and Meusel in left. Now that Ruth had completely recovered his health and been won over to Huggins, that was once more the best outfield in the league. Pennock was at the very top of his effectiveness. Some of the other pitchers had slowed down, but Hug had added two promising youngsters: Myles Thomas, a right-hander, and Garland Braxton, a southpaw. The catchers—Pat Collins and Benny Bengough—seemed capable enough.

He was chiefly concerned with the infield. That was a real danger spot. Dugan, at third base, was the only one on whom, it seemed then, he could depend absolutely. Gehrig, although a terrific hitter, still was a green hand at first base, almost as awkward as he was powerful. At short stop, Koenig had behind him only twenty-eight games as a major-league ball player. At second base was a young man who not only never had played in a major-league game but never had seen one. And yet, when the race started and the chips were down, he was the one who held the infield together and made the pennant possible.

His name Anthony Michael Lazzeri, and he came from the sandlots of San Francisco—the latest of the San Francisco Italians to come swinging out of Golden Gate Park to make his mark on the big time. He was tall, lean, square-shouldered, and, for all his comparatively slight build, exceedingly strong and durable. He had a face like those in the paintings of the Italian masters—olive-skinned, oval, with high cheekbones and smoldering eyes. He spoke seldom, and when he did his voice had an angry quality, although he was seldom angry.

"Interviewing that guy," one of the writers said, "is like trying to mine coal with a nail file and a pair of scissors."

But he was a ball player. He had never seen a major-league game, but from the day he walked into the camp he was a major-league player. Gehrig at times was uncertain on defense—although never at the bat—and Koenig, a high-strung kid, was inclined to be jittery. Between them, Lazzeri had the poise of an old stager and a wisdom that must have been born in him, since he had had so little time in which to acquire it. As a hitter he belonged with the Yankees, too. His main hitting strength lay in his forearms, developed by his work as a riveter in his father's boiler shop.

Well, there they were. A great outfield, one great pitcher, the best third baseman in the league—but apparently carrying a crushing handicap in the form of an inexperienced second-base combination. This seemed so glaring a weakness that none of the critics could overlook it, and all but one of them thought it would be fatal. Only one, Fred Lieb, thought the team could win in spite of it. He nodded when Huggins said, as the team broke camp for the journey north:

"I believe we will win the pennant. We'll either do that or fall apart. And I don't think we'll fall apart."

Lieb, alone among the writers, picked the Yankees to win.

As usual, the Yankees hooked up with the Dodgers for a series of exhibition games on the way north. The Dodgers had had a bad season in 1925, too, winding up in a tie for sixth place. They evidently hadn't recovered, and the Yankees, who were hot, won the first four games. After the fourth, played in Montgomery, Ruth said:

"If we keep on going and beat these fellows in every game, we'll win the pennant."

No one could see any connection between beating the Dodgers in the spring and combatting the Senators, the Indians, and the other American League contenders through the long summer ahead, but it seemed like a sensible notion to the Babe and he kept repeating it as the Yankees went on winning.

In Atlanta they were called upon to face Dazzy Vance, the Dodger ace, and undoubtedly a great pitcher. For some reason or other, the Yanks usually could hit Dazz in the spring; but that made not the slightest dent in his ego, and he was sure the time had arrived for him to check their string of victories. A youthful cousin of his had come in from the country to see him and, in the hotel lobby before the teams set out for the ball park, Dazz amused himself by introducing the Yankee players to his cousin and telling him what he intended to do to them.

"This is Lazzeri," he said. "I'll strike him out.... This is Combs. He'll pop up.... Meet the Babe. He'll break his back swinging at my fast one...."

And so on. The Yankees grinned. The cousin was awed at the very thought of the havoc Dazz was about to work on them.

When the game began, he was in a box seat near the Dodgers' dugout, where Dazz had planted him.

"You wait right there for me," Dazz said. "I'll pick you up after the game, and we'll go back to the hotel together."

Combs, leading off, popped out, as Dazz had promised. The cousin blinked. It was wonderful, he must have thought, to be a great pitcher like that—and to make $25,000 a year which Dazz, the most highly paid pitcher in baseball, was getting that year. Then, all of a sudden, things began to happen. Koenig doubled. Gehrig tripled. Ruth hit one over the right-field wall. Meusel tripled. Lazzeri hit one into a tree back of the left-field wall, and three little Negro boys toppled in fright from its branches.

Vance, seething, was hauled out by Wilbert Robinson. Unmindful of his cousin, he stalked out of the park, got into a cab, and was driven back to the hotel. Later, when the cousin overtook him, he had cooled off.

"Well," he asked smiling, "how did you like it?"

The boy shook his head. "Cousin Dazzy," he said, "that's the easiest way to make $25,000 I ever saw."

The teams moved on, the Yankees still winning. When they wound up the series at Ebbets Field, the Yanks had won twelve games in a row.

"Don't forget what I've been saying all along," the Babe bellowed in the clubhouse after the last game. "We'll win the pennant now, sure!"

2

With the opening of the season, the Yankees won a few, lost a few, and then won eight games in a row. By the end of April they were in first place. The Indians pursued them closely, and the Athletics, being rebuilt by Connie Mack, were not far behind, but the Yankees hung on. The weeks passed and there they were—rocking, reeling, skidding sometimes, but still in front.

Ruppert was happy again. He was in his box at the Stadium every day the team was home, usually accompanied by friends to whom he extolled the players and explained the game. One day he and his party arrived late. It was the fifth inning, and the visiting team was at bat. Apparently the Colonel had been talking about the team on the way to the park.

"There, see?" he said excitedly. "That's Gehrig now. A great boy. Some day he will be a great player. At second base, that's Lazzeri. 'Poosh 'Em Up,' we call him. Great player, great player. At short stop, there's Koenig. He's pretty good, but sometimes the ball rolls up his sleeves."

At that moment the hitter drove a sharp grounder to Koenig. As Mark tried to field the ball, it took a bad hop, skipping over his glove and spinning up his sleeve. It never had happened before, of course. The Colonel was delighted.

"See?" he exclaimed. "Up the sleeves! 'Up the Sleeves Koenig' we call him!"

His friends were impressed. The Colonel certainly knew his ball players.

Barrow held his breath, and Huggins kept his fingers crossed as the Yankees went on winning. Ruth, Gehrig, Meusel, and Lazzeri were powdering the ball. Lazzeri was superb at second base. The other players, who for so long had looked to Ruth to lead them, now were looking to this amazing busher. Around the league the other players were talking about him. The umpires, too.

"I shouldn't be saying this, being an umpire," Tommy Connolly, dean of the staff, said one night in Cleveland, "but I can't help it. That Italian is a great ball player. And he's got a surprising head on his shoulders. I never saw a young fellow like him."

"A ball players' ball player," one writer called him.

He wasn't fast, but he always seemed to be in front of the ball, and he had a strong arm and his aim was deadly. His batting average wasn't high, but he hit a long ball and he made most of his hits in the clutch. He was good all the time, but he was at his best under pressure. And when, as it frequently did, the team faltered, he was the one who pulled it together and sent it on its way again.

He was almost as big a drawing card as Ruth. Italian societies in New York, Boston, Detroit, almost wherever the Yankees played, held banquets in his honor and showered him with gifts. The first time he went to Detroit he was fêted at a huge dinner in the Book Cadillac Hotel. At the speakers' table were the Mayor, the Italian consul, and distinguished members of the faculty of Detroit University. That afternoon he had won the game with a home run over the left-field fence with two men on the bases in the tenth inning. The diners cheered every time his name was mentioned by the speakers.

Called upon to speak after the others had spent hours telling what a great man he was, he rose and said, his voice huskier than ever and his hands nervously gripping the edge of the table:

"Reverend fathers, Mr. Mayor, ladies and gentlemen. I can't make a speech. I'm only a ball player. But I promise you that out at that ball park I'll give you the best I got every day." He sat down.

The ball room rocked with cheers. Later, one of the newspapermen said:

"Tony, that was a remarkable tribute to you, that dinner."

And Tony said: "You're —— —— right."

The Yankees rumbled on. They won six games in a row, lost a couple, won twelve in a row, lost a couple, won five in a row. Pennock was the greatest left-handed pitcher in baseball. Once so badly hampered by lack of control that he had been tempted to quit, he was now almost perfect. He pitched so easily that he was deceptively fast and he had an assortment of curve balls that began with a wrinkle and ended in a jug handle. His control was so good that hitters faced him with assurance—and then popped out or struck out.

One day in Cleveland he was warming up with Bengough, and a fan seated in a field box directly in line with him called out to Benny:

"How does he get anybody out?"

Benny held the ball and turned to the fan. "What makes you ask that?"

"Why," the fan said, "he pitches so easy I think I could hit him myself."

"Come on," Benny said. "Get a bat and try it."

The fan shook his head.

"Oh, no," he said. "I'm too smart for that. But it sure looks easy."

"That's the way it looks to the hitters," Benny said. "But they have trouble with him, too."

Shocker, past his physical prime as a pitcher but pitching with the accumulated wisdom of his long years in the major leagues and with control that matched Pennock's, was another consistent winner.

"Pitching," Shocker said, "is this and that."

He illustrated by a wave of his hand: A few inches this way, a few inches that. Just that much off the beam where, as the ball players say, a hitter can get only a piece of the ball.

Hoyt had a lame arm part of the time, and Shawkey and Jones had lost some of their stuff. But Thomas and Braxton were useful as spot pitchers. Bengough's throwing arm had buckled and, with the catching burden resting squarely on Collins, Huggins got the veteran Hank Severeid from Washington to help out.

There were days when the team wasn't impressive. Sometimes there would be a string of those days, and around the circuit the baseball writers tried to explain the Yankees.

"They aren't a good ball club," some of them said.

But they were. Not a great club. Not yet. But a good one. And they went on winning.

Late in August, Huggins claimed Walter (Dutch) Ruether, veteran left-hander, from Washington. The Dutchman wasn't as good as he had been back in 1919, when he

HERB PENNOCK

TONY LAZZERI

LOU GEHRIG

BILL DICKEY

had helped to pitch the Cincinnati Reds to the pennant. He had been around considerably, drifting from one club to another, and the years were beginning to get him down. But when his assignments were spaced properly, he was a good man to send after a badly needed game because he was a great competitor.

As the teams rolled on to September, the Yankees' lead dwindled. The Indians, driven tirelessly by Tris Speaker, closed in on them swiftly. In mid-September they went west for the last time. They must win—or lose—the pennant on the road.

When they reached Cleveland they were four games in front, and the schedule called for them to play six games in five days. The Indians had been on a winning spree, and the town was churned up by excitement at the arrival of the Yankees. The excitement died down somewhat as the Yanks won the opening game but flared again the next day when the Indians won both games of a double-header. The Indians won the fourth game, and the fifth.

The Yankees were reeling. Headlines in the Cleveland papers screamed that they were through; the Indians would trample them in their rush to the flag. The furrows in Huggins's brow deepened. Some of the younger players were so dazed they could scarcely eat, and it is unlikely that they slept well.

"I would offer to buy their World Series shares cheap," Hoyt said, "but I am afraid some of them might take me up on it."

As is usually the case when a team is losing in a spot like that, there was some snarling among the players as their sorely tried tempers cracked. At dinner in the Hollenden Hotel after the fourth straight defeat, Mike Gazella, utility infielder who had been an all-round athlete at Lafayette, was about to sit down when one of the other players, probably

trying to get his mind off the situation, asked, inanely
enough:

"How's the old college spirit, Mike?"

Mike looked at him coldly.

"You fellows have been kidding me about the old college
spirit ever since I have been on this ball club," he said.
"If you gutless —— had a little of it you wouldn't have quit
as you did out there this afternoon."

He said it loudly enough for the players at several tables
near by to hear him. No one had anything to say in reply.

The final game was played before a crowd that packed the
ancient League Park to overflowing. Huggins called on
Ruether to pitch. The Dutchman had lost, 2 to 1, in the
first game of the double-header three days before, and he
wasn't used to pitching that often, but Huggins was desperate and he figured that Ruether was the best man he
could have in there in the crisis. He also made one change
in his line-up, sending Gazella in to play short stop in
Koenig's place.

His judgment—his hunch, if you will—was vindicated.
Gazella played a bang-up game, and the Indians were held
in check by Ruether as the Yankees hammered the ball. The
Dutchman was so tired when he reached the ninth inning
that he couldn't quite get through it, and Hug had to send
a pitcher to his rescue, although the score was 8 to 3 in his
favor. He was so tired he almost had to be trundled off the
field. But for eight innings he had been magnificent.

The Yanks, escaping from Cleveland with a lead of two
games, absorbed a couple of other shocks in Chicago, but the
fire had died out in the Indians and they were losing, too.
And then Hoyt pulled the Yanks up with a well-pitched
game, and they moved on to St. Louis.

The day they arrived, the Cardinals clinched the National
League pennant by beating the Giants in New York. It was

the first time they had ever won and the first time any St. Louis team had won since 1888, in the days of the long-defunct American Association, which had no connection with the present minor league bearing that name. That night there was a city-wide demonstration. As part of it, truck-loads of Cardinal rooters descended upon the Buckingham Hotel (now the Kingsway) in the West End where the Yankees were quartered, beating drums and yowling defiance.

The Yankees, from darkened windows, replied in kind— and the next day clinched the pennant by winning both games of a double-header with the Browns, Pennock pitching the first game and Hoyt the second. The long haul was over. They were champions once more. Ruth, hitting .372, had made forty-seven home runs. Gehrig, Lazzeri, and Koenig had been hardened in struggle. Lazzeri had capped his great first year as a major-league player by hitting eighteen home runs.

3

Outside of St. Louis, the Yankees were favored to win the World Series, but there was considerable sentiment through the country for the Cardinals. Rogers Hornsby, playing manager and one of the greatest hitters of all time, had hurled his forces to the top in his first full season as manager. Grover Cleveland Alexander—the likable, colorful Alexander the Great—obtained from Chicago when Joe McCarthy had tired of his didoes, had been of considerable help to Hornsby, who wasn't interested in the great man's private life as long as he was ready to pitch every fourth or fifth day.

It was an unforgettable series, with Ruth smashing out four home runs, Alexander rising heroically in the pinches, Tommy Thevenow, at short stop for the Cardinals, hitting .417 and a heart-tugging, breath-taking climax to the final game. It was a series in which previous records for crowds and gate receipts were broken, the largest crowd, 63,600, seeing the second game, played in New York.

The Yankees won the opening game, 2 to 1, behind the three-hit pitching of Pennock, who triumphed over Bill Sherdel and Jess Haines. Alexander won the second game for the Cardinals, 6 to 2, taking a decision over Shocker. The teams moved to St. Louis, and the Cardinals took the lead when Haines pitched a five-hit shutout as his teammates slammed Ruether, to win by a score of 4 to 0. The next day the Yankees evened the count. Ruth made three home runs, two of them in succession, as Flint Rhem was slaughtered and Hoyt breezed in, 10 to 5. Pennock came back to win the fifth game from Sherdel, 5 to 2.

The teams surged back to New York. The Yankees had to win only one more game to end the series; but Shawkey, starting at the Stadium, quickly was batted out. Shocker, who relieved him, was slugged hard in the seventh inning, and the Cardinals won, 10 to 2. Alexander, having made his second appearance and with two victories to his credit, took it for granted that he wouldn't be called upon again; and that night—it was a Saturday night—he put on a personal celebration. It ended in the early hours of Sunday morning, when some of his team mates, who admired him not only for his pitching but for his capacity for enjoying himself, saw him safely to bed.

Sunday dawned bleakly. A light rain fell through the morning. About noon a chill wind from the west swept the rain from the town, and word went out that the game would be played, although the skies over the Stadium were gray and threatening.

As the Cardinals left the clubhouse, Alexander said to Hornsby:

"I'm going down to the bull pen. If you need me, I'll be ready."

There is a myth, grown through the years, that Aleck stretched himself out on the bull pen bench and went sound asleep—but it is just that and nothing more. He was watching the game closely, had begun to warm up when he saw Haines, the starting pitcher, was in trouble and, as he had promised, was ready when Hornsby called him.

As the Yankees went to bat in the seventh inning, the score was 3 to 2 in favor of the Cardinals. In the third, the Yankee defense had cracked, and three errors behind Hoyt, plus a couple of fly balls that fell safely, had yielded three runs. In the same inning, Ruth had hit a home run, and the Yanks had scored once in the sixth. Now Pennock, hurled in as a replacement for Hoyt, was the Yankee pitcher.

Haines, who had been pitching steadily, was bothered now by a blister on the second finger of his pitching hand that marred his control. Combs, leading off in the seventh, singled and reached second on a sacrifice by Koenig. Haines walked Ruth intentionally with the tying run in scoring position, and the Babe was forced by Meusel. Gehrig walked and the bases were filled.

Hornsby held up the game, walked part way out into left center, and beckoned Alexander from the bull pen as Lazzeri advanced to the plate.

"I wanted to look at his eyes," Hornsby explained, later.

He looked and saw that Aleck's eyes were clear.

"All right," he said. "Get in there."

Aleck's first pitch to Lazzeri was outside; his next was a low fast ball that Tony took for a called strike. Aleck whipped in another fast ball, and Lazzeri drove it to left field, but it curled just inside the foul pole. It was a cruel break for Lazzeri. A yard or two the other way, and the smash would have been a home run and he would have been the hero of the series.

Now, with the count two and one, Aleck poured another

fast ball down the slot. Lazzeri swung savagely at it—and missed.

The veteran still had two innings to go to clinch the game. In the eighth, he retired the Yankees in order. Two were out in the ninth when the Babe loomed at the plate. Aleck pitched carefully to him, knowing that he could tie the score with one swipe of his bat, and wound up by walking him. Then the Babe, with Meusel, always a dangerous hitter, at bat, tried to steal second; but Bob O'Farrell nailed him with a throw to Hornsby.

The game was over. The Cardinals were champions of the world.

It was a dismal end to the rush the Yankees had launched in April. Ruppert was bitterly disappointed; Barrow was unhappy. Huggins hid his chagrin under a promise to build a better team for 1927. As the players were collecting their World Series checks a few days later, Dugan said to Hoyt:

"After the exhibition we put up in the last game, I feel as though I was picking somebody's pocket."

And yet there was balm for their wounds. The club had made money, the players had received $3,417.75 each as their share of the prize money. And, after all, they had come from seventh place at the end of the 1925 season to top the league once more, and just around the corner was another season.

X · Five-O'clock Lightning

1

THE DEFEAT in the 1926 World Series was a dark interlude between the Yankees' unexpected triumph in the pennant race that year and their rise in 1927 to a peak which many believe they never have surpassed. This, they say, was the team. Greater than any that had gone before, greater than any that has followed.

The training season was uneventful, because there was little for Huggins to do. Born of their eagerness to redeem themselves for the loss of the series, a new spirit burned brightly in the players. New bonds had been forged in the crises they had met. Huggins had no need to demand their loyalty. It was his completely.

With few changes, the make-up of the team was the same as 1926: Ruth, Combs and Meusel in the outfield; Gehrig, Lazzeri, Koenig, and Dugan in the infield. Johnny Grabowski, a good journeyman catcher, had been purchased from the White Sox to work with Bengough and Collins. Cedric Durst and Benny Paschal were the extra outfielders. For protection in the infield, there were Gazella, Roy Morehart, and Julian Wera. The brunt of the pitching would be borne by Hoyt, Pennock, Shocker, and Pipgras, who had been brought back from St. Paul, where he had finished his schooling for the majors. To help out there were Ruether, Thomas, Braxton, Shawkey, and Joe Giard. And to the staff had been added one of the most amazing players ever to wear a Yankee uniform.

His name was Wilcy Moore, and he was a dirt farmer from Hollis, Oklahoma. Nobody knew exactly how old he was. He said he was twenty-eight, but nobody believed him. The chances are he was at least thirty. He was big, broad-shouldered, slow-moving, good-natured, and a great favorite with the other players. For six years he had toiled in the minor leagues with no thought or hope of getting to the majors. He had good years and bad ones. When he picked up a little money, he went home and put it in the bank or bought new tools for his farm.

So far as he was concerned, the 1926 season had been just about the same as other good ones he had had. Pitching for Greenville in the South Atlantic League, he had won thirty games and lost only four. When it ended, he packed his stuff and said good-by to the other players. Good-by forever, he thought to himself, for he had about made up his mind that the time had come for him to quit trouping around the country and stay in his fields. And then, the night before he was to leave, he learned that he had been sold to the Yankees.

"I didn't know anybody from the Yankees had looked at me," he said later. "I didn't know they'd ever heard of me. And nobody in our front office ever had said anything to me about me being sold. Maybe it just happened—or maybe they were keeping it as a surprise for me. Anyway, I thought I'd come up and see what it was like up here."

His equipment for pitching in the major leagues was limited but sound. It consisted of a sinker—a low, fast ball that broke sharply downward as it reached the plate—almost flawless control, and nerves of steel—or no nerves at all. He also had, or thought he had, a curve ball, and he used to beg Huggins to let him throw it once in a while, but Hug always shook him off.

"Your curve ball," Hug said, "wouldn't go around a button on my vest."

He was used almost exclusively as a relief pitcher. By common consent of those who played with him or against him, he was the best they ever saw.

The other players, admiring him for his pitching, laughed at him as a hitter. And with reason. He had the perfect stance at the plate and the perfect swing. The only trouble was that he always swung in the same spot, no matter where the ball was, so that if he hit it, it was by accident. Ruth, after one look at him in batting practice at the training camp, bet him $300 to $100 that he wouldn't make three hits all season. He made five. When he got home he wrote the Babe a letter.

"The $300 come in handy," it said. "I used it to buy a fine pair of mules. I named one Babe and the other Ruth."

2

Once the season opened, there never was any doubt that the Yankees would win the pennant. Ruth, Meusel, Gehrig, and Lazzeri daily terrorized the opposing pitchers; and there wasn't a man in the batting order, down to the pitcher's spot, who couldn't break up a ball game by hitting one out of the park. Hoyt's arm, which had bothered him the year before, was strong again. Pennock was—well, Pennock. Shocker, with proper rest, was a hard man to beat, although by now he was pitching mostly with his head. Huggins picked assignments carefully for Pipgras, and the youngster won regularly. Braxton, Thomas, and the others filled in effectively. When any of the pitchers faltered, there was always Moore. The power of the team blinded the onlookers to the skill and smoothness of its fielding.

Enemy teams cracked and broke wide open before their

assaults. When one of them did strike back and put a Yankee pitcher to rout, Moore ambled in from the bull pen, and the struggle was over. There was an incident one night in Detroit when Mike Gazella said something that indicated how the rest of the Yankees felt about Moore. The players were watching a big fire in an office building near their hotel. Flames roared and dense black smoke poured from the stricken building as the constantly augmented ranks of firemen poured water on it from every angle. At last the flames died down and thin white smoke rose from the seared walls.

"We can go home now," Mike said. "They got Wilcy Moore in."

The race virtually was decided as early as the Fourth of July. The Senators, in a June spurt, had moved up on them, and the holiday double-header between the teams packed the Stadium. But when the games were over, the departing crowd knew that never again would the Senators be dangerous. The Senators knew it, too; for the Yankees had won the first game 12 to 1 and the second 21 to 1.

Ruth, with his genius for rising to every occasion, was having his greatest season. When he had hit fifty-nine home runs in 1921, it had seemed that no one, himself included, ever would approach that mark. Now he was slamming the ball out of every park on the circuit, and his total was mounting. Gehrig wasn't far behind him. They were the Home Run Twins. Babe and Lou. The greatest combination of power hitters the game had ever known.

The team struck so often in the late innings that Combs called this delayed attack "five-o'clock lightning." The phrase caught on, spread through the league and seeped into the consciousness of opposing pitchers. They began to dread the approach of five o'clock and the eighth inning.

Always in demand for exhibition games in the minor-league towns during the season since Ruth had been a member of the team, the Yankees were in even greater demand now, so that they scarcely had a day off. Open dates found them in St. Paul, Dayton, Buffalo, Indianapolis. Even Cincinnati and Pittsburgh, having no American League teams, booked them.

Sometimes the players grumbled about this, but actually they enjoyed it. And no one enjoyed it more than the Babe. He snarled traffic and jammed the parks wherever he went. His progress through the countryside was like that of a president or a king. Even in the smallest towns, no matter how late the hour, there would be crowds at the station hoping to catch a glimpse of him. And the Babe never failed them. He would leave his dinner or a card game, even get up out of bed, to go out on the platform and greet his admirers and shake the hands stretched up to him.

"How did you know he was coming through?" a reporter asked a grinning section hand at one crossroads village where, for some reason, the train had stopped one night.

"The station agent told us," he said. "Every station along the line knows he's coming."

One of the secrets of the Babe's greatness was that he never lost any of his enthusiasm for playing ball, and especially for hitting home runs. To him a homer was a homer, whether he hit it in a regular game, a World Series game, or an exhibition game. The crack of his bat, the sight of the ball soaring against the sky—these thrilled him as much as they did the fans.

In Indianapolis one day—this was when the ball park was down by the railroad tracks—he went to bat three times without hitting a ball out of the infield, and the overflow crowd was having a fine time razzing him. But on his fourth trip, he really got hold of one. He hit it high and far over the right-field fence where, as those in the press box on the roof of the grandstand could see, it went bouncing and rolling among the boxcars in the freight yard. The crowd howled. They had seen many a home run, but never one like that. And the Babe? He was as happy as though the world championship had hung on that drive.

"I guess I didn't show those people something!" he said, on his return to the dugout. "Make fun of me, will they?"

In Toronto—the Babe usually played first base, with Gehrig in right field in these games—a crowd of small boys piled down out of the bleachers in the eighth inning, crowded around the big guy, and refused to be driven back by the umpires or even the police. Seeing the situation was hopeless, the umpires called the game, whereupon the kids leaped on the Babe joyfully and bore him to the ground.

"I had the presence of mind," the Babe said, "to put my cap between my teeth and hold onto it like a dog. Otherwise, one of those little suckers would have stole it for a souvenir."

Once the Yankees went to Sing Sing to play the prison team. The Babe hit one over the right-field wall in batting practice, then hit one over in center, where the yard is deepest. The prisoners roared.

"Well," one of them yelled, "there's something goes out of here, anyway!" And another: "Oh, boy! I'd like to be riding on that one!"

The Babe had a great time. When a convict umpire called one of the prison players safe in a close play at the plate, he boomed:

"Robber!"

When the Yankees, clowning, permitted a prison player to steal a base, he wanted to know if there weren't any cops in the joint. Turning to the first-base bleachers, he asked what time it was, and when a half dozen inmates eagerly told him, he roared:

"What difference does it make to you guys? You ain't going any place."

The prisoners thought that was wonderful, although if someone else had said it they might have felt differently.

But those were diversions. The serious business of clinching the pennant remained—although it must be said for them that the Yankees attacked that with as much relish as they put into the fun making. The decisive game took place in Boston on Labor Day. Up to that time they had, for the most part, strictly adhered to the training rules. But that night the lid was off. All Huggins asked them to do was to show up at the Back Bay station in time to get the 1 A.M. train for New York, and they all made it.

There were some passengers on the train who will never forget that they rode with the Yankees that night. The three cars for the players were at the head end of the train, which was unusual. The players clambered aboard near the rear end and marched through. Two of the cars through which they had to pass were compartment cars, and the shoes of the occupant had been placed in front of each closed door for the porter to shine. Someone kicked one of the shoes. The others thought it was a great idea. When the Yankees had passed, there in the forward end of each car was a pile of shoes that must have taken hours to sort the next morning.

Having clinched the pennant, the Yanks kept right on hammering. They wanted to win—and did—every game they possibly could. They set an American League record which still stands by winning 110 games and losing 44. They won the pennant by seventeen games. Ruth smashed his own record for home runs by hitting sixty and had a batting average of .356. Gehrig hit .373 and made forty-seven homers. Hoyt, with twenty-two victories, was the league's leading pitcher in games won and lost. Moore, with an average of 2.28, was the best in the matter of earned runs allowed.

3

In the National League the Pittsburgh Pirates, under Donie Bush, had won the pennant after a terrific struggle with the Cardinals. This was a good team, with Clyde Barnhart and the Waner brothers, Lloyd and Paul, in the outfield, Joe Harris at first base, George Grantham at second, Glenn Wright at short stop, the great Pie Traynor at third base, Earl Smith and Johnny Gooch to divide the catching, and such pitchers as Ray Kremer, Vic Aldridge, Lee Meadows, Carmen Hill, and Johnny Miljus.

The series opened in Pittsburgh. Hotel accommodations were inadequate for the crowds that poured into the town. For a while, nobody seemed to know where the Yankees could be housed. Just in time Barrow received word that a new hotel, the Roosevelt, had been completed and would throw open its doors to the Yankees as its first guests. On the bulletin board in the clubhouse at the Stadium the day the team left New York was a notice:

"The Yankees will open the Hotel Roosevelt in Pittsburgh."

And under it a player wrote, in pencil:

"And how!"

All was confusion in the hotel when they arrived early in the morning of the day before the first game. The lobby was packed with fans eager for a close-up of Ruth, Gehrig, Lazzeri, Pennock, and the other famous players—so packed that Huggins, his short-stemmed pipe in his mouth and his dinky traveling bag in one hand—almost was trampled in the rush as the players made their way to the desk.

Arrangements had been made for the Pirates to work out about ten o'clock that morning and then withdraw, leaving the field to the Yankees. By the time the Yankees appeared, the Pirates had dressed and were in the stands. Also in the stands or hovering back of the plate were the newspapermen and photographers sent from all over the country to cover the series.

"You're starting tomorrow, Waite," Huggins said to Hoyt. "Go out there and take about ten minutes of batting practice. Just lay the ball in there."

Straight as a string, Hoyt laid the ball up to the plate. Combs, Koenig, Ruth, Gehrig, Meusel, Lazzeri, Dugan, Collins, Grabowski, walked up and hit it. Up against the stands. Into the stands. Over the fences. It was a terrifying demonstration of power hitting.

In the stands the Waner brothers, great ball players in their own right but little men, stood talking with Ken Smith, *New York Mirror* reporter, as the Yankees slugged the ball. Ruth hit one over the fence in center field, Gehrig hit one high in the seats in right field, Meusel hit one over the fence in left field. Lloyd turned to Paul.

"Jesus," he said fervently. "They're big guys!"

Paul shook his head. The Waners walked out. Most of their team mates followed them. They had seen enough. It is undoubtedly true that right there the Yankees won the series. Before a ball had been pitched in actual competition, they had convinced the Pirates that theirs was a losing cause.

The Yankees won the first game, 5 to 4, with Hoyt taking a decision over Kremer. Hoyt failed to finish the game, however. He got in trouble in the eighth inning and was hauled out, whereupon Moore stalked in from the bull pen to turn the Pirates back and sew up the game.

Pipgras hooked up with Aldridge in the second game, and the Yankees romped in, 6 to 2. There were some who thought Huggins was taking a long chance in starting Pipgras, but the youngster vindicated his manager's judgment by yielding only seven hits scattered over as many innings.

Now the series moved to New York. As the Yankees were riding down to the station that night, a newspaperman in a cab with Lazzeri and three other players said:

"If you fellows don't wind this series up in these next two games, I'll shoot you."

And Lazzeri said: "If we don't beat these bums four in a row, you can shoot me first."

The other players nodded. That's the way everybody on the ball club felt.

Huggins called on Pennock in the opening game in New York, defying the dope that no left-hander could beat the Pirates. For seven innings, pitching against Meadows, Pennock did not allow a hit and, the way he was going, it looked as though he would be the first pitcher in World Series history to hang up a no-hit game. Ironically, he was stalled by his own team mates, for in the eighth inning the Yankees, runless since the first, when they had scored twice, set upon Meadows savagely, drove him from the box, and scored six runs, one of which was a homer by Ruth. Sitting on the bench through that long half inning, Pennock cooled out. He got rid of Wright, the first man to face him in the eighth, but Traynor singled and Barnhart doubled, Traynor scoring. In the ninth Lloyd Waner singled to left. Pennock had missed a no-hit game and a shutout as well. But his three-hit performance, the score of which was 8 to 1, still stands as one of the finest ever seen in a World Series.

Later, in the clubhouse, the taciturn Meusel was moved to ask:

"Who said a left-hander couldn't beat the Pirates?"

And a reporter, to whom the question was addressed, said:

"Plenty of guys. But they meant the left-handers in the National League. They haven't any like Pennock in that league."

The outcome of the series now was assured. The Yankees not only would win but would win in four games, as they had promised themselves. They did it, too. But not without a few chills and shakes along the way. The Pirates, probably reckoning that all was lost anyway, were free of the tension which had gripped them through the three preceding games and put up a stubborn struggle against Moore, who was allowed to pitch a game of his own as a reward for his great relief work during the season. Ruth, who had driven in the Yankees' first run in the first inning, made his second homer of the series off Hill in the fifth with Combs on base. But the Pirates, who also had made a run in the first, made two in the seventh, and the game went into the last half of the ninth still tied.

Hill had been removed for a pinch hitter in the seventh, and Miljus was pitching for the Pirates. He walked Combs, leading off, and Koenig, intending only to sacrifice, beat out the bunt he had rolled toward third base. With Ruth up, Miljus let go with a wild pitch and the runners moved up. Miljus then purposely passed the Babe and the bases were filled. With Gehrig and Meusel coming up, Miljus really was in a jam; but, pitching desperately, he fanned both. There still was Lazzeri. In his eagerness to get rid of Tony, Miljus turned on too much stuff. A fast ball, sailing, whizzed over Gooch's head as the catcher tried frantically to knock it down, and Combs crossed the plate with the winning run.

Ruppert, trembling in his box next to the dugout as the struggle went on, was almost incoherent with joy as he saw Combs racing home and realized that once more his team was the best in the world. The disappointment of the previous October had been forgotten.

XI · "Break Up the Yankees!"

⊖

W ITH CONTRACT signing time in early February of 1928 came repercussions from the pennant-winning in 1927 and the smashing of the Pirates in the World Series. The players on the greatest team in baseball—well, that's what they had read in the papers almost every day, wasn't it?— wanted more money. Much more.

The contracts were mailed out and were returned unsigned. The task of satisfying the players' demands—or getting them to meet the club's terms—naturally was Barrow's. He hammered at the players through the mail and they hammered back at him. One of the first to capitulate was Gene Robertson, utility infielder. The letter accompanying his signed contract drew a chuckle from Barrow. Ed had written him that the club really couldn't afford to pay him any more than the sum offered, since operating expenses, including the cost of maintaining the Stadium, were extremely high and, in spite of the glorious season of 1927, the margin of profit had been astonishingly slim. Thus, much as he appreciated the aid Robertson had rendered, he felt that the club was in no position to do any more for him, etc., etc.

"All right," Gene wrote. "I give up. I just can't stand the thought of walking around New York next summer and having people point at me and say:

" 'There goes the guy who broke the Yankees.' "

Players living in or near New York called on Barrow to plead their cases in person. If he couldn't come to terms with them, Barrow would suggest that they go up to the brewery and see Ruppert. Some of them, thinking the Colonel might be a softer touch, went gladly. But as soon as the door closed behind them, Barrow would have Ruppert on the wire telling him not to yield or, now and then, to yield—but only a little.

One of the holdouts was Hoyt. He called on Barrow but got nowhere with him. At last Barrow said, with a shrug:

"It's Ruppert's money. Go up and see him."

The pitcher found the Colonel at his desk in the brewery, going over a sheaf of papers. At a nod from Ruppert he sat down. And then:

"What's the matter with the contract, Hoyt?"

"I'd like the amount I asked for," Waite said.

Ruppert went back to his papers. Hoyt looked around him at the dark oak paneling of the room. There seemed to be no door except the one by which he had entered, but a panel behind the desk slid back noiselessly. A secretary entered and laid some correspondence before his employer. They talked quietly, and the secretary departed as silently as he had come. Ruppert turned to Hoyt.

"We have a great team, Hoyt," he said. "Maybe you know that. You can make lots of money with this team of mine."

Hoyt nodded. He went on nodding as Ruppert enumerated the virtues of each player on the roster—with the notable exception of Hoyt. Finally:

"Now will you sign?"

"No."

Ruppert was irritated. "Well," he said, sharply, "cool off in the other room until you come to your senses."

Hoyt went into an outer office and began to examine the photographs on the wall. They consisted chiefly of buildings and other properties owned by the Colonel, who was the largest single owner of real estate in New York. A little later the Colonel came out.

"I see you like my pictures," he said, smiling for the first time.

"Yes," Hoyt said. "They're very interesting."

Ruppert beamed.

"This one is the Ruppert Building on Fifth Avenue," he said. "It cost me $4,500,000. That's my estate at Garrison. Valued at $750,000. That—over there—that's another piece I got not long ago. That's worth $1,000,000. There's a factory I just bought in Long Island City. It set me back $1,000,000. But come in."

As they sat down Ruppert shook his head.

"I can't understand what has got into you fellows," he said, peevishly. "One wants this, another wants that. There's Ruth. He wants $80,000. Dugan asks for $20,000—and he has a trick knee. You want $20,000—what do you fellows think I am—a millionaire?"

In time all the holdouts were settled. Everybody was satisfied, including the Babe, who got his $80,000. No ball player had ever received that much money before. Far from being envious of him, the other players, not only on the Yankees but all over the leagues, major and minor as well, were delighted. In the first place, he was as popular with them as he was with the kids in the bleachers—and just as much of a hero. In the second place, his salary set a standard by which their own salaries could be measured. In other words, they felt that, with the top man in their field getting a record-breaking salary, they all would be moved up in the financial scale—which was what happened.

Huggins also had a problem as the Yankees went to St. Petersburg to train—to provide an incentive for his players. Most of them were old hands at reaping the laurel. To talk to them of winning another pennant just for the sake of seeing it fly from the flagstaff at the Stadium would have been to waste his words. Nor would it do just to hold out to them the prospect of getting another World Series check. The value of money—the things it could buy, rather than its mere possession—was the theme he struck.

It worked wonderfully. He talked to them of raising their standard of living. Of making better homes for their families, of providing better schooling and other advantages for their children. He talked to them of their investments. A sound student of finance, he warned them against the increasing lure of the stock market, which seemingly everyone, in all walks of life, was playing in the spring of 1928.

"If you're in the market, get out," he dinned. "It can't last."

Most of them, fortunately, took his advice. When the crash came in the fall of 1929, very few of the players were affected, and those few but lightly.

Meanwhile, the team was moving through its training paces. There had been few changes. Wera, the young infielder, had been sent to Hollywood. Lyn Lary and Jimmy Reese, the sensational second-base combination of the Oakland club, had been purchased for $100,000, but were not to report until the following spring. There was a long-legged young catcher named Bill Dickey from Little Rock in the camp. Huggins liked him, but he wasn't quite ready for the major leagues and was tagged for shipment under option to Buffalo. There was also a young infielder named Leo Durocher, who had been with the Yankees briefly in 1925—so briefly that, with all the comings and goings of players in that dark year, no one had noticed him. Durocher had been with Atlanta and St. Paul since then. Now he was ready.

The season opened, and the Yankees started with a rush, then skidded, went out of first place by losing to the Red Sox on April 19, but quickly regained their stride and, with it, the lead.

Lazzeri had suffered a back injury and was unable to play, and Durocher was posted at second base. He was a remark· able fielder but a streaky hitter. For a week he would hit at a .300 clip. The next week he scarcely would hit a ball out of the infield. Once, when he was hitting, a reporter asked Huggins:

"If he can hit that way part of the time, why can't he do it all the time?"

"If you can tell me," Hug said, "I'll give you $50,000, because a fellow who can field like that would be worth that much more to this club if he could hit consistently. I've watched him, studied him, and talked to him. And between us we can't figure him out."

Durocher's presence in the line-up enlivened every game the Yankees played. Not yet twenty-two years old and full of zing, he was undoubtedly the freshest busher who had come up to the big leagues in a long time. He went out of his way to ride opposing players, and the more famous they were, the greater delight he took in insulting them. One object of his attentions was Ty Cobb, then with the Athletics and in the last year of his fabulous career.

Leo took a fiendish delight in riling him.

"Why don't you give yourself up?" he asked Cobb one day. "What are you waiting for them to do—cut your uniform off?"

Cobb snarled threats at him and he laughed.

"Go home, Grandpa," he said. "Get wise to yourself. If you keep on playing with us young fellows, you might get hurt."

Another time, Cobb was on first base with two out, and the next hitter singled to right center. Cobb, running as the ball was hit, was headed for third base; but as he rounded second, Durocher, standing close to the bag, gave him the hip. Ty stumbled, caught himself, kept on—and was thrown out at third base by a yard. Durocher laughed and, tossing his glove back of him, started for the dugout.

Cobb, in a rage, stopped him on the third base line.

"The next time you try that," he said, "I'll cut your legs off."

Durocher wasn't laughing now.

"You'll cut nobody's legs off," he rasped. "You've been bulldozing young ball players in this league for years, but you can't frighten me. I'll give you the hip every time you come around that bag, if I can. And if you try to cut me, I'll stick the ball down your throat."

Cobb could have killed him and looked as though he was going to try it when other players and the umpires got between the pair.

George Moriarty, who had been an umpire—and later returned to the blue uniform—was managing the Tigers that spring. Durocher deliberately picked on him, too. There seemed to be no reason for this, since Moriarty, from his place in the dugout or on the coaching line, had said nothing to him. But Moriarty had a well-earned reputation as a fighter, and it pleased Durocher to taunt him. Moriarty, who made almost two of Leo physically, was in an awkward spot. He couldn't throttle his tormentor, greatly as he was tempted to do so; and Durocher, knowing this, drove him almost frantic every time the Yankees and the Tigers met. It was not until Huggins called him off that he desisted.

The Yankees swept along, but the Athletics, who had been in first place for those few days in April, pounded right along behind them. Connie Mack had been rebuilding his team for years. Now he almost—but not quite—had the team he wanted. He had Cobb in right field, Speaker in center, the youthful Al Simmons in left, Eddie Collins on second base, Mickey Cochrane back of the plate, and Lefty Grove, with his dazzling speed, in the box. He had to make more changes, and did with the coming of another year as some of his older players faded. But the A's were a menace now.

Ruth was pounding the ball. So were Gehrig and Meusel —and Lazzeri, who had returned. But Shocker had been ailing through the spring and into the summer, and early in July he retired and went to Denver in an effort to regain his health. To replace him, Huggins brought Lefty Heimach up from St. Paul. On July 29 the Yankees had their biggest day of the year at bat, making 27 hits as they beat the Indians, 24 to 6. Two weeks later Pennock pitched a three-hit game against the Red Sox but strained his arm. When Herb was unable to take his regular turn in the box, Huggins bought Tom Zachary, veteran southpaw, from the Senators. Three days later Lazzeri was on the bench again, this time with a shoulder injury.

Still the Yanks were in front and getting a great deal of enjoyment out of life, on the field and off. As long as they were winning, there was little Huggins could say. One day in Chicago, however, he called a meeting, much to the surprise of the players, since he hadn't called a meeting in years. He looked them over coldly as they assembled. When they were all there, he told Doc Woods, the trainer, to shut the door. He paced up and down before them for a few moments, and they looked at one another, wondering when the storm was going to break and what form it would take. Then he stopped pacing and said:

"Chicago is a bad town for you fellows. Be careful." He walked out.

It was the shortest meeting on record. The players, greatly relieved, followed him out—and mauled the White Sox.

On another visit to Chicago, Hug decided that a few words of remonstrance would do Ruth no harm.

"I don't like to do it," he said to Mark Roth, "but it's for his own good. I'll talk to him before the game today."

But when he reached the clubhouse, he decided to wait until after the game. That afternoon, the Babe hit two homers, one off Red Faber, the other off Ted Lyons. That evening, after dinner, Huggins and Roth were sitting in the lobby of the hotel when an elevator door opened to reveal the Babe. He wore white pants, a brown sport jacket, a Panama hat with a brown sash band. His feet were encased in brown and white sport shoes. "Jidge," as the players called him, was stepping out.

Roth who knew that Hug hadn't spoken to the Babe at the ball park, nudged him.

"Now?" he asked, grinning.

"Shut up," Huggins said.

"Go on," Mark said. "Talk to him."

Hug got up.

"Shut up," he said, again. "Come on. Let's go to the movies."

The Yanks were still in front. Their lead had lengthened to seventeen games. And then the law of averages—and the Athletics—caught up with them. Injuries spread. Ruth had a bad leg. Combs was taped from head to foot. Pennock's pitching arm still bothered him. Lazzeri was in and out of the line-up. They began to lose, and the Athletics pressed on. The Yanks' lead dwindled at a breath-taking pace. The break the Athletics had been looking for had come. On they came, battling furiously. On September 8 they went into first place.

Then, on September 9, came the memorable double-header at the Stadium between the Yankees and the Athletics with a crowd estimated at more than 80,000 in the stands. The checks were down now. The Yankees knew that unless they won, the jig was up. Rousing themselves, they brought the A's crashing down in both games, Pipgras pitching a shutout in the first and Hoyt winning the second. A home run by Meusel with the bases filled was the decisive blow in the second game.

They were in first place again. They knew the threat of the Athletics had been smashed, but there was no celebration in the clubhouse. There would have been but, as they trooped in after the second game, yelling and laughing, they were met by Roth with the news, withheld from them during the afternoon, that Shocker had died in Denver.

Two days later, they beat the A's again, this time on a home run by Ruth. Now the pennant was within clutching distance. Still hobbling—but still game—and with eyes blazing, they stormed on. Only one of them failed to go the route. On September 27 Wilcy Moore, whose arm had been bothering him all year and who had made the weary rounds of the doctors, the bonesetters, and the muscle manipulators, asked to be retired for the year and went home to Hollis, Okla.

The pennant was clinched in Detroit on September 28. Ruth, in another great year, had made fifty-four home runs. Gehrig had led the team in batting with an average of .374. Hoyt had won twenty-three games and lost only seven. Pipgras had won twenty-four and lost thirteen. Garland Braxton led the league in the earned-run averages with a mark of only 2.52. Pennock, for all the trouble he had had, was second with 2.56 and had won seventeen games, losing six.

2

The Yankees almost literally were held together by wires, pins, string, and sticking plaster as they moved into the World Series with the Cardinals. Tony Lazzeri's right shoulder was in such shape that he suffered every time he threw a ball or swung a bat. Joe Dugan was hampered by an old knee injury. The other catchers were lame and battered, and Benny Bengough was doing all the receiving. Herb Pennock couldn't pitch at all. The Babe had a bad charlie horse and limped every time he thought of it, although when a ball game was on he didn't think of it. The busiest man on the ball club was Doc Woods, the trainer. Doc had all the regulars ready for the bell except Earle Combs. The Kentucky schoolmaster had to sit that one out, except for a single appearance as a pinch hitter, while Cedric Durst and Benny Paschal divided the assignment in center field.

The Cardinals were inclined to believe that, in their crippled state, the Yankees could not reach anything approximating their full stride. And the Cardinals were pretty good. The team, now managed by Bill McKechnie, had been made over considerably since 1926. Frank Frisch was at second base; the colorful Rabbit Maranville, who had played in his first World Series with the Braves in 1914, was back after fourteen years, still playing short stop. George Washington Harper was in the outfield with the holdovers, Taylor Douthit and Chick Hafey. Jim Bottomley was still at first base, and Tommy Thevenow was Maranville's understudy. Jimmy Wilson was the first-string catcher. Grover Cleveland Alexander, Bill Sherdel, and Jess Haines would do most of the pitching in the series.

The first game was played in New York, with Hoyt pitching against Sherdel. Curiously enough, the scoring of a run by the Yankees in the first inning was, from the Cardinals' point of view, grimly foreboding, since it was fashioned on doubles by Ruth and Gehrig, who plagued the St. Louis pitchers throughout the series. In the fourth inning, after Ruth had doubled and Gehrig had been thrown out by Sherdel, Meusel hit a home run into the right-field bleachers. Bottomley hit a home run off Hoyt in the seventh. In the eighth, successive singles by Koenig, Ruth, and Gehrig ac-

counted for the Yankees' final run. And so the game ended
with the score 4 to 1. Hoyt had yielded only three hits, and
Bottomley was the only Cardinal to get as far as second.

Pipgras, opening the second game against Alexander, got
a three-run lead to work on in the first inning, when Gehrig
hit one into the bleachers with Durst and Ruth on the bases.
But George was unsteady, and the Yankee dugout was in a
tumult when the Cardinals tied the score in the second inning. Some of the players obviously felt that Huggins should
change pitchers, but Hug was stringing with Pipgras and
his faith in the young man was vindicated. The Yanks went
ahead once more with a run in their half of the second, and
in the third hammered Alexander out and scored four runs.
They scored once again in the seventh and won the game,
9 to 3, Pipgras having got a grip on himself after the first
inning. All told, he gave up only four hits.

The teams went to St. Louis, and there Hug called on
Zachary, the ancient left-hander, to oppose Jess Haines. The
Cardinals were off to a flying start, scoring two runs in the
first inning; but in the second inning Gehrig smashed a ball
into the right-field pavilion, and in the fourth the Yankees
took the lead, Ruth smacking a single to center and Gehrig
hitting his second home run, this one within the playing field
on a drive over Douthit's head. The Cardinals tied the score
in the fifth, but in the sixth the Yankees scored three runs.
Ruth, carrying one of these runs, actually was tagged out at
the plate, but he slid high into Wilson, knocking the catcher
down so hard that the ball was dislodged from his grasp;
and so, of course, the Babe was safe. Another Yankee run in
the seventh made the final count 7 to 3.

The fourth game was the setting not only for a tremendous
show by Ruth, but also for the episode of the quick pitch,
in which the Babe was one of the principal actors.

Hoyt, starting his second game, drew Sherdel as his opponent. The Cardinals slapped Hoyt for a run in the third inning, but in the fourth Ruth hit a homer. Another Cardinal run crossed the plate in their half of the fourth, and the score stood at 2 to 1 as the Yanks went to bat in the seventh. And then came the quick pitch and one of the most bitter quarrels in World Series history.

Koenig had been retired when Ruth went to bat. Sherdel quickly blazed two strikes over on the Babe and then caught him napping. With his foot still on the rubber as the ball was returned to him by Wilson, Sherdel fired another strike right through the middle. Then the row popped.

"You can't do that!" the Babe roared.

Huggins and most of the Yankee players rushed from the dugout and swirled around Charlie Pfirman, the National League umpire back of the plate. Wilson whirled on Pfirman. Sherdel charged in to the plate with Frisch and Maranville at his heels. The Yankees were yelling that the pitch was illegal, the Cardinals that Ruth had been struck out. Pfirman, pushing the players away from him, said:

"Ruth isn't out. Sherdel will have to pitch over to him."

The Cardinals were in a frenzy. The Yankees backed off. They had gained the decision. The quarrel belonged to the Cardinals now.

"But it is legal!" McKechnie and his players screamed at Pfirman. "It is legal in the National League and this is a National League game!"

The other umpires—Cy Rigler, Brick Owens, and Bill McGowan—rushed to Pfirman and corroborated his judgment. It was, they agreed, a legal pitch in the National League but not in the American. Before the series, in conference with Judge Landis, they had agreed that it would be barred from the series. It happened, however, that they had neglected to inform either the rival managers or the pitchers.

When the row, which delayed the game for almost ten minutes, had subsided, the Babe stepped to the plate again —and hit the next pitch into the right-field stand, tying the score. Gehrig followed with an even longer smash and the Yankees were in front. The Yankees hammered on, making two more runs in the inning. Sherdel was derricked, and Alexander came in to pitch for the Cardinals. In the eighth, Durst, leading off, hit a home run. Koenig was retired, and the Babe hit his third homer of the game—in his third successive time at bat.

This brought on a demonstration seldom matched by a crowd watching its heroes hurtling to defeat. Their disappointment had been overcome by their admiration of the Big Guy, and they cheered him wildly as, grinning, he circled the bases. And then, just to make the show complete, he brought the game to a close by making a spectacular one-hand running catch of a foul fly at the end of the left-field stand and, without breaking his stride, ran to the clubhouse, still clutching the ball.

The score was 7 to 3. For the second year in succession, the Yankees had won the series in four straight games. Ruth had hit .625 and made three home runs. Gehrig had hit .545 and made four home runs. Durst, with .375, was the only other player to hit over .300, but the combination of the Babe and Lou had wrecked the Cardinal pitchers. Hoyt was the pitching star of the series with two victories.

The Yankees departed for New York almost immediately after the game. It was a wild ride, the celebration culminating in a movement, started by the Babe, to rip the shirts off all the players, club officials, and newspapermen. To the Babe fell the distinction of stripping Ruppert to the waist. The Colonel, happy, bewildered, was docile in the Babe's grasp. All he said was:

"Is this usual, Ruth?"

3

The roar of the series crowds had barely died away when the cry was heard for the first time:

"Break up the Yankees!"

It was loudest in the rival cities, of course. But it had a faint echo even in New York. The Yankees had won three pennants in a row—and then two World Series in four games each, something no other team ever had been able to do. Even when they were crippled, as they were through the last month or so, the other American League clubs were no match for them. Even without Pennock and Combs, and with Lazzeri in such shape that he shouldn't have been playing at all, they had beaten and all but demoralized the Cardinals. And, as a final touch, had cost Bill McKechnie his job.

There were many who felt that the presence of the Yankees as now constituted removed the element of doubt from the pennant race and the World Series alike. They were like men playing against boys. Agitation was begun to compel Ruppert—just how this was to be effected nobody seemed to know—to sell some of his players to the other American League clubs. A heavily scored point in the clamor was that Ruth and Gehrig should be split up. One such Titan was enough on any club. Two were too many. It was conceded that Ruppert would not sell Ruth; but he could get $150,000 or more for Gehrig.

The clamor became so insistent that Ruppert, merely impatient with it at first, felt called upon to silence it.

"I have no intention of selling Gehrig or any of my players who, in the judgment of Miller Huggins, can help the team to win another pennant, if possible, in 1929," he said. "I not only have no thought of breaking up the Yankees, but Ed Barrow, Huggins, and myself will exert our best efforts to strengthen them. I do not believe that any of the other club owners is in sympathy with this movement. If any of them is, I advise him to leave the direction of the Yankees to us and to do the best he can to build up his own club. Baseball is a sport as well as a business. In every sport the object should be to win on your own merits and not ask the other fellow to weaken himself deliberately to aid your cause."

Barrow, when asked to comment on the matter, merely pointed to Ruppert's statement. Privately he scoffed at those who would tear down the team in whose construction he had been a major factor. Huggins said simply:

"It won't be necessary to break up the Yankees. No matter what we do, the law of averages will take care of us. We can go on, trying to improve the team to the best of our ability. But the time will come when we will crash."

That December Barrow and Huggins conferred on player changes to be made. Waivers were asked on Dugan, and he was claimed by the Braves. Gazella was released to Newark. It was decided to bring Lary up from Oakland, but to leave Reese there for another year. Sammy Byrd, purchased the year before and sent on option to Albany, was recalled. Ed Wells, a left-handed pitcher who had been with the Tigers, was purchased from Birmingham. Dickey, who had rejoined the team in the last few weeks of the 1928 season, obviously was ready.

It was decided to put numbers on the players' uniforms. In St. Louis, Branch Rickey had put small numbers on the Cardinals' sleeves in 1924, but since the fans had paid little or no attention to them and none of the other clubs followed his lead, Rickey had the numbers removed two years later. Now the Yankees revived Rickey's idea and improved upon it. The numbers were to be placed on the backs of the play-ers' shirts, and large enough to be visible from any point in the park. The original set, by the way, corresponded to the batting order, so that Combs drew Number 1, Koenig Number 2, Ruth Number 3, Gehrig Number 4, etc. Once the season got under way, the numbers were so popular with the fans that the other clubs quickly adopted them.

Meanwhile, in Philadelphia, Connie Mack had reformed his ranks for a new assault on the Yankees, who had repelled him in September. He had Jimmy Foxx on first base; Max Bishop on second; Joe Boley at short stop; Jimmy Dykes on third base; Al Simmons, Mule Haas, and Bing Miller in the outfield; Mickey Cochrane back of the plate; and Lefty Grove, George Earnshaw, and Rube Walberg to carry out most of the pitching assignments. It was a young club, full of hustle and fight and zing and power. It wanted the glory and gold the Yankees had monopolized for three years. And Connie, too, was eager. He hadn't won a pennant since 1914.

4

With the opening of the season the Yankees broke fast, then lagged, then came on again. But the Athletics, after a slow start, were right with them. In the second week of May, the A's went into first place. The Yankees dropped back to third, moved up to second—and the race was on in earnest. They swept through June and into July. Ruth was hitting a terrific pace, sinking his drives deep into the stands or clearing the fences with them, staving off defeats, clinching victories, sending runners clattering over the plate ahead of him. But the A's clung to the lead.

Then the Yanks began to stagger and would have fallen except for the Babe. The left side of the infield was the main trouble spot, although not the only one. Robertson had failed to hold up at third base, and Huggins shifted Koenig to that post, sending Lary in at short stop. Lary, however, still was green, and Hug pulled him out and replaced him with Durocher. Leo's fielding was superb, but he couldn't hit. A year before, his weakness at the plate would have been no drag on the ball club; but now Meusel, in left field, was slowing down on both offense and defense, and Gehrig, after a great season in 1928, was swamped in a series of batting slumps. Hug switched Koenig back to short stop and tried Lary at third, but there was no improvement. Pennock's arm still bothered him, Hoyt was ill part of the time, and Pipgras had lost the effectiveness of the year before. Bengough, whose catching had been a feature of the World Series in 1928, could hardly throw a ball as far as second base and didn't catch a game until late in June.

But Ruth still was hammering the ball, old Tom Zachary was doing a heroic job in the box, and the decline of Bengough was more than offset by the rise of Dickey. This long-legged kid from Arkansas was terrific. As Lazzeri had been, three years before, he was a big leaguer from the time he got his first chance in the Stadium. For a kid, he had done a tremendous amount of work in the minors, having caught 101 games one year with Jackson in the Cotton States League when he was only twenty, and averaging 60 games a year in his other years. Even as a kid—he was only twenty-two now—he wasn't fast. Too much bending down and getting up back of the plate had taken the spring out of his legs, he said; but he was a fine receiver, had a wonderful arm, hit major-league pitching as though it had been made to his order, and was like an old hand under fire.

Late in July the Yanks put on a sustained drive, winning seven games in a row. They battled their way into August, and on the eleventh of that month Ruth hit the five-hundredth home run of his career, with Willis Hudlin of Cleveland pitching. Then came the downbeat. They were shut out three times in a row—on August 22, 23, and 24—by the

Browns in St. Louis, with Sam Gray, George Blaeholder, and Alvin Crowder doing the pitching.

Still in second place, but losing ground to the Athletics, they returned to the East. After a losing game one day, Huggins followed them into the clubhouse and said:

"I don't want anybody to leave. I have something to say to you."

When they had dressed, he began to talk. He talked to them for twenty minutes. He began mildly, analyzing their faults and weaknesses. He told them how he had tried, by shifting the batting order, even the line-up, to pull them out of the slump into which they had fallen. He reminded them that time was short, and if they were to overhaul the Athletics, they must start immediately. He reminded them of the things they could do with the money they would get out of another World Series.

They were looking at him, but he knew his words were making no impression. Nor his tone. So he stepped up the pace and heated the words. Solely with a view to rousing them to a fighting pitch, he began to call them names, to say things he didn't mean, to call up old incidents. They still looked at him blankly.

"All right," he said quietly. "That's all. You can go now."

Silently they walked out of the clubhouse, leaving him alone. He filled his pipe and walked up to the offices between the lower deck and the mezzanine. Ruppert and Barrow were waiting for him, as he had asked them to do. He sat down, hunched himself back in his chair, put his legs up on a desk, and puffed away at his pipe.

Ruppert broke the silence.

"What's the matter with the boys, Hug?" he asked.

"They're through, Colonel," Hug said.

"But we still have a month—"

"Forget about it," Hug said. "Start getting ready for next year. These fellows are through."

Ruppert looked at Barrow, who nodded. Still he couldn't believe it. He turned again to Huggins.

"But how do you know?" he asked.

"I just finished talking to them," Hug said. "I talked to them for twenty minutes. I talked to them calmly, I pleaded with them. Then I abused them. No matter what I said, or how I said it, it didn't make the slightest difference. I couldn't make them mad. I couldn't even make them laugh. When I realized that I might just as well have been talking to that wall over there, I quit."

"But why?" Ruppert asked. "Why should they be through?"

"I guess they're just tired, Colonel," Hug said.

He got up and walked to the door.

"I'm tired myself," he said. "I'm tired out—and I can't sleep."

5

For some years Huggins had been an almost constant sufferer from neuritis. Now his condition was aggravated by the worries piled upon him as the Yankees stumbled in their hopeless pursuit of the Athletics. There were times when his right leg shook in nervous spasms. Lack of sleep and loss of appetite had lowered his resistance.

On September 20, when he appeared at the Stadium an hour or so before game time, there was an ugly red blotch under his left eye. Fletcher looked at him with concern.

"What's the matter, Hug?" he asked.

"I must have picked up some kind of infection," he said. "I first noticed it last night. I'll have a doctor look at it after the game."

"It looks like a boil to me," Charlie O'Leary said. "You're

all run down, Hug. That's what's the matter. Why don't you go home and take it easy this afternoon and then see a doctor and have that thing taken care of?"

"I'll be all right," Hug said.

He forced a smile.

"You don't think I would trust the ball club to a couple of clowns like you, do you?"

They laughed and went out to the field, and Huggins slowly got into his uniform and followed them. But just before game time he said to Fletcher:

"Art, I'm going home. Look after the ball club."

"I think you're wise," Fletcher said. "See a doctor, get a good night's sleep, and you'll be all right tomorrow."

Huggins went slowly down the steps from the dugout to the runway under the stand.

Hoyt started the game that day. He was knocked out in the fifth inning. Impatient with himself because he had reached a point where, it almost seemed to him, he couldn't get anybody out, he stalked angrily into the clubhouse and hurled his glove into his locker. He had thought he was alone in the room, and then he heard behind him the pain-racked voice of his manager.

"What happened out there, Waite?"

Huggins was seated by a rubbing table, the rays of a heat lamp beating on the red and now swollen spot on his face. In the glare of the lamp he was ghastly, and Hoyt was shocked.

"Joe Hauser just hit one into the stand," he said.

"How did you pitch to him?"

"High and outside. The way I always pitch to him."

Hug tinkered with the lamp for a moment.

"How old are you, Waite?" he asked.

"I was thirty the other day—three days ago."

Huggins nodded slowly.

"I'm going to tell you something, Waite," he said. "I never want you to forget it. In baseball especially, you can't do after thirty what you've done before. I told Colonel Ruppert this spring that you weren't in the shape you should be in— that you'd probably have an off year. Every year from now on, if you live soft in the winter, as you have been doing, you'll find it harder to get in condition in the spring. You and Pennock are finished for the year. I've already told him. Go down to the office tomorrow and get your check. I'll see you in the spring. And keep in shape this winter."

This was the last time Huggins talked with one of his players. He left before the game was over, and his doctor diagnosed the spot on his face as a carbuncle. He ordered him at once to a hospital, but the poison spread rapidly through his weakened system, and on September 25, he died.

News of his death stunned the players. They had known, of course, that for a long time he had not been well. But even on the day he left the dugout they had no thought that he was so gravely ill. In some ways they were a pretty hard-boiled crew, those Yankees of 1929; but they cried in the clubhouse when they heard that he was gone.

His body was taken to Woodlawn Cemetery in Cincinnati for burial. Ruth, Gehrig, Lazzeri, and some of the other veterans accompanied the Little Miller on his last journey. None of them had any heart for the rest of the season. Lazzeri was so affected by Huggins's death that he did not play again that year, but went from Cincinnati to his home in San Francisco.

Thus Huggins passed as the Yankees crumbled and the Athletics rushed on to the pennant and a subsequent triumph over the Cubs in the World Series. His death, keenly felt by Ruppert, Barrow, and the players, had taken from baseball one of its greatest figures. His triumphs never had come to him easily nor, so far as the public was concerned, had he towered over his players or had the glamour of a John McGraw or a Connie Mack. But through the long, hard years he had earned the respect of his players, his rivals, and all who knew of him. He had come a long way from the days when, as a boy, he had played on the sandlots of Cincinnati—using the name of Proctor, on Sundays, by the way, so that his father, a strict observer of the Sabbath, wouldn't know where he had spent the afternoon. Now the cycle was ended, and he slept under the quiet trees not far from where he once had played.

XII · The Quest for a New Manager

R UPPERT AND BARROW faced the task of selecting a successor to Huggins.

"Well, Ed," the Colonel asked one morning, "what about it? What about a manager?"

"I called Donie Bush this morning at his home in Chicago," Barrow said. "I got his mother on the phone, and she told me he'd gone to Chicago for the day. She didn't know where I could reach him there, but she said he'd be back tonight and she'd have him call me at my home."

Bush, a great little short stop with the Tigers a few years back, had managed the Senators in 1923, had gone back to the minors, then returned to the majors in 1927 to manage the Pirates. It was his team which had won the pennant in 1927 and then been frightened and run down by the Yankees in the World Series. He had hung on through 1928 as the Pirates finished fourth, and then had driven them up to second place in 1929. But he and Barney Dreyfuss had reached a point, late in the season, where they couldn't agree on anything, especially the line-up of the team from day to day, and at the end of the campaign Donie was released. Barrow liked him because he was a dead game little guy and a hustler.

That night Bush called Ed.

"You want me for something?" he asked.

Barrow is a very direct person. He doesn't waste any time on preambles.

"Yes," he said. "I want you to manage the Yankees."

There was silence on the other end of the wire.

"Hello!" Barrow said. "Are you there, Donie?"

"Yes."

"Did you hear me?"

"Yes," Donie said. "I heard you. But I wish I'd heard you a few days ago. I signed today to manage the White Sox. I'm sorry, Ed. I'd sure like to have the job you just offered me."

"Well—I'm sorry, too. But we can't do anything about it. Good luck, Donie. I hope you beat everybody but us."

He hung up.

"Well?" the Colonel wanted to know, after Barrow had made his report the next morning. "What now?"

"Eddie Collins," Barrow said.

Collins, after a brilliant career as second baseman for the Athletics and the White Sox, had managed the Sox in 1925 and 1926, then gone back to Philadelphia to play again for Connie Mack. He lacked Bush's aggressiveness, but he was smart and he had demonstrated in Chicago that he could handle players.

"I'd like a few days to think it over," he told Barrow when Ed called him that day. "I'd like to talk to Connie about it, too."

Two days later he was on the telephone again.

"I talked to Connie," he said, "and he thinks I'm not quite ready for the job—and I'm inclined to agree with him. So my answer is no, but thanks for asking me."

The reason for his refusal offered an interesting slant on the respect in which the Yankees were held by their rivals. Collins had done a good job in Chicago, considering the mediocre material with which he had to work, and generally was rated as having been touched with genius as a player, yet so keen a judge as Mack didn't think he was capable of managing the Yankees—and Collins himself was of the same opinion.

Ruppert was beginning to worry.

"Take it easy," Barrow said. "I asked Fletcher to stay in town for a few days until I had a chance to go into this situation. I want to talk to him today. I think he might be our man."

Fletcher had learned his baseball from McGraw when he was the short stop of the Giants. He had been with the Giants from 1909 until June of 1920, when he was traded to the Phillies. He had managed the Phillies from 1923 through 1926 and then had resigned to join the Yankees as Huggins's first lieutenant. He was perhaps better qualified than either Bush or Collins to lead the Yankees. The regard in which Huggins had held him was shared by all the players. A firebrand, almost constantly embroiled with umpires and enemy players, and frequently fined and suspended in his National League days, he had calmed down on entering the American League; but he was still a positive, aggressive figure on the coaching lines. His appointment would have been popular in the dugout and the stands as well. But he, too, rejected Barrow's offer.

"No, thanks, Ed," he said. "I feel that this is the greatest honor that has ever come to me—but I can't accept it. I had too many headaches and heartaches in Philadelphia, and I never want to manage a team—even this team—again. If it's all the same to you, I'll stay on the third-base coaching line."

That afternoon, when he went back to his apartment, he said to Mrs. Fletcher:

"I just turned down the best job in baseball."

Mrs. Fletcher knew what he meant.

"I'm glad," she said.

Now Ruppert really was worried. The days were rolling by, and he still had no manager for his team. And then Barrow called him.

"I'm bringing your new manager up to see you," he said.

"Who is it?"

"Bob Shawkey," Barrow said.

"Shawkey? Good! He'll be a good manager. Why didn't we think of him before?"

"I don't know," Ed said. "I guess he'd been around so long I sort of got used to him—and looked right past him at first."

Shawkey was thirty-seven years old. Born in Brookville, Pa., and, after a brief minor league experience, purchased by the Athletics from Baltimore in 1913, he had been obtained by the Yankees on waivers in 1916 and had been with them continuously. He had been a good pitcher, but by 1929 he had slowed down considerably. He was a sound student of baseball from the time he began to play professionally. And he was a Yankee.

It seemed to be a wise choice. Perhaps it was. But Shawkey was burdened from the start with two terrific handicaps. One was that he was following Huggins; the other, that for a long time he had been, in every sense of the word, one of the group that he now commanded. It is probable that Barrow took these circumstances into consideration, yet banked on Shawkey's ability to overcome them.

At any rate, there he was, the manager of the Yankees. There had been other candidates, nominated by themselves or others, in the field. There had been reports that the appointment would go to Ruth, and his selection had been urged in some of the newspapers. But Barrow, although admiring him greatly as a ball player, never had considered him as a manager. Now it was settled, and Ruppert and Barrow looked ahead to another season.

Meanwhile, a few days before the engagement of Shawkey as pilot, Barrow had announced the sale of Bob Meusel to the Cincinnati Reds. The disposal of the veteran apparently had been decided upon before the death of Huggins, for Bob had slowed down woefully in 1929, playing in only 100 games and hitting only .261.

Meusel had been one of the greatest—and most misunderstood—players ever to wear a Yankee uniform. Joining the club in 1920, he had been a major factor in its rise to greatness. He and Ruth and Gehrig had formed the most feared three-man combination at the plate that baseball had known since Cobb, Crawford, and Veach were terrorizing enemy pitchers in Detroit. He had the most powerful throwing arm in the league, and, although not especially fast, he was a fine base runner, being the best base-stealer the Yankees had over a long stretch.

And yet, sharing the burden carried by Ruth and Gehrig, he had no share in their popularity. The fans respected him but never could warm up to him. The baseball writers, even those traveling regularly with the team, found him cold, uncommunicative, almost hostile. Recognizing him as a great competitor when the checks were down, they accused him of being lazy.

To the attitude of the fans, the writers, and even the majority of his team mates, he was completely indifferent. It didn't seem to make the slightest difference to him whether the fans cheered him or booed him—and they did both. Of the newspapermen with whom he came in contact, he cared for only one, the late Bobby Boyd, for whom he had a genuine affection and whose death shocked and saddened him. His companionship among the players was limited. Pennock, with whom he roomed, Dugan, and Hoyt were the only ones whose company he sought. He had little to say to the others at any time. In the beginning, he seemed to have

EDWARD GRANT BARROW

JOE McCARTHY

an active dislike for Huggins. Later he learned to like the little manager, but even so he was capable of passing him in the lobby of a hotel without so much as a nod to him. It was Huggins, however, who had a better understanding of him than anyone except Pennock, Dugan, and Hoyt.

"You fellows," Hug said to a group of newspapermen one night, "have the wrong slant on Bob, and so you never have given him credit for being the ball player he is. If you knew him as I do, you would know that he is a fine young man. His nature, however, is such that he simply can't warm up and be as cordial as he would like to be. Nor is he lazy on the ball field. He's just—well, he just rates himself out there. You'll never see him giving the old college try in a play he figures is hopeless. But when it counts most—when there is a catch to be made, a hit beaten out, or an extra base to be got in a pinch—there are few ball players I've ever seen on whom I'd bank so heavily."

The record was on Hug's side—and Meusel's. In ten seasons with the Yankees, he hit over .300 seven times. In one of the years that he missed, he hit .297, and in another .292. But in 1929 he was thirty-one years old and no longer the player he had been. And so he passed from the Yankees and from the American League.

Curiously enough, at the training camp in the spring of 1930, the Yankees came up with another great player who was the direct antithesis of Meusel. This was Vernon Gomez, a left-handed pitcher from Rodeo, Cal., purchased from the San Francisco club. Tall, light-haired, and blue-eyed, although the blood of Castile flowed through his veins, he became a great favorite with the other players and the writers the day he walked into St. Petersburg because of his ready smile and his nimble wit.

He wasn't quite ready that year. He was amazingly fast for one of his slight build, deriving his speed from his

tremendous nervous energy, but with only two years of professional experience behind him he still was green. Moreover, he had to be built up physically in order to withstand
the rigors of major-league pitching. So, after a brief fling, he
was sent to St. Paul for seasoning and put on a milk diet—
which he was ordered to continue through the winter—to
increase his weight. But in time he was to be a great man
for the Yankees and a delight to the newspapermen who, as
the years rolled on, chuckled as they recorded his observations on baseball and life in general or pointed to him as
the inventor of, among other things, the revolving bowl for
tired goldfish.

2

Shawkey's troubles began early. His first mistake, from the
effects of which he never recovered in full, lay in being too
lenient with the players. He outlined to them frankly the
difficulties that he faced and asked their help. Where some
of the young men were concerned, that was asking too much,
or at least the approach was wrong. They were the ones
from whom he should have asked nothing—and demanded
everything. They weren't slow to take advantage of him.
They stayed out late at night, did as they pleased, and almost
openly scoffed when he attempted to discipline them.

There were frequent rumbles in the clubhouse and the
dugout. Bob was reminded by some of the older players of
the days—and nights—when they used to knock around
together. When he replied that he didn't need any reminders
but that things were different now, they laughed at him.
Many of his friendships were broken. He knew that he
would have to make some changes.

In Philadelphia one day, Al Simmons hit a home run off
Hoyt, the drive going into the upper deck of the left-field

stand. At the end of the inning, Shawkey asked Waite what he had pitched to Simmons.

"A fast ball," Hoyt said.

"Well, don't do it again," Shawkey said. "After this, make him hit your curve ball."

"If I ever threw him my curve ball, he'd hit it over the stand," Hoyt said. "Don't tell me how to pitch to Simmons. I'll go on pitching to him my way."

"You'll pitch the way I tell you to," Shawkey said angrily, "or you won't pitch for me at all."

Hoyt was through as a Yankee, and he knew it. Two weeks later Shawkey traded him and Koenig to the Tigers for Owen Carroll, a pitcher; Harry Rice, an outfielder; and Harry Wuestling, an infielder. Waite always had said that the secret of success in pitching lay in getting a job with the Yankees, and that a Yankee pitcher never should hold out or rile the manager because if he did he might be traded and then he would have to pitch against those murderous hitters. He was to prove the soundness of these observations. The first time he pitched against the Yankees they knocked him out in the second inning.

Beset by troubles, unable to overtake the Athletics, but gamely sticking to his assignment, Shawkey pushed on, making changes in his team as he went along and bringing so many strangers into the ranks that one of the veterans was moved to remark, looking the squad over in the clubhouse one day:

"The trouble with this club is that there are too many fellows on it who aren't Yankees."

But Bob made one change that was to benefit the Yankees for years to come: he traded Cedric Durst, an outfielder, to the Red Sox for Charlie Ruffing.

Ruth had a good year in 1930, hitting .359 and making forty-nine home runs. Gehrig hit .379 and smashed out forty-one homers for one of his greatest years. Combs was tops in center field and Lazzeri at second base. Dickey, although only in his second year, already was recognized as the best catcher the Yankees had ever had, and the mark of future greatness was plain upon him. But Wuestling was not an adequate substitute for Koenig at short stop—nor was any of several other young men Shawkey tried at that position—and the infield further was weakened by the bungling of Ben Chapman, a misplaced outfielder, at third base. The pitching, good at times, was uncertain.

Shawkey, all things considered, did a good job in bringing the team home into third place behind the Athletics and the Senators. But Ruppert and Barrow had come to the conclusion that, after all, Bob was not the man they wanted. And so, as the season waned, Ed was casting about again.

His quest ended abruptly when, so to speak, a manager figuratively was tossed at him. Word came out of Chicago that Joe McCarthy, manager of the Cubs, had been released.

XIII Up From the Minor Leagues

⊖

J

OSEPH VINCENT MCCARTHY had never played a game of ball in the major leagues. He was born ir Philadelphia on April 21, 1887, attended grade schools and high school there, played ball on the sandlots, went to Niagara University at Buffalo for a while. Then he quit his books to join the Wilmington club of the Tri-State League in 1906. Square-shouldered, square-jawed, tenacious, he made the most of his limited ability as a ball player by the thoroughness with which he studied the game and the zeal with which he played it. A year and a half with Wilmington, a half-year with Franklin in the Inter-State League, and he made the jump to Toledo in the American Association.

He spent three and a half years in Toledo, playing the infield mainly, being used in the outfield now and then, and in 1911 was sold to Indianapolis. Failing to hold on there, he drifted back to Wilkes-Barre in the New York State League, where he was appointed manager in 1913. Buffalo, in the International League, bid for him in 1914, and he went there to play second base. After two years he was sold to Louisville, where he also played second base. There, too, he first began to be heard of beyond the confines of the league in which he was playing.

He was a good fielder, a quick thinker, a fair hitter, and he took himself and his job very seriously. In 1919 he became the manager of the team but continued to play second base.

His retirement came suddenly in 1920, precipitated by a play on the line between first and second. McCarthy had never pondered the question, but when it came up he had the answer for it in a split second.

The first baseman of the Louisville club was a fabulous character by the name of Jay Kirke, a big, free-swinging, hard-hitting country boy from Fleischmanns, N. Y., of whom a hundred tales are told. He could hit .300 in any league—and did in a number of them—but he was a clumsy fielder, slow of foot and sometimes a little slow on the mental up-take. One day he and Joe had an enemy runner hung up between first and second, and as the runner made a break for second, Joe yelled:

"Give me the ball! Give me the ball!"

Jay hesitated. Before he let the ball go, the runner was right in on McCarthy. The runner hit Joe in the chest and the ball hit him on the chin. The runner, of course, was safe and Joe was blazing. He called Kirke everything he could think of, and in a spot like that he was never at a loss for thoughts or words. Jay looked at him, wide-eyed, half-smiling, and then blandly said:

"I guess you're right, Joe. I guess I'm all the things you say I am. But, do you know, come to think of it, you ain't looked so good to me yourself lately."

Stunned, Joe walked back to his position—and never played another game of ball.

"I knew," he has said, in telling of the incident, "that if the time had come when I didn't look good to Jay Kirke, the only thing for me to do was to quit."

In 1921, with the Yankees winning their first pennant in New York—and New York must have seemed very far away to him at the time—he won his first pennant in Louisville. Soon baseball men around the country began to talk of him. They said that he was one of the best managers in the minor leagues, perhaps the best. His teams were well disciplined, well managed on the field and off. He had major-league ideas and, although he couldn't always put them into practice, he stuck to them. Players he sent up to the major leagues had been schooled in every department of the game. He had two fetishes. One was the double play; the other, that a pitcher must know how to field his position. He had smooth workmen at second base and short stop, and while all the pitchers who went from Louisville to the majors didn't last, there wasn't one of them who wasn't practically a fifth infielder in his handling of thrown or batted balls.

The best player he developed was Earl Combs, who was a rural school teacher when he joined the Louisville club as an outfielder from Pebworth, Ky., in 1922 and was sold to the Yankees at the close of the 1923 season. Combs, now a coach with the Yankees, tells a story that illustrates Mc-Carthy's way with a young ball player.

"The first day he put me in center field," he says, "I was so nervous I could hardly see straight—and I muffed the first ball that was hit to me. Joe never said a word to me when I went to the bench at the end of the inning, and he didn't say a word when, a couple of innings later, I booted a single into a couple of extra bases for the hitter. Finally, in the eighth inning, with the score tied and a couple of men on the bases, a hitter singled to center. As I saw the ball coming out to me, I said to myself:

" 'I will stop this ball if it kills me.'

"Well, it didn't kill me. But it went through my legs to the fence. As I went after it, I was tempted to keep right on going, climb the fence and not stop running until I got back to Pebworth. But I couldn't do that. I had to get the ball, throw it in, finish out the game—and then go in the clubhouse and get dressed. But my mind was made up. I was through. If McCarthy didn't fire me, I'd quit.

"He didn't say anything to me until I reached the clubhouse after the game. I guess he could tell how I felt by the way I looked. He came over to me and said:

"'Forget it. I told you today that you were my center fielder. You still are.'

"And then he laughed and said: 'Listen. If I can stand it, I guess you can.'

"I think I can say that from that minute on I was a ball player."

In 1925 McCarthy won the pennant again. And in 1925 William Wrigley, Jr., chewing-gum millionaire and owner of the Chicago Cubs, was looking about for a manager to succeed Walter (Rabbit) Maranville, who had the club in last place and was giving off no signs of improving his position. John B. Foster, who had been secretary of the Giants, was editor of *Spalding's Guide* and wrote for newspapers and magazines, and was a recognized authority on the game, suggested to Wrigley that he engage McCarthy. On asking other baseball men, Wrigley found that McCarthy was highly regarded by all of them.

"He's a major-league manager in a minor-league town," they said.

McCarthy considered Wrigley's offer for some time before accepting it. He had been very successful in Louisville, and he was extremely popular there. He knew that he could stay there for the rest of his life if he wanted to. Now, with the major leagues beckoning, there were a lot of things for him to consider. After all, he had never played in the major leagues, and because he had been kept busy in the minors all his life, he had seen few major-league games. Going to Chicago would be a gamble, in which he would be risking security. But one night, having thought it all out carefully, he made his decision. He would go. Sure, it was a gamble. But the stakes were high.

Under McCarthy, the Cubs finished fourth in 1926, fourth again in 1927, third in 1928. He was on solid ground now. He had been, almost from the first. In 1926, new to the major leagues, he had made a daring move. He had asked for waivers on Grover Cleveland Alexander, one of the greatest pitchers who ever lived and a hero to Chicago fans. It took courage for a manager fresh from the sticks—a manager who was constantly being reminded that he never had played in the majors—to do a thing like that. But McCarthy felt that it wouldn't be his team and that he couldn't enforce his ideas of discipline on the younger players, especially so long as Alexander, somewhat faded though still a great pitcher in spots, could go his own way, taking his fun where he found it. McCarthy knew he couldn't reform Aleck. Therefore, the only thing to do was to get rid of him. He asked for waivers on him, and the pitcher was claimed by the Cardinals. There was some commotion in Chicago over that, but it soon died down. Chicago was beginning to learn that, whatever his background, McCarthy was a major-league manager.

With the 1929 season approaching, Joe put himself squarely on the spot with Wrigley.

"Get me Rogers Hornsby," he said, "and I'll win the pennant this year."

Hornsby, a great hitter, a great second baseman, hard-boiled, blunt, had won the pennant and the world championship with the Cardinals in 1926. Sold to the Giants the following winter, he had spent one year in New York and then had been traded to the Braves, where, shortly thereafter, he had succeeded Jack Slattery as manager of a hopeless seventh-place ball club. He was a trouble maker, those who didn't know him said. They said he had fought with Sam Breadon in St. Louis and with Charles A. Stoneham in

New York. They said, which was untrue, that he had wanted John McGraw's job in New York and had undermined Slattery in Boston.

"I'll take a chance on him," McCarthy said. "He can hit, and he can play second base. I'm not afraid of him—and I know I can win with him."

He got Hornsby—and he won with him. Won the pennant and then lost to the Athletics in the World Series. Near the end of the 1930 season, he was out—and Hornsby was in. Joe blamed Hornsby and the late William C. Veeck, former baseball writer, at that time president of the Cubs, for his dismissal. He was very bitter about it then and for a long time afterward. But it was the best break he ever got, for it put him at liberty when the Yankees were seeking a manager.

2

McCarthy was no stranger to Barrow. When Joe was playing in Buffalo, Barrow was the president of the International League. As a matter of fact, Ed had once tried to interest the Yankees in Joe as a player, but without success. In the years between, he had watched Joe's progress as a manager. He knew that Joe was ready for what Fletcher had called the best job in baseball.

He called Ruppert and told him he wanted to engage McCarthy, and Ruppert told him to go ahead. The World Series between the Cardinals and the Athletics was about to open in Philadelphia, and Barrow called McCarthy and asked him to meet him and Ruppert there. The night before the first series game they were together in a hotel room. It was the first time McCarthy and Ruppert had met. Barrow did most of the talking. Here and there Ruppert asked a question. McCarthy had very little to say, but when Barrow asked him if he would take the job he said:

"With pleasure."

Few of the many newspapermen covering the series knew that Joe had been hired. Those who did were pledged to secrecy, for Barrow wanted to withhold the announcement until the series was over. As soon as the Athletics had scored their final victory, the story broke. McCarthy, appearing at the Yankees' office for the formal signing, was so nervous that when the newsreel microphone was placed before him and he was asked to say something to his new employer, he began:

"Colonel Huston, I—"

Ruppert joined in the shout of laughter from the assembled baseball writers and the newsreel man had to start all over again.

McCarthy was warmly received in New York. The writers covering the Giants knew him well; and those who, spending most of their time with the Yankees, had had very little opportunity to judge him at first hand, were willing to accept him on his record. Yet he knew that once more he was taking a gamble, with the odds, perhaps, running strong against him. He was entering a new league again—but that was only a part of it. He knew that, high as the standard was he had met in Chicago, in New York it would be even higher.

There was something else that bothered him. He had been assured by both Ruppert and Barrow that Fletcher, having declined the job the year before, hadn't changed his mind. But he wanted to hear that from Fletcher, too. He didn't know Fletcher very well. When he was managing the Cubs and Fletcher was managing the Phillies, they had yelled insults across the field at each other, but that had been the limit of the conversation between them. Fletcher had been as loyal to Shawkey as he had been to Huggins, but Joe couldn't be sure that Fletcher wouldn't regard him as an interloper. He wouldn't know until he had had a talk with him.

On his return to Buffalo, where he made, and still makes, his home, he called Art at Collinsville, Ill., and asked him to meet him in Chicago a few days later. There, any doubts about Fletcher's loyalty to him were cleared up. Moreover, they spent two or three days together, and Fletcher gave him all the information he could about the players whom he was to command and the players and managers on the other clubs in the American League.

At St. Petersburg that spring, McCarthy spent most of his time with Fletcher and Jimmy Burke, who had been his lieutenant in Chicago and whom he had taken with him to the Yankees. He had very little to say to the players, aside from telling them what he wanted them to do. Some of them didn't know quite what to make of him in the beginning. Most of them were ready to go along cheerfully—Combs, of course, was delighted to be playing under him again—but others resented his presence, believing that Ruth, having been passed over the year before, should have been appointed when Shawkey was released. If McCarthy knew this he gave no sign of it, but went quietly about his task of putting together his strongest team.

Ruppert and Barrow, as was their custom, arrived at the camp to stay for a week or so and look on as the team rounded into shape, and the baseball writers gave a dinner for the purpose of bringing them together socially with their new manager. Ruppert made a speech that night. He told of how happy he was over the signing of McCarthy. He smiled, laughed, made up jokes about himself and his team, and then, suddenly serious, he looked straight at the manager and said:

"I will stand for you finishing second this year because you are new in this league. But I warn you, McCarthy, I don't like to finish second."

And McCarthy, looking straight back at him, said:

"Neither do I, Colonel. I like to win, too."

A few days later, McCarthy gave the players their first jolt. They had just beaten the Milwaukee club by a score of 19 to 1 in their first exhibition game, and they were feeling pretty good about it. They didn't usually maul minor-league foes like that, especially so early in the spring. But they had wanted to impress McCarthy, and they believed they had done so. As they climbed, laughing and chattering, into the bus that was to take them back from Waterfront Park, where they had played the game, to their clubhouse at their own park, now called Huggins Field, Jimmy Reese, the young second baseman from the Coast League, piped:

"Well, Joe, how did you like that one?"

Joe almost snarled at him. "Against a bunch of bums like that," he said, "you should have made fifty runs."

There was an abrupt silence in the bus. The players looked at each other. What did the guy want, anyhow? Huggins hadn't been like that. Hug would let them take it easy for the first couple of weeks. Nobody liked to win any better than Hug did, once the bell had rung to send the teams on their way in the pennant race. But he would stand for a little loafing in the spring as long as he was sure the players were behaving themselves and getting into condition. But this guy—why, he wanted them to go out and murder everybody, right from the start! It was all right with some of them. Others didn't like it, especially the older players, who thought they ought to have a little more time to get ready before they were set to ripping and tearing. But he was the boss. If that was the way he wanted it, that was the way it had to be. At any rate, they had a better line on him than they had had before.

They completed their spring training and moved into New York to start the season with McCarthy's grip on them tightening. The day he first walked into the clubhouse at the Stadium, he looked about and saw a round table in one corner of the room.

"What's that?" he asked Fred Logan, the clubhouse man.

"Why," Logan said, "that's the card table."

The players, arranging their stuff in their lockers, stopped to listen.

"Take it out of here," McCarthy said.

Logan and one of the clubhouse boys began to lug the table toward the door.

"Wait a minute," McCarthy said. "Get an ax."

One of the boys went out and came back with an ax.

"Break it up."

Logan smashed it to pieces.

"Now take it out," McCarthy said.

At the door of his office, McCarthy turned, his gaze sweeping the players.

"This is a clubhouse, not a clubroom," he said. "Do your card playing in your homes. When you come in here, I want you to have your minds on baseball."

Nobody said anything.

3

The Yankees were good that year, but not quite good enough. As the basic strength of their club, they had Ruth, Gehrig, Lazzeri, Combs, Dickey, Ruffing, Gomez, Pennock, Pipgras, and Chapman, who had been moved to the outfield. Chapman was exceptionally fast, was a good fielder, and had a strong arm; but it was what the ball players call a scatter arm, meaning that on short throws especially, his aim was likely to be bad. McCarthy believed that, at longer range, his throwing would be just as strong and much more often on the beam. McCarthy juggled his pitchers, made switches in the infield and outfield, gave to the team a force and drive it had lacked the year before. Ruth made forty-nine home runs, and Gehrig forty-six. Their games were enlivened by Chapman's base stealing. Enthusiastic baseball writers, mostly young ones who never saw the Georgian at his best, called Chapman a second Ty Cobb. He wasn't quite that, nor ever would be. But he was fast and daring and spectacular. He ran, very often when there was no excuse for running. But the main thing was that he ran, and to a generation of fans who had seen little base stealing, he was a revelation as he raced and slid to a total of sixty-one stolen bases.

But the Athletics, still at the peak or close to it, won the pennant for the third time in a row, and the Yankees finished second. Ruppert and Barrow were satisfied. McCarthy had improved the team and moved it up one peg in the standing. The fans were satisfied, too. But McCarthy wasn't. He had hoped, almost wildly, to win a pennant in his first year in New York, and he had failed. He promised himself that he would not fail in 1932.

4

That promise was fulfilled. With Ruffing and Gomez leading the pitchers and Ruth hitting .341 and hammering out forty-one home runs to lead the attack, the Yankees drove the Athletics from the top of the league and swept to the pennant with 107 victories.

The way hadn't been easy for McCarthy, however. He had not settled on his regular line-up when the training season opened. The arrangement of his infield was a subject to which he had to give considerable thought and some experimentation. He started with Jack Saltzgaver, up from Newark, at second base, Lazzeri having shown signs of wear as the 1931 season waned. He posted Lary at short stop and Frankie Crosetti, purchased from San Francisco, at third base in place of Sewell. For a while that worked out all right. But when the championship season got under way, Saltzgaver didn't hit, and Crosetti plainly wasn't a third baseman. So McCarthy shifted Crosetti to the short field, restored Sewell to third base, and Lazzeri to second—and the team began to move.

Joe had no worries, of course, at first base with Gehrig, back of the plate with Dickey, nor in the outfield with Ruth, Combs, and Chapman. In the box, his main strength lay in Ruffing, Gomez, Johnny Allen, up from Jersey City, and Pipgras. Danny MacFayden, later obtained from the Red Sox, helped. So did the aging Herb Pennock and Wilcy Moore, retrieved from Boston. Gomez, however, made the most important single pitching contribution. He won seven games from the Athletics.

To win, McCarthy had to meet and overcome other problems. There were some players on the team he had to drive hard. There were others who disliked him, still believing that Ruth should have been the manager. Ruth himself was one of these. The Babe's feelings were in no way reflected in his playing, but there was a marked coolness between him and McCarthy. Joe quietly tagged some of the young men for shipment elsewhere when the opportunity arose. But the team was winning, and he bided his time—and drove on toward the pennant.

One day, when the Yankees were in Washington, he was alone in the clubhouse, the players having gone out to take batting practice. The door opened and a player came in, still in his street clothes, reporting nearly an hour late. He was one of the group that didn't like McCarthy, and although Joe had never said anything to him about it, he was fully aware of the young man's attitude.

Now he almost leaped at him.

"Who do you think you are?" he yelled. "And what do you think I am? A dope? What do you mean by coming in here at this time, when you should be dressed and on the field?"

Before the player could answer, Joe roared on. He never talked to a player before, or since, as he did then. Lazzeri, coming back for a new bat he had put in his locker and forgotten, walked right into the scene. McCarthy, ignoring him, continued to abuse the hapless player, who was fumbling into his uniform. Tony hadn't been quite sure whether he liked McCarthy or not, although he admired him as a manager. Now he was sure he didn't like him. He couldn't like any manager who talked that way to a ball player. And, being a very forthright young man, he was going to tell him so as soon as the player had left the room.

As the door closed on the player, Lazzeri wheeled on McCarthy.

"That was a fine thing to do," he said, coldly. "You ought to be—"

The anger had died out of McCarthy's eyes.

"I'm glad you were here, Tony," he said. "I'm glad you heard what I had to say to him. Now I want you to understand why I said it. I know that boy doesn't like me. I'm not interested in whether he does or not. But I am interested in him as a ball player. He could be one of the best ball players in this league, but he isn't because of his attitude. He thinks he's been getting away with something around here, just to spite me. But he hasn't. I took this opportunity to tell him so because I hope that, by scaring him—as I think I did—I can wake him up. I didn't like to do it that way. But I had made up my mind it was the only way. I wasn't in here by accident when he came in an hour late. I was waiting for him. Do you understand now what it was all about?"

Tony nodded. "I do, Joe," he said. "I've known all along how he felt about you—and how some of the others feel. I didn't know just how I felt about you myself. But I do now. I want you to know that from now on, I'm on your side."

Tony not only was on McCarthy's side from then on, but let the other players know about it. And since they had a great regard for him and a profound respect for his judgment, those who, like himself, had wavered in their loyalty to their manager, followed him into McCarthy's camp.

It was an exciting year for the Yankees as once more they hammered their rivals into submission. They had regained their power, their pitching was good, and Chapman, although no longer as reckless as he had been the year before, still was running and hitting the dirt as he led the league in stealing bases.

In Philadelphia on June 3 of that year, Gehrig hit four home runs, three off George Earnshaw and the other off Leroy Mahaffey. Only twice before in the history of baseball had that feat been performed—by Ed Delehanty of the Phillies on July 13, 1896, and by Bobby Lowe of the Boston club on May 30, 1894. That should have been the baseball story of the day, of course. But it wasn't. Baseball writers covering the Yankees were winding up to give the Gehrig story full play when their desks wired them:

"Take it easy. John McGraw has just resigned as manager of the Giants."

There was a slightly amusing sequel to Lou's performance. A few days later the Yankees were in Boston and one of the writers with them saw in a late edition of an evening paper a picture of Gehrig shaking hands with Lowe at the park before the game.

"Why didn't you tell me Lowe was out there today?" he asked, meeting Lou in the dining room. "I would liked to have written a story about him."

Lou looked bewildered.

"Lowe?" he said. "Who's Lowe?"

"The fellow who hit four home runs in a game in 1894."

"Was that who that was?" Lou exclaimed. "I wish I'd known that myself. All I knew was they asked me to pose shaking hands with an old gentleman. Honestly, I hadn't the faintest idea who he was."

The Yankees plunged on, never out of first place after the middle of May, and won the pennant in a romp. In Chicago the Cubs won the National League flag. This provided an added incentive for McCarthy. What he wanted more than anything in this world was to go back to Chicago at the head of the Yankees and beat the Cubs at Wrigley Field. That would make his revenge complete—or nearly so. It would have been perfect if Hornsby still was managing the Cubs, but Rog had been released and Charlie Grimm, a good friend of McCarthy's, had been chosen to succeed him. Even so, there was a great day coming—and Joe pressed forward to meet it.

The series opened in New York, and before the game a row was precipitated that was to thrive as the series lengthened and provide the setting for one of the greatest performances ever seen on any field of sport—and then to die out as suddenly as it had begun.

In August, with the Cubs' infield staggering, Grimm had reached out to the Pacific Coast League to get Mark Koenig who, having drifted back to the minors from Detroit, had taken on new vigor. It was a wise move. Koenig, actually a better ball player than he had been when he was with the Yankees, steadied the infield and accounted for a number of victories with his timely hitting.

"He made it possible for us to win the pennant," Grimm said, as the season ended. "He was a real life saver."

Yet when the Cubs met to decide on how their World Series money was to be divided, they allotted only a quarter of a share to Koenig. The Yankees resented this fiercely. Koenig now wore the uniform of another club and, in the impending series, they would be trying their hardest to thwart him. But he had been a Yankee. He had been one of them and, in the sentimental sense, he always would be. They talked, not only among themselves, about what they deemed to be scurvy treatment accorded to Koenig, but were more than willing to be quoted in the newspapers on that point.

Meanwhile, they looked forward with relish to telling the Cubs to their faces just how they felt about it. They were determined that no one could deal as niggardly as that with an old team mate of theirs and get away with it. Not while they had tongues in their heads.

Now, in the Stadium, as in some other major-league parks, the visiting players must pass through one end of the home club's dugout on their way from the clubhouse to the field; and on the opening day of the series, as the Cubs made their first appearance, coming in single file up the narrow steps, the Yankees were waiting for them. Not a word was said until Koenig, reaching the top of the steps, paused to greet his former team mates. They yelled to him.

"Hello, Mark! How are you, boy?"

And then, in the booming voice of the Babe:

"Who are those cheap skates with you, Mark?"

The Cubs just ahead of Koenig and those crowding up the steps behind him heard the Babe very plainly. Koenig, embarrassed, started on his way again, and the line of players moved rapidly but the shouts of the Yankees followed them:

"How does it feel to be with a lot of crumb bums like that when you've been on a real ball club?"

"Nickel nursers!"

"If it hadn't been for Koenig, you wouldn't have won the pennant, you misers!"

The Cubs remained silent under the verbal barrage. There wasn't anything they could have said, as a matter of fact. But once the game got under way, with Charlie Ruffing pitching against Guy Bush, they opened fire from their dugout, particularly at Ruth. But the Yankees hurled it right back at them and chortled in almost ghoulish glee as they knocked Bush out, hammered Burleigh Grimes, and won by a score of 12 to 6. Vernon Gomez outpitched Lon Warneke in the second game, and the Yankees won, 5 to 2, as the players rode each other savagely.

By the time they reached the third game, in Chicago, the exchange of insults had become terrific, with Ruth still the main target of the Cub bench warmers. It was in this game that the Babe contributed his astonishing achievement of calling his shot on Charlie Root, the Cubs' starting pitcher. In the third inning, Root ripped a fast ball across the plate; and the Babe, without waiting for the umpire, called a strike on himself, holding up one finger in derision as he grinned at the Cubs' bench. Another fast ball split the plate, and the Babe called that, also, holding up two fingers. Now the crowd was howling, and the Cubs in the dugout were jeering. And now the Babe, with a wave of his right arm, indicated that he would hit the next pitch over the wall in right center.

Root, a smart pitcher, was too smart for his own good. Instead of wasting a pitch with a count of 2 and 0 on the Babe, he thought to catch the big guy napping with another fast ball across the plate. But Ruth, timing it perfectly, smashed it squarely—and it roared on a line over the fence in right center!

No one ever had seen anything like that before nor, probably, ever will again. The fact that he had hit a home run against the home club made no difference to the crowd, and the cheers for him were deafening as, grinning and thumbing his nose at the Cubs, he trotted around the bases. In their dugout, the Yankees were wild with delight.

That blow softened up the Cubs and hastened their defeat. With Pipgras and Pennock dividing the pitching, the Yankees won the game, 7 to 5. The following day, they spotted the Cubs a 4-to-1 lead in the first inning and then swarmed all over five Cub pitchers, led by Bush, to win by a score of 13 to 6.

It was a great series for the Yankees. Gehrig hit for an average of .529 and made three home runs. Ruth and Lazzeri each made two homers. The club had run its string of consecutive victories in World Series games to twelve.

It was a great series for McCarthy, too. Having won his first pennant in New York, he had completed the triumph by beating the Cubs. The Yankees were on top of the world again, and Ruppert was supremely happy.

XIV · The Farm System

$\ominus$

NOTHER IMPORTANT development between the arrival
of McCarthy and his first pennant was the beginning of the
farm system which, in the years since then, has yielded most
of the players who have won pennants and made crowds
roar at the Stadium.

In itself, the founding of this system was not an accident,
but the way for it was paved by chance. In 1931 the attention of all the other major-league clubs was focused on the
chain of minor-league clubs that Branch Rickey had forged
for the Cardinals. This was no longer in the experimental
stage. It was sending a stream of players up to the parent
club, and the Cardinals were winning with them. Rival club
owners, having scoffed at Rickey's idea, now paused to examine it, believing there might be something in it after all.
Among those who stopped, looked, and listened, were Ruppert and Barrow but, having given considerable thought
to the possible benefits to be derived by a similar chain of
Yankee outposts, they decided against it.

Two weeks after they had reached that decision, Max
Steuer, the lawyer, walked into Ruppert's office in the brewery. Ruppert was a client of his. So was Paul Block, newspaper publisher and the owner of the Newark club of the
International League.

"Paul wants to sell his ball club," Steuer said. "I thought
you might like to buy it."

Ruppert shook his head.

"No," he said. "I'm not interested."

But Steuer, as judges, juries, and discomfited rivals knew, was an eloquent pleader. Within fifteen minutes he had persuaded Ruppert to change his mind. The Colonel didn't even have a chance to call Barrow and consult him. The first Barrow knew of it, his phone rang and there was Ruppert on the wire.

"Ed," he said, "I just bought the Newark ball club from Paul Block."

"You what?" Barrow exclaimed.

"I bought the Newark ball club. Steuer sold it to me."

That was on November 12. Barrow, with the club dropped into his lap, immediately began to look around for someone to run it for him. He found him at the minor-league meeting, which he and Ruppert attended, at West Baden, Ind., in December.

"There he is," he said to Ruppert in the lobby of the hotel the night they arrived.

"There's who?" Ruppert asked, surprised.

"The man we want to run the Newark club."

"Who is he?"

"George Weiss."

Ruppert had never heard of him.

"Who's Weiss?" he asked.

Barrow told him. Weiss was born and reared in New Haven, Conn., and had managed the high-school baseball team. Joe Dugan was the third baseman on that team, which undoubtedly was one of the best high-school teams ever put together. Later, almost intact and still under Weiss's management, the team had played as the Colonials, an independent professional outfit and a highly profitable one. From that beginning, Weiss had branched out. He had obtained the New Haven franchise in the Eastern League, had operated it very successfully, and had become known as one of the ablest figures in the minor leagues. Upon the death of Jack Dunn in Baltimore, the directors of the Orioles had induced him to sell his holdings in New Haven and to take over in Baltimore.

On one occasion, Barrow told Ruppert, George very nearly had been killed. It was an odd story. At the time, 1923, Bill Donovan was managing the New Haven club, and he and George were on their way, riding the Twentieth Century Limited to Chicago for the major-league meetings in December. Weiss, retiring before Donovan, had settled himself in the upper berth in their drawing room. When Donovan entered the room, he said:

"Come on. Get down out of there. I'm sleeping in the upper."

"No, you're not," George said, laughing. "I'm comfortable here, and I'm going to stay here."

"But it isn't right," Bill said. "After all, you're the boss. And who am I to be sleeping in a lower when the boss is sleeping in an upper? Besides, I've been climbing in and out of uppers all my life. Come on down."

George turned over, yawning.

"Stop annoying me," he said. "Go to bed."

Bill, still arguing, undressed and got into the lower berth. Two hours later, the train was wrecked. Weiss was so badly injured that he was in the hospital for months—but Donovan was killed outright.

"He knows as much about minor-league baseball as anybody in the country," Barrow said. "He knows the International League especially."

Ruppert wanted to meet him. Following the introduction, Barrow said:

"Look out for him, Colonel. He's a tough man. I know. I've had some dealings with him."

He laughed when he said it, but he was only half fooling. As a matter of fact, he and George were not particularly cordial at the time. On two or three occasions they had clashed and, over one period of two years, they had not spoken to each other. But, as Barrow had indicated to Ruppert, in his mind there was no one as well equipped as Weiss to look after their property in Newark. Ruppert, having talked at some length with Weiss that night, concurred in Barrow's appraisal of him and offered him the job. Weiss, liking Ruppert and sure that he and Barrow could get on as long as they were on the same side, took it.

Weiss hadn't been in the organization very long before he began to preach to Ruppert and Huston the virtues of the farm system. They weren't impressed in the beginning. They told him they had been through all that and intimated that since he had been hired to run the Newark club it might not be a bad idea for him to stick to his last. But George wouldn't give up.

"You have some small minor-league connections now," he said. "Tie them in with Newark, get a couple more to fill in the spaces in between, and the first thing you know you'll have a system that will be feeding players right up the line to the Yankees, with the Newark club as the proving ground."

Barrow snorted.

"What's the difference between that and Rickey's farm system?" he asked.

"There isn't any," George acknowledged. "I just happen to think it's the best idea that's been advanced in baseball in a long time. I believe Rickey has proved it, and I also believe that, with our resources, we can do an even better job than he has done. What are you going to do with all those ball players your scouts are digging up? It's got so the scouts for the other clubs are complaining that every time they try to sign a young ball player they find he belongs to either the Yankees or the Cardinals."

Ed chuckled at that. He was proud of his scouting staff, as he had good reason to be.

"You've got to have a place for them to develop," Weiss continued. "Would you rather have them on minor-league clubs of your own, being taught by managers you have selected—or on some clubs managed by fellows you don't know much about and that might ruin a good prospect for you overnight?"

Ruppert and Barrow finally agreed with him that they needed a farm system. He gave them one that, in time, exceeded that which Rickey had designed. Judge Landis, who doesn't like farm systems anyway, has poked around in this one—as he has in the others—from time to time. But whereas he has found something wrong with most of the others, he has found no flaw in this.

To skip ahead a few years, just for the moment: From year to year, Weiss has added to his farm chain—or cut it down. Three years ago there were fifteen clubs in it. Last year there were only nine. The base of it was three Class D clubs: Butler in the Pennsylvania State Association, Wellsville in the Pony League, and Fond du Lac in the Wisconsin State League. Ranging just above were two in Class C leagues: Amsterdam in the Canadian-American and Joplin in the Western Association. Then came Norfolk in the Piedmont League, Class B; Binghamton in the Eastern League, Class B; and, at the top, the two Class AA clubs, Newark in the International and Kansas City in the American Association. Newark, Kansas City, Binghamton, and Norfolk are owned outright. Working agreements with the other clubs gave the Yankees free rein with their players.

The managers of these clubs were picked, for the most part, from the ranks of former players on Yankee farm teams.

They have been extremely successful, not only in the development of players for the home office—which, after all, is their main job—but in the winning of pennants. Moreover, the chain has been financially independent almost from its inception. Some of the smaller clubs occasionally need help, but this is supplied by the Newark and Kansas City clubs, so that Weiss never has to draw on the Yankee strong box. Part of the revenue taken in by these clubs is from the sale of players. Those sold to the Yankees—and under baseball law they must be sold or exchanged for other players—go at purely nominal rates, usually just enough to cover the cost of their baseball education. But surplus material is disposed of to other major and minor league clubs at prices that sometimes are astonishing.

Weiss spends a good part of his time on the road, checking up on players and managers. At the end of a season he and Barrow settle the fate of the farmhands for another season, moving some of them up, holding others over, moving still others back. Sometimes, although not often, McCarthy is consulted. As a rule, he has nothing to add to a conference between Barrow and Weiss because he hasn't seen the players under discussion. However, his is the main voice when, at the end of a training season, the squad is being cut.

The scouting staff to which Weiss so wisely referred, back in the early months of 1932 to help swing Barrow to his way of thinking on the farm system, undoubtedly is the most complete that any ball club has ever had.

It is headed by Paul Krichell, who has the rotund, slightly bowed frame and rolling gait of an ex-catcher and is one of the keenest seekers of talent in the raw, although he played only one major-league engagement himself. That was a two-year hitch with the Browns in 1911 and 1912. The rest of his playing career, which began on the sandlots of New York around the turn of the century and ended in Toronto in

1916, was spent in the minors. He was with Barrow in 1910, when Ed was managing the Montreal club. It was Ed who sold him to the Browns—and Ed never forgot him. When Barrow was managing the Red Sox in 1920, he sent for Paul, then coaching at New York University, and hired him as coach and scout. When Barrow moved down to New York, Paul moved with him.

Krichell's regular beat is in the East, but he may be sent anywhere—and frequently is, usually to give the final word on a player dug up by another scout—and he assists Weiss by regularly visiting the farm clubs and reporting on the progress of the players. The Pacific Coast is covered by Bill Essick and Joe Devine, although occasionally Essick is sent on a flying trip to the American Association and Devine to Texas. Steve O'Rourke and Johnny Haddock operate in the Middle West, Johnny Nee in the South, and Gene McCann in the East.

They have accounted for most of the players who, coming up through the farm system so ably managed by Weiss, have won seven pennants in the years beginning with 1932.

XV · A Three-Year Pause

⊖

MᶜCᴀʀᴛʜʏ ʜᴀᴅ ʜɪᴛ the top in a sustained drive which carried across two seasons. Now, as 1933 came on, the drive slowed, and he was to know three years of disappointment before he reached the top again.

The team, of course, was very largely that which had ripped the American League race to pieces in 1932 and crushed the Cubs in such impressive style. Gehrig was at first base and Lazzeri at second, with Eddie Farrell as Tony's understudy. Crosetti, after a doubtful spring in which it seemed he might be sold or traded, had clinched the job once more at short stop. The veteran Sewell, in his third year with the Yankees after his long service in Cleveland, was at third base. Lary acted as replacement for either Crosetti or Sewell. Ruth, Combs, and Chapman were the regular outfielders, with Dixie Walker and Sammy Byrd for utility service. Dickey would do most of the catching, with Arndt Jorgens to relieve him now and then.

For pitchers, McCarthy had Gomez, now recognized as the best southpaw in the league and with a great season in 1932 behind him; Ruffing; Russ Van Atta; Charlie Devens, late of Harvard; Allen; Don Brennan; big Walter Brown; Pennock; Danny MacFayden, obtained from Boston; and Moore. He sold Pipgras to Boston in May, and later on picked up George Uhle, who had been almost a great pitcher with

Cleveland a few years before but now, a shop-worn wanderer, had been with the Tigers and the Giants.

Early indications were that the 1933 race would be three-cornered, with the Yankees drawing their strongest opposition from the Athletics and the Senators, who had finished second and third, respectively, in 1932. But it soon was seen that the A's had been so weakened by their winter deals with the Red Sox that they would not be dangerous, and the Yankees need look only to the Senators as a threat.

For almost two months, it seemed they had nothing to worry about, even from that quarter. Moving into June, they were playing at a clip close to .700. Then they began to spin alarmingly. They lost thirty points in eight days as their pitchers faltered. Ruth's hitting fell off, and even Gehrig, although slamming along well beyond .300, could not hold to the pace he had set through 1932.

Meanwhile, the Senators were rushing at them. It was Joe Cronin's first season as manager; and his players, catching his youthful, fighting spirit, were hustling at top speed for him. Earl Whitehill was a consistent winner. Goose Goslin and Heinie Manush were slugging the ball. On June 24 they passed the Yankees and went into first place. The Yankees, rallying swiftly, drove them back; but they came on again, and this time there was nothing the Yanks could do about it. From there on it became increasingly plain that they were going to win the pennant.

On August 3 the Yankees were shut out by Robert Moses Grove of the Athletics. This was notable because it cracked their record of having gone through 308 consecutive games without being blanked. Whether they realized it at the time or not, it was a symbol of the waning of their power.

On August 17 Gehrig broke Everett Scott's endurance record by taking part in his 1,308th game. Oddly enough, the day Scott's record ended, Gehrig was in the Yankee dug-out—and the day Gehrig set a new record, one of his team mates was Sewell, who, as a member of the Indians, had set the mark of 1,103 games that Scott had shattered.

So far as the Yankees were concerned, the season dragged on. They couldn't overtake the Senators, and they had second place securely locked up. They were playing now only for their pay checks on the first and fifteenth of the month. On the final day of the season, as a means of luring customers to the ball park, Ruth pitched a full game, beating Boston by a score of 6 to 5—and, which was quite in character, winning the game with his thirty-fourth home run of the season.

There are figures to show, tersely and clearly, what happened to the Yankees that year. Ruth hit .301, a drop of forty points in his average from 1932. Gomez, who had won twenty-four games in 1932, won sixteen. Ruffing, who had won eighteen the year before, won nine. There were, of course, other factors. But if Ruth hadn't slowed down at the plate—and, incidentally, in the field as well—and if Gomez and Ruffing had not, between them, produced a deficit of seventeen victories as compared to their 1932 total, the Yankees and not the Senators would have faced the Giants in the World Series that fall.

2

In 1934 McCarthy overhauled his material, lopping some of his veterans from the squad, bringing in some rookies, and reshaping his infield.

Two of those who departed were Pennock and Sewell. Pennock had come almost to the end of his effectiveness as a pitcher, although, upon being unconditionally released, he was signed by the Red Sox. For a year or so he had been of scant use to the Yankees as a pitcher, but he had helped considerably in the coaching of the younger men on the staff. "The club pro," Ford Frick had called him. Sewell had served the Yankees well, but he had slowed down to a walk. The time had come for McCarthy to begin a rebuilding; and, high as was his personal regard for Pennock and Sewell, they were not the type he could use in the process.

On the opening day of the season at Philadelphia, the Yankees had Gomez pitching, Dickey catching, Ruth, Combs, and Chapman in the outfield, and Gehrig at first base. But Lazzeri had been moved from second base to third, and there were two strangers in the infield: Don Heffner at second base and Robert (Red) Rolfe at short stop. Heffner, purchased from Baltimore, had been tabbed as a fielding wizard, and in his four seasons at Baltimore he had constantly improved as a hitter. Rolfe had been signed in 1931 while a student at Dartmouth and had spent one year in Albany and two years in Newark being schooled for the big leagues. Crosetti had been relegated to the bench, there to sit with Lary and Saltzgaver, the latter recalled from Newark.

Myril Hoag, who had been with the team in 1931 and 1932, also was back from Newark to help out in the outfield. Jimmy DeShong had been added to the pitching staff. So had Johnny Murphy, signed out of Fordham University and trained in the minors, who developed into a first-rate relief pitcher.

A rather general expectation was that the Yankees would reclaim the title wrested from them by the Senators the year before, and that they had most to fear from the Senators and the Red Sox, strengthened by further deals with the Athletics. The Tigers were lightly regarded, and scant attention was paid to them even when they moved off to a flying start under the fiery leadership of Mickey Cochrane, in his first year as manager.

But when the teams had straightened out and settled down, with the Yankees out in front and swinging along, it was seen that the Tigers were the ones they would have to beat. Schoolboy Rowe was hanging up victories at a breathless clip, and the whole team seemed to have caught fire from Cochrane.

Up through June and July the Tigers came clawing. And as they clawed the Yankees began to weaken. Ruth had reached a point where he was hitting only in spots, and his fielding was pitifully weak. Realizing fully the extent of his shortcomings, he began to take himself out of the line-up frequently, to call on Hoag or George Selkirk, brought up from Newark, to spell him, even to talk about retiring at the end of the season.

McCarthy, grimly watching the decline of his team and powerless to check it, as grimly watched the decline of the Babe. The pretense of friendliness for each other that they had sought to maintain was worn so thin now that it was transparent to even the most casual observer. Had Ruth been just an ordinarily good player who was wearing out fast, McCarthy would have benched him. But he was Ruth, who had become a tradition in his own time, and Joe watched him silently, giving him enough rope, confident that he would hang himself in the end. He put the Babe in the line-up when he said he wanted to play, took him out when he said he wanted to rest. They spoke to each other only when it was necessary, and then but briefly. But the Babe, sometimes only to the newspapermen, sometimes in the hearing of the other players, was sharply critical of the way things were going and of McCarthy's failure to correct them.

On July 23, at Sportsmans Park in St. Louis, where for some curious reason so much Yankee history has been written, the team suffered a crippling blow in an almost fatal accident to Earle Combs. In pursuit of a fly ball, Combs crashed into the concrete wall of the bleachers in left center, fracturing his skull and tearing the muscles of his right shoulder so badly it seemed that, if he lived, he never would be able to play ball again. The accident naturally had a depressing effect on the other players, not so much because they had lost the services of their center fielder for the balance of the season, but because they feared for the life of the schoolmaster. Rushed to a hospital and placed under the care of Dr. Robert F. Hyland, he was in a coma for hours; but Hyland not only brought him safely through but so skillfully operated on his injured shoulder that with the coming of another season he was able to return to the outfield.

In August the showdown between the Tigers and the Yankees, weakened further by the loss of Combs, took place before a crowd that jammed the Stadium. Cochrane—with Rowe, Hank Greenberg, Charlie Gehringer, and the rest of his crew riding high—moved in for a double-header on August 14. The season still had six weeks to go, yet everyone —the players, the writers, the fans—had a feeling that if the Tigers won those two games they would, in effect, clinch the pennant. And that was precisely what happened.

McCarthy struggled along, shifting his players about. He moved Lazzeri back to second base, shunted Rolfe to third, and posted Crosetti at short stop. He had Selkirk and Byrd in the outfield with Chapman on days when the Babe didn't play, Selkirk and the Babe on days when the Babe felt the urge to go out there. An injury to Allen had lessened the effectiveness of the pitching staff.

Gehrig was hitting—he hit .363 that year to lead the league, made forty-nine home runs and received the award as the most valuable player in the league. And Gomez was back in his best form, winning twenty-six games and losing only five, and having the lowest earned-run average, 2.35. But Lou and Lefty couldn't put the Yankees across, and the pennant went to Detroit for the first time since 1909.

3

Ruth had hit only .288 that year and had made only twenty-two home runs. He had failed to start—or having started, had taken himself out of—perhaps fifty games. He was thirty-nine years old and he was tired. Moreover, he was constantly tormented by the thought that McCarthy had not done a good job with the team and that he would have done better—and would do better in the future if the opportunity came to him.

Near the end of the season, he walked into Ruppert's office in the brewery.

"Well, Ruth," the Colonel said, "this is a surprise. What's on your mind?"

The Babe wasted no words. "Are you satisfied with McCarthy as your manager?" he asked.

Now Ruppert was even more surprised. "Why, yes," he said.

"Well, I'm not," the Babe said.

Ruppert was nettled. "Ruth," he said, "I know you would like to manage this ball club. Don't think I haven't considered the matter. I have. But this is a big business, Ruth, and you are untried as a manager. No one has a greater admiration for you as a player than I have. As a manager—I don't know."

They looked at each other in silence for a moment. And then Ruppert asked: "Would you go to Newark, Ruth?"

"To Newark!"

"Yes. As manager. It would give you an opportunity to prove to your own satisfaction—and mine—that you are capable of managing a ball club. If you are, and the time comes when I want to make a change on the Yankees, you would be in line for the job."

The Babe was angry.

"No," he said. "I won't go to Newark or any other minor-league club. Why should I? I'm a big leaguer. Why should I go to the minors?"

Ruppert shrugged. "I think you are foolish," he said.

"Maybe. But that's the way I feel about it."

"Then I can do nothing for you," Ruppert said.

The interview was over. As the Babe walked out of the office, the Colonel looked after him thoughtfully. He knew in that moment that the Babe's usefulness to the Yankees had ended. He had offered him a way out, but the Babe had refused to take it.

When the World Series, at which he was a spectator, was over, the Babe, with Gehrig and Gomez, went to the Orient with a team of major-league players for a series of exhibition games. From there he completed a circuit of the globe, reaching New York from Europe in February of 1935.

The news that awaited him was not pleasant. Ruppert and Barrow not only had not weakened in their support of McCarthy, but had prepared what they called a provisional contract for the Babe. This called for only a nominal sum, with the provision that if he could prove at the training camp that he had rounded into such condition as to warrant a belief that he would have a better season than he had had in 1934—or, for that matter, in 1933—his salary could be fixed on terms suitable to him and the club. The Babe promptly announced he wouldn't sign such a contract and wasn't even interested in seeing it. Merely to offer it to him was an insult, he said. By way of reply, Barrow pointed out that the Babe had admitted he had had a hard time of it for two years and seriously had considered retiring, adding that it was unreasonable to expect the club to gamble on him, especially as he had spent the off season playing ball and traveling and might find it difficult, if not impossible, to get into top form at St. Petersburg.

And now, with the Babe providing the impetus, his dissatisfaction with McCarthy as manager and his ambition to succeed Joe were thrown into the open. The Babe, asserting that he had earned the right to manage the Yankees, vowed that he would not wear a Yankee uniform again unless he received the appointment. At this, Barrow went into a deep silence, and the Colonel followed him.

Yet both Ruppert and Barrow were troubled. They felt that they were dealing justly with the Babe, but they wished mightily for an escape from a situation that, they feared, might be misunderstood by those who, with an eye to the Babe's great qualities as a player and his expansive personality, would think they were dealing with him callously. The means of escape came unexpectedly.

At that time, the Boston Braves were controlled by Emil Fuchs, a former New York City magistrate and a great baseball enthusiast. In his struggle for patronage with the Red Sox, rapidly being built up by the youthful and wealthy Tom Yawkey, Fuchs had sought to lure the customers by recapturing some of the heroes of another era, such as Johnny Evers, Rabbit Maranville, and Hank Gowdy; but that had failed and now he was struggling along with a collection of mediocre players managed by Bill McKechnie.

On a Sunday night, late in February, the Babe called Ruppert on the telephone at his estate near Garrison.

"Judge Fuchs is having dinner at my house," he said. "He wants to talk to you."

"Put him on," Ruppert said.

"Hello, Colonel," Fuchs said excitedly. "I want the Babe for my team! Will you let me have him? Name your terms right now, and I am sure I can meet them."

"Wait, wait," the Colonel said. "I don't do business this way. Come to—"

"But we can fix it up right now," Fuchs insisted. "I want your word that I can have him so that I can go back to Boston tonight and announce it to the newspapers there tomorrow."

"Come to my office tomorrow morning," Ruppert said. "We can talk about the matter there."

Fuchs continued to press him, but he was obdurate.

"Tomorrow morning," he said. "I don't do business over the telephone."

Ruth and Fuchs arrived at the brewery the next morning. Ruth entered Ruppert's inner office alone, leaving Fuchs in the anteroom.

"You're still satisfied with McCarthy as your manager?" he asked.

"Yes," Ruppert said.

"And there is no chance that you will change your mind?"

"No."

The Babe went to the door.

"Come in, Judge," he said.

Fuchs walked in briskly, shook hands with Ruppert and sat down.

"Well?" he asked.

Ruppert handed him a form which had been filled out and which he had signed.

"There is Ruth's unconditional release," he said. "After you called me last night, I sent wires to all the other American League club owners asking for waivers on him. I received them this morning."

Fuchs stared at him, almost unbelieving.

"But the price?" he asked. "What do you want for him?"

The Colonel shook his head.

"Nothing," he said. "Ruth has been a great ball player for this club. I am sorry we could not satisfy him now. But I do not wish to stand in his way nor to make any profit from his opportunity to better himself."

XVI · Never Another Like Him

T HUS, ON FEBRUARY 25, 1935, the Babe passed from New
York. His subsequent experiences in Boston and Brooklyn
are now all but forgotten—and happily so. But no one ever
will forget him in the time when he was a Yankee. It is trite
to say that there never was, and never will be, another like
him. But it must stand as the big guy's accolade.

Departing, he left behind him a thousand stories. Of his
skill and power and courage on the field, his good nature,
his boisterous humor, his streaks of stubbornness and flares
of temper, his generosity, his genuine love of children and
his solicitude for them, especially the poor or the ill or the
neglected, his escapades by candlelight, his utter naturalness
in all things.

One story, which has almost all of Ruth in it, goes back to
the day before the opening of the World Series with the Cardinals in 1926.

In Essex Fells, New Jersey, there was a little boy by the
name of Johnny Sylvester, who had been very ill and whose
convalescence was so slow as to be a cause for alarm on the
part of his doctor.

"I have done all I can for him," the doctor said to the
boy's father. "What he needs now is a mental pick-up of
some kind. What is he interested in, particularly?"

"Baseball," the father said. "And he thinks Babe Ruth is
the greatest man that ever lived."

"That's it!" the doctor said. "Call the Babe up or write to him, explaining the situation, and ask him to send Johnny an autographed ball."

"But I don't know the Babe," the father protested.

"Neither do I," the doctor said. "But from what I hear of him, that isn't necessary. Anyway, give it a trial. It may work—and if it does, I'm sure Johnny will get well in a hurry."

The father called the Stadium the next morning and told the Babe his story.

"Where do you live?" the Babe asked.

"Essex Fells, New Jersey."

"How do you get there?"

Mr. Sylvester told him.

"I'll be out this afternoon," the Babe said.

Nobody told Johnny that the Babe was going to visit him. Try to imagine his feelings as he looked up to see his hero, bearing not only an autographed ball but a couple of bats and a glove, standing in the doorway of his bedroom. The Babe pulled up a chair alongside the bed and sat with the boy for an hour, telling him stories—and Johnny got well, of course.

The following spring, the Yankees were opening the season in Philadelphia, and on his way to the park the Babe stopped in the lobby of the hotel to talk to a couple of newspapermen. As he stood there, an elderly man approached.

"Mr. Ruth," he said, extending his hand, "I'm Johnny Sylvester's uncle."

The Babe wrung his hand.

"Is that so?" he boomed. "I'm glad to know you. How's Johnny?"

"Oh, he's fine now—thanks to you."

"I'm glad to hear that, sir."

"We can't ever express our gratitude to you, Mr. Ruth. But I want you to know we'll never forget it."

"Don't mention it," the Babe said.

The man shook hands with him again.

"I didn't mean to interrupt you in your conversation with these gentlemen," he said. "But I did want to say hello to you. I'll tell Johnny I saw you, and I know he'll be glad."

"Fine! Give Johnny my best regards."

The Babe looked after the retreating figure for a moment and then, turning to the newspapermen he said:

"I wonder who the hell Johnny Sylvester is?"

One of them laughed.

"That's the little sick boy you went to see in Essex Fells last fall," he said.

"Oh, sure," the Babe said. "I remember now."

Well, there it is. He didn't know who Johnny Sylvester was and hadn't the faintest notion of what he had done for him, but whatever it was, he was glad. Reminded of the incident, his memory of it was clear enough. He simply had forgotten the name.

Johnny, had he known that, needn't have felt badly about it. The Babe was—and remains—utterly indifferent to names. To him, any male, regardless of age, is "Kid." A young woman is "Sister," an elderly woman "Mother." Incredible as it may seem, there were times when he didn't know the names of some of his team mates. One day, when Paul Whiteman visited the Yankees in their dugout at the Stadium, the Babe took him down the line of players, introducing him.

"This is Herb Pennock," he said. "And this is Bob Meusel. This is Lou Gehrig and this is—er...er..."

"Wera," the player said.

"Oh, sure! Wera...and this is Earle Combs and this is—er...

"Braxton."

"Of course! Braxton. And this is . . ."

Wera and Braxton and a few others. Their proper names simply never had registered with him. He had his own names for them, however. Wera was Flop Ears and Braxton was Chicken Neck. And, incidentally, Shocker was always Rubber Belly.

Word was received in Baltimore one early spring day that the Babe would pass through on his way to the South about noon. Paul Minton, a newspaperman, asked Alphonse Thomas, now the manager of the Orioles but then a pitcher with the White Sox but residing in Baltimore, if he wouldn't like to go down to the train to say hello to him.

"Sure," Thomas said. "And I'll lay you a little bet he doesn't recognize me or, if he does, he can't call me by name."

Minton thought he was fooling. But he wasn't. When the train stopped and the Babe got off to walk up and down on the station platform for a few minutes, Minton, with Thomas at his side, greeted him.

"How are you, kid!" the Babe said, shaking his hand.

"You remember Alphonse Thomas," Minton said.

"Sure I do," the Babe said, still talking to Minton as the grinning Thomas stood by, completely unnoticed by him. "How are you, Tommy?"

There was the time when, after an extra-inning ball game, he showered and dressed in even greater haste than usual.

"I nearly forgot I had a dinner date," he explained.

"With whom?" Pennock asked.

"That man and woman in the movies," the Babe said.

"What man and woman?"

"Oh, you know. They just got back from Europe."

"Douglas Fairbanks and Mary Pickford, by any chance?"

"That's right," the Babe said, struggling into his coat and

rushing for the door. "I never can remember their names."

The chances are that, in the course of the dinner, Doug and Mary were somewhat puzzled at being addressed as Kid and Sister.

There was the fan who stuck his head around the corner of the dugout one day when the Babe was sitting there waiting his turn in batting practice.

"How are you, Babe?" he yelled.

"Fine, kid. How are you?"

"Swell! You don't remember me, do you?"

"Well," the Babe stalled. "Your face is familiar but I just can't place you."

"Remember that party Joe Banks gave for you in Mobile a couple of springs ago?"

"Sure."

"Well, I was at that party."

"That's right," the Babe said. "I remember you now."

The fellow beamed.

"How are you hitting, Babe?" he asked.

"Pretty good."

Still beaming: "I knew you'd remember me when I told you about Joe's party."

"Oh, sure. Give my regards to Joe."

"I will! So long, Babe! I thought you wouldn't remember me at first."

He ducked back out of sight.

The Babe sprayed the dugout floor with a jet of tobacco juice.

"I don't remember the —— —— —— now," he said.

One of the reasons why he was a great ball player was that he thought like a champion. About nine o'clock on the night of the day on which he called his shot on Root in the World Series game in Chicago, Joe Williams said to him:

"That was the greatest thing I ever saw, Babe. But if you'd missed that ball, you sure would have looked like a sucker."

"By God, that's right, Joe!" the Babe exclaimed. "I sure would have, wouldn't I?"

In other words, it had occurred to him at nine o'clock at night that he might have missed a swing in the early afternoon.

Once, after he had retired, he was talking with Frank Frisch about hitting, and he said:

"I could have hit .600 every year if I'd wanted to. The way they used to play for me, with the infielders back on the edge of the grass and the outfielders out by the fences and everybody swung around to the right, I could have rolled a bunt anywhere in the infield or popped the ball into short left field and walked to first base."

"Why didn't you?" Frisch asked.

"Because," the Babe said, "the people paid to see me hit home runs."

So they did, of course. He could make two doubles, two singles, and a triple, drive in six runs, make a couple of great catches in the outfield, throw a runner out at the plate and, what with one thing and another, bring the enemy down practically single-handed. And yet, when the game was over, there would be those in the departing crowd to growl:

"What a bum! He didn't hit a home run all afternoon!"

No other ball player ever had to meet such a terrific and incessant demand. It is doubtful if any other could have withstood the strain of it year after year.

It has been said, sometimes in ignorance, sometimes in malice, that the Babe's visits to the bedsides of sick or crippled children in hospitals or private homes were arranged solely for the publicity they afforded him. No one who knew the Babe or traveled with him could say such a thing nor, hearing it said, fail to resent it.

It was natural that, in some cases, pictures should be taken and stories written of such visits. They were news, after all. They really were news because the Babe was always on the level. But after a while, hurt by the charge that they were but publicity dodges, he exacted promises from his friends among the newspapermen not to mention them, and these promises always were kept.

Once, on a holiday in Boston when the Yankees were playing morning and afternoon games with the Red Sox, Jack Malaney of the *Post* said to a New York baseball writer during the morning game:

"There's a kid out here in one of our hospitals who is on the danger list, and in his delirium he keeps calling for the Babe. The doctors and nurses think that if the Babe goes to see him it will save his life. How do you think I could go about getting him to go out there?"

"That's easy. Just ask him."

"When?"

"As soon as the game is over."

Now, between morning and afternoon games, the ball players do not leave the clubhouses. Their lunch is sent in to them, and they spend the intermission lounging about, reading, playing cards, listening to the radio, or napping. But when Malaney told the Babe about the delirious boy, the Babe hurriedly showered, dressed, went to the hospital with him, saw the boy, and hurried back to the park in time to take batting practice for the afternoon game. He made the trip on one condition, however: Malaney had to give him complete assurance that not a word of it would get into the newspapers. It didn't. This is the first time the story has ever been told.

There was another charge of publicity seeking by the Babe, frequently made and even more widely believed, that irked him. It irked Ruppert, too. This was that the Babe's almost annual holdouts were feigned. They weren't. They were on the square, too. Doubtless the Colonel and the Babe could have agreed upon terms without the fanfare that always accompanied their dickerings, and there is reason to believe that the publicity attendant upon them generally—although not always—was pleasing to them. But there never was anything spurious about the difference of opinion between them on the matter of the salary to be paid to the Babe.

That the Babe always wound up with the Colonel, while the lesser heroes usually signed with Barrow was, more than anything else, a matter of pride on the Colonel's part. He felt that it was his prerogative, as president of the club, to have the final word on Ruth and to sign him in person. It also was more than agreeable to the Babe, who liked to think —which probably was true—that he could get more out of Ruppert than he could out of Barrow. One year, at least, he proved his point.

In 1933 the salary offered to him was $50,000, and he promptly rejected it. He went to St. Petersburg for some golf ahead of the rest of the players and was still unsigned when, as the training season began, Ruppert and Barrow arrived. Barrow had primed the Colonel to stand fast. Or, at least, he thought he had. Meanwhile, the Babe was telling his friends that, while he realized $50,000 was a lot of money, it had become a matter of principle with him, and he positively would not sign for that amount.

"I'll take $50,001," he said, "but I won't take $50,000."

He and the Colonel met in his penthouse apartment. Barrow, confident that the Colonel would not relent, remained at the hotel where the team was quartered. There was a long argument behind closed doors. When it was over, the Colonel—rather glumly—announced that the Babe had signed. The Babe was grinning.

"For how much?" a reporter asked Ruppert.

"That is a secret between Ruth and me," he said.

But as far as the Babe was concerned it was no secret.

"I got $52,000," he said.

It would be interesting to know how the Colonel brushed that one off when he rejoined Barrow.

Now the big guy was gone from the Bronx. Most of the fans accepted his departure as inevitable and resigned themselves to the absence of his bulky, spindle-legged figure from right field. A few of them, however, hooted George Selkirk when he took his place in right field on opening day and they saw that he had inherited the familiar Number Three. They had nothing against Selkirk, of course. They simply wanted him—and the world—to know that they were still loyal to the Babe.

XVII · Another San Francisco Italian

⊖

M 1

EANWHILE, IN San Francisco, a young Italian by the
name of Joseph Paul DiMaggio had set fire to the Pacific
Coast League. His father and an older brother, Tom, were
fishermen. But Joe and another brother, Vince—and a very
little brother named Dominick—wanted to be ball players;
and every time they could get away from the boats or the
fish wharves, they played in Golden Gate Park or on the
neighborhood playgrounds. Vince and Joe played with ama-
teur and professional teams, and in 1932 Vince was signed as
an outfielder by the San Francisco club and farmed out to
Tucson in the Arizona-Texas League. Recalled by the Seals
late in the season, he arranged for a trial for Joe, who was
then an infielder. Joe played in three games, made a couple
of hits, and at the end of the season was ordered to report
in the spring.

Later, Lefty Gomez said in the Yankee clubhouse one day
in Joe's presence:

"Nice boy, this DiMaggio. His brother gets him a trial
with the Seals—and he beats his brother out of his job."

"I didn't," Joe said.

"No," Gomez said. "I guess not. You were together on the
club in the spring of 1933, weren't you?"

"Yes."

"Vince was a regular in the outfield, wasn't he?"

"Yes."

"And after a while you were a regular?"

"Yes."

"And whose place did you take?"

"Well, but . . ."

"But what?"

"I don't know."

"You don't know! What happened to Vince?"

"Hollywood bought him."

Gomez howled.

"How do you like that! 'Hollywood bought him!' You mean the Seals sold him to Hollywood to make room for you."

Turning to his amused listeners he said: "You see? He is nothing but an ungrateful bum who beat his brother out of a job."

Seriously, by the spring of 1934, Joe DiMaggio was the most talked-of player in the Coast League or, for that matter, in any minor league. Major-league scouts looked at him, were entranced with what they saw, and promptly wired to their employers, urging them to buy him. He had hit safely in sixty-one consecutive games while rolling up an average of .340 in 1933. Now he was hitting .360 or better. The major-league clubs began to bid for him. Charles Graham, owner of the Seals, was in no hurry to sell him. The longer he waited, the more hits Joe got, the higher the bids would go. Up they went—$50,000, $60,000, $75,000.

One day the Seals were playing in Seattle where Dutch Ruether was managing the club. Before the game, the Seattle trainer said to Joe:

"Dutch wants to know if you ever had any trouble with your left leg."

"No," Joe said. "Why?"

"He says you drag it a little when you run."

"Tell him he's nuts," Joe said. "I never hurt it, and I don't drag it."

The trainer returned to the Seattle dugout. In a few minutes he was back.

"Dutch says he ain't nuts," he said.

Joe looked across to where the veteran sat, peering at him. "I still say you're nuts!" he yelled.

The Dutchman shrugged.

A week later the Seals were at home.

"I had a date for dinner at my sister's house," Joe recalled, a couple of years later, "and the game dragged, so I was in a hurry to get there. As my cab pulled up at her door, I jumped out—and my left knee popped like a pistol. I swear you could have heard it down the block."

They heard it in New York ... in Boston ... in Chicago ... in Cleveland ... in all the towns whence the bids on him had come. They wanted no part of him now. The great young ball player had a trick knee that popped like a pistol.

He had to be helped into his sister's house, and from there to a hospital. It was a couple of weeks before he returned to the line-up. When he did, he was playing for Sweeney, so far as the scouts were concerned. All, that is, save one.

Bill Essick watched him closely, saw that his speed was unimpaired, that he ran not only as swiftly but as easily as before, that he pivoted smoothly at the plate.

"Don't give up on DiMaggio," he said to Barrow over the telephone one night. "Everybody out here thinks I'm crazy, but I'm not. I still think he's all right. Let me watch him for a couple of weeks more, and I'll have the final answer on him."

Barrow had great faith in the scout.

"All right, Bill," he said, "Stick with him."

About two weeks later, Essick called him again.

"Buy DiMaggio," he said. "I think you can get him cheap. They're all laughing at me, but I know I'm right."

Barrow called Graham.

"How much do you want for DiMaggio?" he asked.

"Forty thousand dollars."

"I'll give you twenty."

"Not a chance," Graham said.

They went on from there. Graham knew that no other major-league club was willing to take a chance on the boy. He also knew that Barrow knew it. He put up a battle as long as he could for $40,000, but finally settled for $25,000. It was the greatest buy in the history of modern baseball.

In consenting to sell the player, Graham made one proviso to which Barrow readily assented. This was that DiMaggio was to remain with the Seals through 1935 and report to the Yankees in the spring of 1936.

Joe hit .341 in 1934, and in 1935 he fairly roared through the league. He hit .398, and included in his 270 blows were 48 doubles, 18 triples, and 34 home runs. His name was in the headlines not only in the towns up and down the Coast but all over the country. Barrow had hung up another score. He not only had given the boy another year of minor-league baseball to fit him for the majors, but had reaped nation-wide publicity for this fledgling Yankee.

One night in Detroit during the World Series in 1935, a Seattle newspaperman looked up one of the baseball writers from New York.

"Dutch Ruether told me to see you," he said. "He told me that you are a good friend of his and that he wanted you to have the right steer on DiMaggio. He said to tell you not to be afraid to go out on a limb for this fellow, because he is a great ball player.

" 'Tell him,' he said, 'that DiMaggio is more than just a great hitter. Everybody talks about his hitting, but he is the best center fielder since Tris Speaker and can throw better than Speaker could the best day he ever saw.' "

2

But back to New York, and the spring of 1935, and the Yankees moving into a pennant fight without Babe Ruth for the first time since 1920.

McCarthy was easier in mind than he had been at any time since he had taken command of the Yankees. Now—and only now, with Ruth out of the way—could he make this ball club his club. Smart enough to know from the beginning that as long as the Babe was at the Stadium he would be the dominant figure, and much too smart to tangle with him in the open, Joe had waged a silent war of attrition with the Babe. At long last he had won.

Now, however, he had to prove that the Yankees could win without the Babe. The indications were that they could. The Tigers had suffered a terrific loss of prestige in the 1934 World Series with the Cardinals. No one seemed to remember the great fight they had made to win the pennant. All anyone seemed to recall clearly was that they had folded miserably before the charge of the Cardinals, losing the final game 11 to 0, and reeling from the field almost deafened by the booing of their own fans. If that was the only team the Yankees had to beat to win the flag, the odds seemed in their favor. And, as it turned out, that was the only team.

Through the first couple of weeks of the season, the Yanks bobbed up and down, but with the coming of May they were straightened out and by the end of the month they had knocked out the front-running Indians and White Sox and were in the lead. If Gehrig had been hitting and if Gomez had been pitching with his usual effectiveness, it would have looked like a breeze. But Lou was lagging, and Gomez was in and out.

McCarthy was scowling, Barrow was grumbling, and Ruppert was fretful. Both Lou and Lefty had made a trip around the world, setting out with the Babe, campaigning through the Orient with him and then separating, each following his own route in his own time from Yokohama around to New York. The popular verdict, in which McCarthy, Barrow, and Ruppert shared—perhaps, even, inspired—was that the young men had had too much baseball and too much touring and were tired when they reached the training camp. Gehrig tended to smash that theory by quickening his pace at the bat—there never had been anything wrong with his fielding— as the season advanced. But it might have fitted Lefty's case, at that. He never did catch up.

Anyway, that was the way they were as they headed into June. Selkirk, Chapman, and Combs in the outfield. Gehrig at first base. Lazzeri playing most of the time at second but giving over now and then to Heffner or Saltzgaver. Rolfe at third. Crosetti at short stop. Dickey doing almost all the catching, with Arndt Jorgens or Joe Glenn to relieve him. Gomez, Ruffing, Allen, DeShong, Murphy, Johnny Broaca, and Vito Tamulis cutting up the heavy duty in the box.

But now the Tigers were on the loose again. The Yankees held on through June and most of July, but as July faded the Yanks faded with it, and before the month was out the Tigers were on top. Combs had recovered from his injuries of the year before, but he was playing his twelfth season in the big show, and he was wearing out fast. McCarthy benched him and switched Chapman to center field, using Hoag or the speedy Jesse Hill in left. Crosetti floundered at short stop, and McCarthy called up Nolen Richardson and Blondy Ryan (the latter famous for his "We can't lose, I'm on my way" telegram to Bill Terry on rejoining the Giants in

1933) to help out, but neither was an improvement on Crosetti. Pat Malone, who had been the mainstay of McCartry's pitching staff when he won the pennant with the Cubs in 1929, also responded to a call for aid but was unable to contribute much. Van Atta had failed and was released to the Browns.

The rest of the clubs practically were nowhere as the Yankees pursued the Tigers through August and September. McCarthy drove his players hard. Ruppert stamped an impatient foot. Barrow was restless in his mezzanine box seat when the team was at home, restless in his office when it was on the road. The players gave all they had to the chase. But they didn't have enough. When the final returns were in, the Tigers had won by three games.

The figures on the Yankees that year, broken down a little bit, show that Gomez, who had won twenty-five games while losing only six in 1934, had won only twelve and lost fifteen in 1935. Ruffing topped the pitchers, yet he won only sixteen games. Gehrig, in spite of his belated rush, slipped thirty-four points in his batting average and fell off by nineteen in his production of home runs.

Spotty pitching, an attack that lacked sustained power, and fielding that was frequently ragged—these had held the Yankees back through the last two months of the season. It galled McCarthy to know that although the Tigers had fallen off, too—winning eight less and losing five more than they had in 1934—he had been unable to beat them. It was easy for him, looking back, to see how easily the Yankees might have won four or five of the games they had lost and so have won the pennant.

They were dark days for him. It was no consolation to him to know that in five seasons in New York he had not finished worse than second, and that he had won one pennant. That pennant was beginning to look a little tattered to him by

CHARLIE RUFFING

VERNON GOMEZ

JOE DIMAGGIO

© *Cosmo-Sileo*

JOE GORDON

now. All he could think of was that four times he had finished second—he who didn't like to finish second.

Could he have looked ahead, around the bend of winter, to another season, he would have been happy as he sat before his fireplace on Gates Circle in Buffalo, for in 1936 he was to launch an era brighter and more amazing than any major-league manager ever had known—or ever has known, up to now.

3

To begin with there was the long-awaited arrival of Joe DiMaggio at the training camp 'in the spring of 1936. He had made the trip across from San Francisco to St. Petersburg in a car with Lazzeri and Crosetti. That was Tony's idea. Tony didn't know Joe very well. Since Joe was only eleven years old when Tony joined the Yankees, Tony never had seen him play, but he had adopted him because he was another Italian kid off the sandlots of San Francisco, just as he had adopted Crosetti for the same reason, three years before.

It also was Tony's idea that the three of them should share the driving chore on the transcontinental haul. He took the wheel when they set out and drove steadily for four or five hours and then moved over to make room for Crosetti in the driver's seat. After Frankie had piloted the car for four or five hours, Tony motioned to Joe.

"All right," he said. "It's your turn."

"I'm sorry," Joe said. "I can't drive."

Lazzeri and Crosetti looked at each other.

"Let's throw the bum out and leave him here," Tony said.

DiMaggio settled himself more comfortably in the rear seat.

"Get going," he said, with a laugh. "I got a date with the Yankees."

It isn't likely there was much conversation on the trip. None of the three even remotely resembles a chatterbox. One day that summer Jack Mahon, International News sports writer, reported a scene featuring them in the lobby of the Hotel Chase, where the Yankees stop in St. Louis.

"I came down in the elevator," he said, "and the three of them were sitting there, watching the guests coming and going. I bought a paper and sat down near them, and after a while became aware of the fact that none of them had a word to say to the others. Just for fun, I timed them to see how long they would maintain their silence. Believe it or not, they didn't speak for an hour and twenty minutes. At the end of that time, DiMaggio cleared his throat. Crosetti looked at him and said:

" 'What did you say?'

"And Lazzeri said: 'Shut up. He didn't say nothing.'

"They lapsed into silence and at the end of ten more minutes I got up and left. I couldn't stand it any more."

When they reached the clubhouse at Huggins Field the other players looked curiously at DiMaggio as Tony took him around and introduced him. DiMaggio was pleasant but silent, merely smiling as he shook hands with his new team mates. The only one who said anything to him beyond, "Pleased to meet you," was Ruffing. Charlie looked at him quizzically, grinned, and said:

"So you're the great DiMaggio!"

Joe gulped, Tony glared at Ruffing, and the pair went down the line of players. McCarthy, in his office at one end of the clubhouse, also looked at Joe with interest. Lazzeri left DiMaggio there, and player and manager had a brief conversation.

When DiMaggio came out, the newspapermen were there to meet him, and Tony again took over the introductions.

"What did McCarthy say to you?" the newspapermen wanted to know.

"Not much."

"Did he tell you where you would play?"

"No."

"Did you express any preference?"

"No. Wherever he wants me to play is all right with me."

"Left field is the sunfield at the Stadium. Did you ever play the sunfield?"

"No."

"Ruth never would play it."

Joe shrugged. "I'll play it if Mr. McCarthy wants me to."

"More likely he'll play you in center field."

"That's all right with me."

Once in uniform, DiMaggio convinced McCarthy, the players, and the newspapermen that the stories of his skill and power had not been exaggerated. Of course, he was hitting only batting-practice pitching and catching fungoes hit to the outfield, but the stamp of the major-league ball player was unmistakable.

Unmistakably, too, he was the number one man in the camp. Gehrig, who had walked so long in the shadow of Ruth, now walked in the shadow of DiMaggio. It was, however, without envy on Gehrig's part that he saw DiMaggio usurp the place he had held so briefly since the departure of Ruth. DiMaggio moved into it without a swagger.

In good condition when he reached the camp, DiMaggio had only to take a few days of batting practice to adjust his swing and to lope around the park or shag flies to limber up his leg muscles, and he was ready for the exhibition games that the Yankees had scheduled. He had played in four of them—one with the Reds, one with the Braves, and two with the Cardinals—when he injured his left foot.

Earle Painter, the Yankee trainer, examined the injury.

"A couple of days of rest and a little diathermy will fix that up," he said.

The second day, as Joe sat with the foot under a lamp, something went wrong with a gadget. Before he realized it and before Painter was aware of what had happened, the foot was burned. A doctor was called, who shook his head after the examination.

"This man will not be able to play for two or three weeks at the least," he said.

The Yankees were about to break camp.

"You may as well go on to New York," McCarthy said to DiMaggio. "There would be no sense in taking you on the tour with us."

And so the great DiMaggio, a day or two later, limped into New York, his burned foot encased in a carpet slipper, as his team mates hammered their way up along the exhibition trail.

4

The day the Yankees opened the season at the Stadium—they had already played in Washington—there was a fellow seated back of first base who yelled, all through the game:

"Where's Joe DiMaggio?"

No one took the trouble to tell him, but Joe was at the office of the Yankees' physician, having his burned foot treated.

Babe Ruth, in his familiar fawn-colored overcoat, with cap to match, sat in a field box near the dugout, looking on at a Yankee opening for the first time. It was a dismal day, atmospherically and otherwise. The sky was gray, a cold wind swept the stands, and the Yankees couldn't hit Lefty Grove, who was pitching for the Red Sox. They couldn't field, either; and Ruffing, opposed to Grove, never had a chance to win.

There was little reason to believe, that day, that the Yankees could beat out the Tigers, finally accepted as real champions after their defeat of the Cubs in the 1935 World Series. There even was some doubt at the time that they could beat out the Red Sox, strengthened by the presence of Jimmy Foxx on first base. And yet, three weeks later, they were in first place. Almost overnight they had clicked. They were a smash hit. They were terrific.

DiMaggio was in the line-up now. He had never seen major-league pitching before, but he was hitting it as though he had been looking at it for years and had reeled off a string of sixteen consecutive games in which he made one or more safe drives. He had never played a sunfield before, but he was playing the difficult sunfield at the Stadium as though he had grown up in it, Combs definitely having retired as an active player to become a coach with the team and McCarthy having kept Chapman in center with Selkirk in right. This gave the Yankees the best outfield they had had since Ruth, Combs, and Meusel were at the peak—and yet McCarthy was looking curiously at the temperamental Chapman and, perhaps, even then framing in his mind a deal for a replacement for him.

Gehrig, of course, was at first base. Lazzeri at second base and Crosetti at short stop, were in top form once more. Rolfe, a sounder and steadier player than he had been the year before, was doing a grand job at third base. Dickey never had been quite as good and was pounding the ball. Bump Hadley and Monte Pearson, newcomers on the pitching staff, were winning consistently. So were Ruffing, Gomez, Broaca, and Brown. Murphy and the veteran Malone were solid relief men.

The Yankees mauled the Red Sox, the only threat in the East, then went West and mopped up the Tigers and the Indians. As they hurtled through June, there was no doubt that they were going to win the pennant. The baseball writers called them the new Murderers' Row. They hammered the ball against the fences and over the fences. They drove enemy pitchers to cover and frightened the infielders.

Eddie Brannick, secretary of the Giants, saw them play one day, and when somebody asked him what he thought of them he summed them up in two words.

"Window breakers," he said.

DiMaggio's popularity was tremendous. As they had done when Lazzeri had first worn a Yankee uniform nine years before, Italian fans poured into the ball parks all over the circuit to see the new hero. Dinners and parties were given in his honor. Gifts awaited him everywhere he went. One day Barrow, fearing his head might be turned by the clamor, called him to his office and gave him some excellent advice.

"Don't take the applause too seriously, Joe," he said, "and don't become overanxious in your efforts to hold to the pace you have struck."

"Don't worry about me, Mr. Barrow," Joe said. "I never get excited."

Not only his words but his tone convinced Barrow that he needn't go any further.

In June McCarthy traded Chapman to Washington for Jake Powell. On the face of it, it wasn't an even trade, and McCarthy was criticized for it. But he knew what he was doing. Chapman, for all his natural ability, was not McCarthy's type of ball player—and Powell was. Ben was hot-headed, quarrelsome, and at times would sulk. Powell was tough and hard talking, but he played earnestly every time he walked on the field and never got into jams with his team mates. He took orders unquestioningly and slipped easily into the spot McCarthy had prepared for him. This was left field, DiMaggio being moved to center because he covered a wider range of territory than Jake.

By August the other clubs in the league had folded under the impact of the Yankees' continued assaults. And on September 9 the Yanks clinched the pennant, thereby setting an American League record, for never before had a club settled the issue as early as that. Smashing on, they finished the season nineteen and a half games in front of the second-place Tigers.

Dickey led the team in batting with an average of .362. Gehrig hit .354, DiMaggio .323, Rolfe .319, Selkirk 308. Only three regulars failed to hit .300—and Powell missed by only one point, while Crosetti's average was .288 and Lazzeri's .287. The home-run yield was startling. Gehrig accounted for forty-nine, DiMaggio for twenty-nine, Dickey for twenty-two, Selkirk for eighteen, Crosetti for fifteen, Lazzeri for fourteen, Rolfe for ten, and Powell for eight. Besides, DiMaggio and Rolfe each collected fifteen triples.

Ruffing won twenty games and Pearson won nineteen. Hadley won fourteen, and Gomez thirteen. Brown and the somewhat ancient Malone each came up with twelve. Murphy tagged along with twelve, but he had saved a number of games that didn't appear in his won-and-lost totals.

5

That year there was a revival of the World Series on the subway. The Giants had crashed through in the National League. Thirteen years had elapsed since the Yankees and Giants last had clashed with the title hanging on the line, and the town was ready for their meeting. A new generation of fans had grown up at the Stadium and the Polo Grounds, and the excitement was as great, or almost as great, as it had been back in 1921, when the first series between the teams had been played.

This series opened at the Polo Grounds, with Ruffing pitching against Carl Hubbell. It was a miserable day for a game. Rain fell intermittently as the afternoon wore on, but Hubbell pitched so magnificently through the rain and mud that the Yankees never had a real chance to beat him. For seven innings Ruffing pitched well, too, so that going into the eighth the score was 2 to 1 in the Giants' favor. But there Ruffing weakened, and the Giants, aided by errors by Crosetti and Dickey, rushed four runs over the plate to win by a score of 6 to 1.

Hubbell's screwball magic had throttled the Yankee power, and in the second game Bill Terry sent Hal Schumacher to the mound, hoping that Hal's fast ball would be equally effective. But it wasn't. President Franklin Delano Roosevelt was in the stands that day, seated in a box near the Giants' dugout, and the Yankees put on a breathtaking show for him, hammering Schumacher, Coffman, Gabler, and Gumbert for seventeen hits, including home runs by Dickey and Lazzeri—Tony's came with the bases filled in the ninth inning—and winning by a score of 18 to 4. Gomez, who pitched for the Yankees, had such a soft time of it that once he actually ignored the hitter and, stepping out of the box, calmly watched a transport plane flying over the grounds.

Ten World Series records for a single game were broken or tied in this engagement. Lazzeri was the second player to hit a home run with the bases filled, Elmer Smith of Cleveland having achieved that feat in the 1920 series with the Dodgers. Lazzeri and Dickey, each driving in five runs, beat the record held by nine players, one being Lazzeri himself. Crosetti equaled a mark jointly held by Ruth and Combs by scoring four runs. DiMaggio tied Ott of the Giants and Orsatti of the Cardinals by making three put-outs in one inning. No team ever had made as many as eighteen runs, thirteen having been the record. No two teams had ever made a total of twenty-two runs. Every player on the Yankees made a hit and scored a run. The teams gathered a total of sixteen bases on balls. Leiber, with eight, had the most chances accepted by a center fielder. And, which wasn't at all surprising, it was the longest series game ever played, dragging through two hours and forty-nine minutes.

The scene was shifted to the Stadium the following day, and there Fred Fitzsimmons, pitching for the Giants, lost a heart-breaker. Fitz hooked up with Hadley, and the pair of them went to the eighth inning with the score tied at 1-1, Gehrig having hit a homer in the second inning and Jimmy Ripple of the Giants having hit one in the fifth. Then, in the eighth, Selkirk opened with a single to right, Powell walked, and Lazzeri moved them along with a sacrifice. Ruffing was sent up to hit for Hadley and slapped weakly to Fitzsimmons, who threw Selkirk out at the plate. Now came the break. Crosetti hit a high bounder just to the right of the box; and, as Fitz was perhaps the best fielding pitcher in baseball at the time, it seemed an easy chance for him. But the ball glanced off his glove for a scratch hit, and Powell raced home with what proved to be the winning run. Fitz, tears of rage in his eyes, got rid of Rolfe to close out the inning; but Malone, who pitched the ninth inning for the Yankees, turned the Giants back scoreless.

After the game a reporter who covered the Yankees regularly said to McCarthy in the clubhouse:

"I was rooting for you, as you know. But I felt sorry for Fitz."

Joe nodded. "To tell you the truth," he said, "I did, too."

Hubbell came back to pitch the fourth game, drawing Pearson as his opponent, but this time he could not foil the Yankees. A home run by Gehrig, jammed into a third-inning attack that yielded three runs, really sewed up the game, the Yankees winning, 5 to 2.

The Giants struck back in the fifth game, winning 5 to 4 in ten innings as Schumacher, pitching doggedly all the way, took a decision over Ruffing and Malone. Selkirk hit a home run in this game, but it didn't matter. A double by Joe Moore, a sacrifice by Bartell, and a long fly by Terry decided the game in the tenth.

But that was the end of the Giants' resistance, and the series ended in the sixth game, played at the Polo Grounds. For eight innings this combat was a thriller, with Gomez and Murphy tussling against Fitzsimmons and Castleman in the box, but Castleman was removed for a pinch hitter in the eighth and, with Coffman pitching for the Giants in the ninth, there was a sudden outbreak of Yankee power, and seven runs clattered over the plate as the Giants were counted out, 13 to 5.

It was a triumph for McCarthy in more ways than one. Not only had the Yankees established themselves once more at the top of the heap; but Powell, lightly regarded by some of the critics right up to the time of the series, played a whale of a game in the outfield—and hit .455. Rolfe hit .400, and DiMaggio .346. Seven home runs had splattered into the stands, Gehrig and Selkirk getting two each, and Powell, Lazzeri, and Dickey one.

Ruppert was happier than he had been since 1932. Barrow no longer was restless. At his desk in the office on Forty-second Street he hummed an old-time tune as he cleaned up his correspondence preparatory to a hunting trip with Paul Krichell. In the newspapers McCarthy was being hailed as the greatest manager in baseball.

XVIII · The Pace Quickens

⊖

1

IN JANUARY OF 1937 the Young Men's Board of Trade gave a dinner for Lou Gehrig at the Harvard Club in New York and presented the Distinguished Service Key to him in token of its recognition of the fine example he set for the boys and young men of the town. The year before the award had gone to Thomas E. Dewey, now Governor of New York, then the gang-busting district attorney of fiction come to life. Never before had an athlete won it.

That same month Barrow and McCarthy conferred about the team and decided to make no material changes in it. They had not only a winning but a rip-roaring combination. Why disturb it?

Late in February the team went South. Late in March it started back—and around the country the baseball experts almost unanimously picked it to win the pennant again. Baseball experts aren't always right, but they were that time. The Yankees simply couldn't miss. It took them about a month to hit their stride as the Tigers stuck close and the White Sox threatened; but even McCarthy, who worries more than he should, wasn't worried about them. They took the lead on May 23 and held it for the balance of the season.

Two days after the Yankees grabbed the lead a dreadful, almost fatal, accident took place at the Stadium. The Tigers were playing there that day, and Bump Hadley was pitching for the Yankees. In the fourth inning he hit Mickey Cochrane in the head. Bitterly as they fought Cochrane on the field, the Yankees had a tremendous liking and admiration for him and they—and particularly Hadley—were shocked as Black Mike rolled in the dirt at the plate.

For a couple of days it was feared that Cochrane would die. Even when he had passed the crisis, it was obvious that he would not be able to play again that year nor even to manage the Tigers from the dugout. His absence undoubtedly weakened his team greatly, and yet it is unlikely that it had a marked effect on the outcome of the pennant race. There is no reason to believe that even with him in the line-up the Tigers could have overhauled the Yankees.

One of the greatest demonstrations the Yanks put on that year came in the All Star game. From the inception of this game the Yanks had figured prominently in it. Ruth, Gehrig, Chapman, and Gomez played in the first game in Chicago in 1933, and Lazzeri and Dickey also were on the American League squad but did not see action. Fittingly enough, Ruth brought the National League crashing down with a home run, and Gomez was the winning pitcher, the score, by the way, being 4 to 2. In 1934, at the Polo Grounds, Dickey joined Ruth, Chapman, Gehrig, and Gomez in helping to beat the National League, 9 to 7. At Cleveland in 1935 Gomez again was the winning pitcher—the score was 4 to 1—and, Ruth having departed, Gehrig and Chapman again were chosen for the team. DiMaggio was the goat of the 1936 game at Boston, although he could easily have been the hero of it, his failure to make a shoestring catch of a line drive by Gabby Hartnett being the turning point of the tussle.

In 1937 the game was played in Washington, and McCarthy, as manager of the American League team, selected five of his players—Rolfe, DiMaggio, Gehrig, Dickey, and Gomez—in his starting line-up, and they proceeded to steal the show. Gehrig hit a home run off Dizzy Dean in the third inning, Rolfe won the game with a triple in the fourth (the final count was 8 to 3), and once more the winning pitcher was Gomez.

Two baseball writers, both working on the same New York paper, were getting on the train after the game. One said:

"I had a wire from the boss. He says for me to take the Yankee angle on the game and that you can write anything else you please."

The other said:

"Then I guess I will have to write about President Roosevelt because he was the only other guy at the ball game who counted."

That was the way the National League fans felt. They felt that their heroes had been beaten, not by the American League, but by the Yankees. As a matter of fact, they had.

Gomez had one of his best years in 1937. He won twenty-one games and lost eleven and had the lowest earned-run average, 2.33, in the league. But Ruffing had an even better record on games won and lost, winning twenty and losing only seven. Spurgeon Chandler, brought up from Newark, was the most notable addition to the pitching staff, although Ivy Paul Andrews, who returned to the club once more, this time from Cleveland, was useful. Murphy, credited with thirteen victories and charged with only four defeats as he toiled in thirty-nine games, was the best relief pitcher the Yankees had had since Wilcy Moore. That was the year the Yankees first called Johnny "the Fireman."

DiMaggio had a fine season. So did Gehrig. Crosetti was about as good defensively as he had been the year before, but his hitting fell off. Rolfe had established himself as the best third baseman in the League. Only Lazzeri, among the infielders, had slipped. It was Tony's twelfth campaign, and he was showing signs of wear. Selkirk had a pretty good season, but lost a month or so because of injuries. Powell and

Hoag alternated in left field. Dickey, as usual, did most of the catching and hit .332.

Meanwhile, a new favorite had been unveiled at the Stadium. In April Commissioner Landis decided that the Cleveland club had been covering up (that is, holding in the minor leagues too long) a young outfielder by the name of Tommy Henrich, who was with the New Orleans club. He thereupon declared Henrich a free agent, and in the rush by major-league clubs to snare him, the Yankees got there first with the most money. They paid Henrich $25,000 to sign a contract with them, farmed him out to Newark, and brought him back a week or so later when Selkirk was hurt.

Smiling, boyish in appearance, Tommy played the outfield almost as though he were another infielder, coming in fast for ground balls hit to his territory and whipping the ball in, sometimes, to first base to catch an unwary hitter rounding the bag. He hit consistently, and, a left-handed thrower, often worked out at first base before a game.

"If Gehrig ever knocks off," a baseball writer said to McCarthy, "you've got a fellow to take his place."

"That's what I was thinking," Joe said.

But Gehrig showed no signs of knocking off. He had said in the early spring that he hoped to run his string of consecutive games to 2,500 before retiring. And now he was slamming the ball with his accustomed vigor—he hit .351 that year and made thirty-seven home runs—and he was still the top first baseman, challenged for that distinction only by Bill Terry.

The absolute supremacy of the Yankees naturally detracted from interest in the other clubs, and around the league—except in New York—gate receipts fell off. But crowds still stormed the Stadium, still packed the parks in the other towns when the Yankees were the attraction. Everybody wanted to see the wonder team. Nobody tired of watching Gehrig, DiMaggio, and Dickey slam the ball against or over the barriers.

Winning in a romp—their margin over the second-place Tigers was thirteen games—the Yankees once more passed the century mark in victories, with 102 as against 52 defeats.

2

Once more the Giants furnished the opposition in the World Series. The opening game, played in the Stadium, brought Gomez and Hubbell together, and for five innings the edge lay with Hubbell; but in the sixth the Yankees opened up, battered Carl badly, and rolled up seven runs. Lazzeri hit a home run in the eighth to make the final count 8 to 1.

The second game ended with the same score, although the Yanks spread their scoring over three innings instead of two. Charlie Ruffing pitched this one for the Yankees, and Cliff Melton started against him. The Giants were off in the lead, making their run in the first inning; but the Yanks scored two runs in the fifth, four in the sixth, and two in the seventh.

Then they switched to the Polo Grounds, but the Yanks went hammering along. They beat Schumacher this time, 5 to 1. Pearson, pitching for the Yankees, weakened in the ninth, and the Giants loaded the bases. Although two were out and he still had a four-run lead, McCarthy was taking no chances. Out came Pearson, and Murphy stalked in from the bull pen to put the crusher on the Giants.

Up to this time it had been a very dull series, especially from the viewpoint of the Giant fans; but in the fourth game Hubbell hurled the Yanks back as the Giants flattened Bump Hadley. Hadley went down under a second-inning assault that yielded six runs, and the Giants won, 7 to 3, one of the Yankees' runs being a homer by Gehrig.

Heartened by their victory in this game, the Giants continued to fight back stubbornly the following day after a home run by Hoag in the second inning and another by DiMaggio in the third. In their half of the third, with Ott hitting for the circuit, they tied the score, and Gomez and Melton practically started all over; but in the fifth the Yankees won the game and the series. Lazzeri opened with a triple and scored the decisive run on an infield hit by, of all persons, Gomez. Crosetti flied out, Rolfe walked, DiMaggio flied out, and Gehrig slammed a double to right center, scoring Gomez to sew up the combat.

The series had gone strictly to form, just as the season had done. The Giants simply had had nothing with which to combat successfully the American League champions.

A surprise in the series was the magnificent playing of Lazzeri who, for at least those five days, was the Lazzeri of old, a standout at second base and leading the team at bat with an average of .400. Among those impressed by the vigor of his playing was Phil Wrigley, owner of the Cubs. The more Phil thought about it, the more he became convinced that he could use Tony in Chicago, and he finally took up with Barrow the matter of obtaining the veteran's services. This was arranged in characteristic Yankee fashion. Lazzeri, when sounded out by Barrow, having expressed a willingness to go to Chicago, waivers were obtained on him and he received his unconditional release. Whereupon he signed a contract with the Cubs at a fine salary, plus a bonus.

"What I really am trying to do," Wrigley admitted, "is to capture some of that Yankee spirit I admire so much. It seems to me that for a long time Lazzeri has typified that spirit, and I am sure he can impart it to our players."

Regret over the departure of Lazzeri was tempered by a

belief that he was on his way to a managerial job in either the National or the American League within the near future —a belief that, by the way, was blasted. Meanwhile, he left behind him but one survivor—Gehrig—of the team that, in 1927, had rocked both leagues. Now, ten years later, the Yanks were rocking the leagues again.

3

There hadn't been a real holdout among the Yankees since Ruth had left the club. But in 1938 there was one—Joe DiMaggio.

Joe had journeyed from his home in San Francisco to New York early in February for the Baseball Writers' dinner; and there he intimated that he would not sign for less than $40,000—a stiff asking price for a player with only two years in the major leagues behind him. However, no one took him too seriously at the time. It was assumed he would see Barrow—or Ruppert—and reach an agreement before he went home, but he didn't. A month later, as the other players were reporting at St. Petersburg, Joe remained in San Francisco, still asking for $40,000. In New York, Ruppert revealed that he had offered $25,000 and would go no higher. Joe's answer to that was that business in his new restaurant was so good he couldn't afford to leave it for that kind of money.

Possibly as an expression of the changing times, or possibly a mere indication that Joe had jumped the gun by holding out after so short a time in the big show, sentiment was almost wholly against him, where once Ruth or, for that matter, almost any holdout, had everybody on his side. Whatever the reason, nearly everyone, including his team mates, felt that Joe would be well paid at $25,000. There was no desire to minimize the young man's skill, drawing power, or the help he had given in the winning of the pennant in the two years he had been with the club. But twenty-five grand, the ball players were saying, was a lot of dough. And, if anybody wanted to know a little more how they felt about it, they thought he should be at St. Petersburg with them getting into shape. He—in shape or out of it—might mean the difference between another pennant and second-place money.

Meanwhile, to take Lazzeri's place at second base, there was Joe Gordon, up from Newark, where he had put in óne of his two years of minor-league training. The Yanks had taken him out of the University of Oregon in 1936 and planted him that year in Oakland. Now he was ready. Ready? Well, to hear Oscar Vitt tell it, he was just about to set the American League on fire.

Vitt, who became the manager of the Cleveland club that spring, had managed the Newark club the year before.

"Gordon is going to be the greatest second baseman you ever saw," he had said one day during the 1937 season when the Newark club had a day off and he had run over to the Stadium to see McCarthy. He was talking to Joe and some of the baseball writers in Joe's office in the clubhouse.

"Take it easy, Oscar," one of the writers said. "I've been around a long time, and I've seen some pretty good second basemen."

"So have I," Vitt said. "I've seen Lajoie, Collins, Evers, Hornsby, Frisch, Lazzeri, and Gehringer—among others. I don't say this kid is better than they were. All I'm saying is that some day he will be. He is better than anybody in the big leagues now, with the exception of Gehringer—and he'll catch him in a year."

Now Gordon was at St. Petersburg, and everybody was getting a good look at him. It was plain from the day he reported that he was more than just an adequate replacement for Lazzeri. Tony's greatest admirers admitted that the Lazzeri of the last couple of years couldn't come even close to matching this acrobatic kid.

McCarthy, watching Gordon and Crosetti flipping the ball back and forth as they bobbed, weaved, and floated around second base, was delighted. He hadn't had a real double-play combination on the Yankees before. But he had one now.

There were a few other additions to the squad. Steve Sundra, Joe Beggs, Buddy Rosar, and Atley Donald had been brought up from Newark with Gordon. Bill Knickerbocker, veteran infielder, had been obtained from the Browns for Don Heffner. Babe Dahlgren, who had spent a little time, almost unnoticed, with the team in 1937, was back, and McCarthy said he would keep him. Everybody knew Dahlgren. He had been with the Red Sox before the Yankees had got him and sent him to Newark. He was one of those first basemen who were growing old waiting for Gehrig to wear out. (Gehrig had hit .351 and made thirty-seven home runs in 1937; and Dahlgren, being right-handed and no dope, bought a finger glove and worked out around second base, third base, and short stop.)

The team was about to break camp—the date was March 29—when the players read in their newspapers of the death of Cap Huston. The news had no effect on them save to spur the curiosity of a few to ask the older newspapermen about him. It had been fifteen years since Cap and Ruppert had split up, and none of the 1938 Yankees, with the exception of Gehrig, ever had seen him. Some of them, indeed, had never heard of him. In New York there were polite expressions of regret from Ruppert and Barrow. In St. Petersburg the graybeards among the reporters talked of the pleasant times they had had.with him and raised their glasses to him. But even to them the time when he was a powerful figure in this ball club seemed long ago.

Cap had died on his plantation on Butler Island, near Brunswick, Ga., where, except for occasional visits to Atlanta or New York, he had spent most of his time since his retirement from baseball, looking after his extensive gardens, his prize dairy herd, and his game preserve. Only once had he seemed tempted to return to baseball. A few years before, he had offered $1,700,000 for the Dodgers, but the offer had been declined.

He was seventy-one years old and had had a full and richly colored life, in the course of which he had made few enemies and countless friends. Sometimes it was doubtful which afforded him the greater pleasure. Certainly it was a treat to hear him curse his enemies.

The training season dragged on with DiMaggio still in San Francisco. Negotiations between him and Ruppert had been suspended. Each was waiting for the other to give in, now that the opening of the season was approaching. In New York, it was being said along Broadway that Joe Gould, fight manager and friend of DiMaggio's, had advised him to hold out. When Gould heard that he went to the Yankees' office to see Barrow.

"Ed," he said, "I think you know me well enough to know I wouldn't have the impertinence to interfere in your affairs by telling one of your ball players how much money he ought to get."

"I do," Barrow said.

"All right. Just so you and Colonel Ruppert know. I don't care what anybody else says or thinks. Joe is my friend, and I hope he winds up making a million; but how he makes it is his business. My business is managing fighters, not ball players."

As weeks passed and criticism of the player was growing, Gould dropped in to see Barrow again.

"Do you want me to call DiMag' and try to straighten him out?" he asked.

"No. We've made our last offer to him. But he's a friend of yours, and if you want to call him, I can't stop you."

That night Gould called the player.

"I don't want to butt into your affairs, Joe," he said. "I just want you to know what the public and the newspapers are saying."

"I already heard," DiMaggio said. "But I won't budge from here until I get $40,000."

"O.K.," Gould said. "I'm not trying to advise you. I'm only trying to tell you."

The team reached New York at the end of the exhibition tour from the training camp, with DiMaggio still 3,000 miles away. A night or two later, Gould called DiMaggio again.

"How's tricks?" he asked.

"Swell," Joe said. "The restaurant is doing fine."

"Any news from the Yankees?"

"No. And they haven't heard from me, either."

"Well," Gould said, "I was just thinking if you don't open the season with them, every day you lose is going to have an effect on your future. You have a chance this year to break a lot of records and put yourself in a position to demand the kind of dough you want. But you can't break any records in San Francisco."

There was silence on the San Francisco end.

"Are you there?" Gould asked.

"Yes," DiMaggio said. "I was just thinking. How's the weather in New York?"

"Swell. The weather is great, and everybody is steamed up about baseball."

"I'd like to be there," DiMaggio said suddenly.

"There's a lot of people around here who would like to see you," Gould said.

The next day the player called Barrow.

"I give up," he said. "I'll take the $25,000."

Within a couple of weeks after he reported, he was in shape to play and, as far as his team mates were concerned, all had been forgiven. But the fans, curiously enough, hooted the first time he went to bat at the Stadium, and it wasn't long before they were hooting him all over the circuit. After a while, however, they stopped hooting. It is pretty hard to hold a grudge against a fellow who not only takes punishment without complaining—as he did, never making the slightest protest either in public or private—but sticks to his ball playing and keeps slamming the ball out of the lot.

Partly because they missed DiMaggio in the beginning, the Yanks got off to a slow start, and it wasn't until July 12 that they overhauled those chronic front-runners, the Indians. After that, nothing much mattered. Among the high spots, however, there was a no-hit game by Monte Pearson on August 27. Pearson, who generally moaned when it was his turn to pitch that he had a sore arm or was a sick man and should be in bed—and then pitched a grand game—was feeling even worse than usual when he faced his old team mates, the Indians, that day. The result was that he came very close to pitching a perfect game. He struck out seven and walked two and, as the two who walked were swept off the bases in double plays, only twenty-seven men faced him. Behind him, the Yankees were swatting the ball with gusto, so that they won by a score of 13 to 0.

It was a breeze, that pennant race. Off slowly...in front by July 12...never bothered, never hurried,...they clinched it on September 18. In the final reckoning, they were nine and a half games ahead of the second-place Red Sox.

There were some interesting details. DiMaggio, after all

the fuss he kicked up in the spring, led the team in batting with a mark of .324 and hit thirty-two home runs. Dickey rounded out another great year back of the bat by hitting .313 and making twenty-seven home runs. Gordon, in his first year, hit only .255—but made twenty-five home runs and made even Gehringer look slow around second base. Gehrig, hitting .295 and making twenty-nine home runs, ran his string of consecutive games to 2,122.

4

On the train the night the Yankees left for Chicago to open the World Series Mrs. McCarthy said:

"Poor Pie! I felt so sorry for him! But as long as he had to lose, I'm glad Gabby won."

She was talking about Pie Traynor, who managed the Pirates, and Gabby Hartnett, who had succeeded Charlie Grimm as manager of the Cubs in midseason. The Pirates, after leading most of the way and apparently having the pennant right in their mitts, had blown up, and the Cubs had rushed from behind to beat them, with Hartnett, in true storybook fashion, hitting a home run in the gloaming to win the decisive game.

"Stop feeling sorry for Pie and start feeling sorry for Gabby," a baseball writer said. "By the time your husband's young men get through with him, he'll wish he had struck out instead of hitting a home run that day."

Which, after a while, was the way it worked out. But it was a pretty good series, at that. It was a better series than it figured to be because, with the exception of Hartnett, Lazzeri, and Dizzy Dean, the Cubs had started to fold as soon as they clinched the pennant. Being in there with the Yankees meant, so far as they were concerned, the loser's end of the purse—and they were going to be very glad to get it.

The reporters who accompanied the Yankees found that out the day before the series opened. The Cubs were practicing and the reporters were talking to the players, and one of the players asked:

"How do you figure this series? Do you think we can win?"

Another—this one a pitcher—moved into the group a few minutes later and asked:

"How do the Yanks feel about this series?"

One of the reporters said to another: "Let's go talk to Lazzeri and see what he thinks."

Tony was waiting his turn to hit and the reporter said to him: "Well, Dago, do you give up?"

"Give up what?" he demanded.

"On the series."

His face darkened. "Give up?" he snarled. "What for? We're as good as they are."

"Who's 'they'?"

"The Yankees, of course."

"'They!' That sounds funny, coming from you."

"Well, I ain't on their side any more. And we'll beat their brains out."

"It's too bad," one of the reporters said, as he moved away.

"Hey!" Tony said. "Come back here! What's too bad?"

"It's too bad," the reporter said, "that a few other guys on your team don't feel the way you do. If they did, it might be a good series."

Tony didn't say anything. It was his turn to hit, and he moved up to the plate.

Dean made it a good series. That spring Branch Rickey, the super-salesman, had sold Diz to Wrigley for $185,000, plus Curt Davis, Tuck Stainback, and Clyde Shoun. At the time, it was rather widely suspected that Diz couldn't pitch up an alley and, in a general way, Diz confirmed the suspicion. But he did contrive to win seven games while losing only one; and now, with the World Series on and the Yankees in town, he was telling everybody what he would do to them. The Yankees—with Ruffing pitching against Bill Lee—had won the opening game, 3 to 1, and Hartnett had announced he was going to start Dean.

"Good," the Yankees said. "We'll shut his big mouth for him."

"He's not a bad guy, really," somebody said.

"Maybe not," the Yankees said. "But he talks too much."

Diz, pitching against Gomez, didn't have much that day. A dinky curve ball and a lot of soft stuff, instead of the fog and plow ball he threw back in 1934. But the Yanks were so eager to hit him that they were popping the ball into the air or hitting it into the dirt, and they wouldn't have had a run going into the eighth inning if it hadn't been for some crazy fielding behind Diz in the second inning. Even so, he was leading, 3 to 2, when the Yanks went to bat in the eighth.

But he was tired then. With his head and his heart he had stood the Yanks off for seven innings, and now they were crowding him. Selkirk opened with a single to right. Gordon forced Selkirk, and Hoag, batting for Gomez, forced Gordon. Two out now—and Crosetti up—and Crosetti hit one over the left-field wall, scoring Hoag ahead of him and putting the Yanks in the lead. Diz struck Rolfe out, and Murphy, who replaced Gomez in the box, turned the Cubs back in their half of the eighth, and then the Yanks were up again. Henrich led off with a single to right—and DiMaggio hit one over the left-field wall. Hartnett took Diz out then.

Well, he had given the Yanks a tussle. But they beat him, 6 to 3, and that really clinched the series for them. The teams left for New York that night, and in two games there the Yanks wound it up, Pearson beating Clay Bryant, 5 to 2, and Ruffing beating Lee again, 8 to 3, this time. After the last game Diz pushed his way through the jam in the Yankees' dressing room to shake McCarthy's hand.

"Congratulations, Joe," he said. "You got a great ball club."

"Thanks, Diz," Joe said. "I was sorry we had to beat you the other day. You pitched a great game."

"That's all right, Joe," Diz said. "I got beat by a great team."

They were both right.

XIX · 1939: Lights and Shadows

$\ominus$

B   1

ABE RUTH called at Ruppert's home on Fifth Avenue in
January of 1939. When he came out there were tears in his
eyes.

"Jake is dying," he said.

So he was. He had been a sufferer from phlebitis for a
long time. He had been reported gravely ill more than once
but always had rallied strongly. Now complications had set
in. On January 13 he died.

He had a great funeral. St. Patrick's Cathedral was
crowded with mourners, and police lines held back the
curious thousands who struggled to see the cortège. Flags
were at half staff on the City Hall and other public buildings.

The stories about him in the newspapers fascinated the
fans—the stories of his boyhood, his social background, his
many interests, his tremendous wealth. They had known all
these things, of course. But for years they had thought of
him only as the owner of the Yankees, the builder of the
Stadium, the man who hired Ruth and Huggins and Mc-
Carthy and DiMaggio. They never had felt—well, close to
him, as other fans had felt toward other club owners. They
had seen him, yelled "Hey, Colonel!" at him, cheered him
after a victory. On one memorable occasion he had autographed the score cards of those who crowded about his
box and still was scribbling away furiously when he was

rescued by the police. That was the extent of the contacts between the Colonel and his public. But now that he was dead, that public was sorry and spoke well of him and said that he had been a great man for baseball.

The club owners felt that way about him, too. Few of them could be described as warm, personal friends of his, for there was about him a reserve that made such a relationship difficult. But they had a profound respect for him and regarded him as one who, for all his triumphs, had put far more into baseball than he had taken from it.

He never had married. Publication of his will revealed that he had bequeathed his baseball properties to three women: two nieces, Mrs. Joseph Holleran and Mrs. J. Basil Maguire, and a friend, Miss Helen Winthrope Weyant. The trustees were Barrow; the Colonel's brother, George E. Ruppert; his attorney, Byron Clark; and a nephew, H. Garrison Silleck, Jr. Within a short time Barrow was elected to the presidency of the club.

Subsequently there were reports that the Yankees—and the two main farm clubs, Newark and Kansas City—were about to be sold. Actually, James A. Farley was about to buy them. Conditions brought on by the war, however, were discouraging to his associates.

2

The man who had made the Yankees possible was gone—but the Yankees pushed on, heading into another great season, but one strangely marked by shadows.

There was a new pitcher on the staff that spring and a new figure in the outfield. McCarthy had traded Hoag and Joe Glenn, a catcher, to St. Louis for Oral Hildebrand and had brought Charlie Keller up from Newark. Hildebrand never was much of a pitcher before the Yankees got him—

nor afterward, although he managed to win ten games in 1939. But Keller—well, the Yankees had been waiting for him.

Not yet twenty-three years old, five feet eleven, weighing about 180 pounds and put together as powerfully as any man (someone had called him King Kong and Lefty Gomez said he was the first ball player brought back by Frank Buck), he had been a sensation for two years in the International League. Krichell had signed him out of the University of Maryland in 1936, and in 1937 he had led the International in batting with an average of .353. In 1938 he had topped that figure, hitting .365. He was a welcome addition to the team, especially as Gehrig wasn't hitting in the South.

No one could figure out just what was the matter with Lou. He had had—for him—rather a bad year in 1938. He had made a good start, but a terrific slump had gripped him soon after the teams had passed the halfway mark. Nothing he could do would free him of it. His average skidded. His home runs became fewer . . . fewer.

"I don't know what's wrong with him," Jim Kahn said, "but it isn't merely that he is slowing down as a ball player. There is something physically wrong with him—something that is robbing him of his power. He isn't popping up, striking out, or just getting a piece of the ball. He is hitting it squarely—but it isn't going anywhere."

Because of his fine start, he wound up with twenty-nine home runs and a batting average of .295. Not bad for almost anybody else. But bad for him. That was the first time since 1925 he had failed to hit .300 or better. In the World Series he had made four hits—but they'd all been singles. As Kahn had pointed out, he wasn't getting his old power into his swings.

Now, in the spring of 1939, he couldn't hit, and he couldn't field. He was slow getting down for a ball, slow get-

ting up, slow covering the bag, slow getting the ball away.
Nobody said anything to him. The baseball writers, out of
admiration and sympathy for him, were guarded in their
comments. Now and then one of them asked McCarthy a
question about him. When he did, Joe shook it off or answered evasively.

With the opening of the season, Lou looked so bad that
McCarthy obviously was waiting for him to take himself out
of the line-up. He had played eight games when, on the
night of April 30, the team left for Detroit. Since the next
day was an off day, McCarthy stopped off at his home in
Buffalo. When he reached Detroit on the morning of May 2,
Lou said to him:

"I'm benching myself, Joe."

McCarthy was silent for a moment. And then:

"Why?"

"For the good of the team," Lou said. "I just can't seem
to get going, and nobody has to tell me how bad I've been
and how much of a drawback I've been to the team. I've
been thinking . . . the time has come for me to quit."

"Quit? You don't have to quit. Take a rest for a week or
so, and maybe you'll feel all right again."

Lou shook his head and told Joe the story of the last play
he had made. The final play in the game at the Stadium on
the thirtieth. A ball hit between the box and first base, and
Johnny Murphy fielding it and tossing it to him, who got
to the bag just in time to make the put out—and Murphy
saying, as they hurried from the field:

"Nice play, Lou."

"I knew then," Lou said, "that it was time to quit."

"All right, Lou," Joe said. "Take a rest. I'll put Dahlgren
on first base today. But remember, that's your position—and
whenever you want it back, just walk out and take it."

For the first time since June 1, 1925, Gehrig sat in the dugout that day as the Yankees took the field. His string of 2,130 consecutive games had been broken. The story flashed across the country, hit the headlines on every sporting page, was shrilled through the loud speakers.

"Gehrig Benched! Dahlgren on First Base for Yankees!"

Of all the first basemen who had waited for Gehrig to slow up, Dahlgren had hit the jack pot. Less gifted than some of the others, he had been around when Lou stepped down.

But was Gehrig through, after all? Scott and Sewell and others with long streaks of steady playing had broken those streaks—and then, after a brief rest, come back to play again, some of them for a long time. Stories of some of Lou's narrow escapes from previous breaks were recounted. The time he had that attack of lumbago in Detroit . . . the time he was hit in the head in Norfolk . . . the time he had a broken thumb in New York. . . . Well, it had come at last. But maybe the guy was just tired. Maybe when he had loafed for a couple of weeks—

On June 20 the nation was shocked. Gehrig had been to the Mayo Clinic in Rochester, Minn., for observation, and on that date the following report, handed to Ed Barrow by Gehrig, was made public by him:

This is to certify that Mr. Lou Gehrig has been under examination at the Mayo Clinic from June 13 to June 19, 1939, inclusive.

After a careful and complete examination, it was found that he is suffering from amyotrophic lateral sclerosis. This type of illness involves the motor pathways and cells of the central nervous system and, in lay terms, is known as a form of chronic poliomyelitis—infantile paralysis.

The nature of this trouble makes it such that Mr. Gehrig will be unable to continue his active participation as a baseball player inasmuch as it is advisable that he conserve his muscular energy. He could, however, continue in some executive capacity.

It was signed by Dr. Harold C. Harbein.

Well, there it was. Infantile paralysis—or something like it, the doctors said. Letters . . . telegrams . . . messages of cheer and hope and encouragement came to Lou from all over the country. The players, the newspapermen, others close to him had little to say to him and most of that little was kidding.

"Quit stalling," the ball players would say to him. "Take a bat and go up there and hit one."

They laughed with him, made gentle fun of him. But when his back was turned they shook their heads and talked about him among themselves and wondered how long he would live, for most of them had learned from their own doctors that the report from Rochester was a death sentence.

On July 4, at the Stadium, New York paid to Lou Gehrig the finest tribute a ball player has received. It was Gehrig Appreciation Day, and it was the big town's way of saying— or trying to say—with gifts and rolling cheers and laughs and halting phrases and tears how much it thought of the Little Dutch Boy.

Many of the old Yankees were there—the Yankees of 1927. The Babe, Bob Meusel, Herb Pennock, Waite Hoyt, Tony Lazzeri, Benny Bengough, and Arthur Fletcher; Earle Combs, of course; Bob Shawkey, Mark Koenig, Joe Dugan, George Pipgras, now an umpire and officiating in the games that day; and three Yankees from the 1925 team: Wally Schang, Wally Pipp, whose job Lou had taken, and Everett Scott, whose record of 1,307 games Lou had smashed.

Mom and Pop were there, and Eleanor, his wife. And Jim Farley, then Postmaster General, and Mayor Fiorello H. LaGuardia, of New York, and many other brass hats. They made speeches and Lou made one, and no one who heard it ever will forget it, not only the words, such as, "With all this, I consider myself the luckiest man on the face of this earth..." but the sound of his voice and the way he stood out there.

The Yankees rolled on. On May 11 they had taken first place. On June 28 they had given a rather frightening demonstration of their power by making thirteen home runs in the course of a double-header in Philadelphia. DiMaggio, Dahlgren, and Gordon made three each, and Dickey, Selkirk, and Henrich each contributed one. Dahlgren didn't make many base hits—his average at the end of the year was only .235—but he hit a long ball, accounting for fifteen home runs. DiMaggio was hitting at an amazing pace, eventually leading the league with an average of .381 and making thirty home runs. Ruffing was winning relentlessly—twenty-one victories, including five shutouts for the year. Nobody could beat Sundra—he won eleven games and lost only the last game he pitched.

The pennant was won by a margin of seventeen games over the Red Sox. The Yanks had won 106 games and lost 45.

3

Cincinnati had won the National League pennant for the first time since 1919. Bill McKechnie was a hero; and heroes, too, were Paul Derringer, Bucky Walters, and big Botcho Lombardi. The Yankees were favored to win the series, naturally.

"Let them come and take us!" McKechnie said grimly.

His players nodded. They wouldn't die in the clubhouse, as the Cubs had died the year before. This—with Derringer and Walters pitching—would be different.

The series opened in New York, with Ruffing pitching against Derringer. The score was 2 to 1 in the Yankees' favor.

With the score tied in the ninth, Keller had tripled, Der-ringer had walked DiMaggio—and Dickey had sent Keller home with a single to center. Ruffing had yielded only four hits. The Yanks had made only six off Derringer.

In the press headquarters at the Commodore that night a couple of reporters were arguing about who had pitched the better game.

"Why, Ruffing, of course," one said. "He gave only four hits and one run, to six hits and two runs off Derringer."

"Yes," the other said, "but don't forget: *Derringer was pitching against the Yankees!*"

In the second game Pearson—complaining as usual when McCarthy told him it was his turn to pitch—hurled a two-hit shutout, beating Walters 4 to 0. The Yanks really won it in the third inning, but Dahlgren clinched it with a home run in the fourth.

In spite of the two defeats suffered by the Reds, Cincin-nati still was in a high state of excitement when the teams reached there for the third game. The feeling in the town was that the superb pitching standard set by Ruffing and Pearson couldn't be maintained by the other Yankee pitch-ers, and that when they leveled off the Reds would take care of them—and, on top of all that, Derringer and Walters would be coming back for return engagements.

Gomez started the third game for the Yanks, drawing Junior Thompson as his opponent. But Lefty had a torn tendon in his side that couldn't be held in place even by a girdle he wore when pitching, and the pain was so great that he wisely retired at the end of the first inning, Bump Hadley taking over. Bump was effective the rest of the way. So were the Yankee home-run hitters. They knocked Thompson out and, although they made only five hits, got the astonishing total of seventeen bases, Keller making two home runs and DiMaggio and Dickey one each.

That night, in the Netherland Plaza Hotel, a Red fan at the bar said:

"Break up the Yankees, hell! I'll be satisfied if they'll just break up that Keller."

That game had done it. The steam had gone out of the town the next day. Before the game the band on the field was playing the currently popular, "Three Little Fishes," and on a ramp leading to the upper deck of the grandstand a fan said to his companion:

"That song is symbolic of the Reds and the mighty struggle that landed them in the World Series: 'They swam and they swam—right over the dam.'"

The last game was a loose one. McCarthy started Hildebrand and followed with Sundra, but Murphy had to come in to halt the Reds. Derringer and Walters pitched for the Reds. The Reds really should have won the game, but they staggered long enough in the ninth to allow the Yankees to tie the score with two runs, and then staggered again in the tenth as the Yanks rushed three runs across. Keller and Dickey hit home runs. Lombardi, in the tenth, took his famous snooze at the plate.

Snooze? Well, that's the way it was made to appear by the wits later on, and all anybody seems to remember is that for an interminable time Botcho lay on the ground at the plate as Yankee runners skipped nimbly over him or by him to score. It wasn't quite as bad as all that. What really happened was this:

Crosetti walked, Rolfe sacrificed, and Keller hit to Myers, the short stop, who fumbled. DiMaggio singled to right, scoring Crosetti, and when the ball got away from Goodman, Keller also raced for the plate. Goodman retrieved the ball and hurled it in to Lombardi, who failed to hold it as Keller sideswiped him in passing. The ball lay on the ground about four feet from the plate; and Lombardi, apparently stunned, lay right alongside it. DiMaggio, seeing this, kept right on running and scored before the hapless Botcho could pull himself together and find the ball.

That was all—but, of course, it was enough. Especially since the Reds had blown so badly in the ninth. The crash in the tenth started many of the fans on their way to the exits without waiting to see what happened to their heroes in their half of the inning. Nothing happened, as a matter of fact. Goodman and McCormick, the first two men up, singled. But Murphy got the next three in a row. The game was over. The Yanks had won, 7 to 4.

Within a couple of hours they were on their way to New York. They had smashed all records by winning four World Series in a row, the last two in four games each. Those who remembered the shirt-snatching on the return from St. Louis in 1928 expected to see at least a repetition of that. They had forgotten the nature of McCarthy.

Some of the players, having had a couple of drinks, started a parade through the cars. McCarthy, seated in his drawing room with Dickey, Gordon, Dahlgren, Hadley, Knickerbocker, and Henrich, got up and stuck his head out the door.

"Cut that out!" he said sharply. "What are you, a lot of amateurs? I thought I was managing a professional club. Why, you're worse than college guys!"

The celebrants subsided. McCarthy closed the door, sat down and resumed his conversation. He had been telling the players in the room—and they had been listening intently —about lost games they might have won during the championship season.

XX · DiMaggio Goes Swinging Along

A
1

FTER FOUR YEARS like that, there was a let down. There had to be. Even the Yankees, as Miller Huggins had pointed out twelve years before, couldn't lick the law of averages.

The make-up of the team in 1940 was the same as the one which had crashed to the last of the four flags in a row. But the players weren't quite the same. Bill Dickey had an off year at the bat. So did Red Rolfe. Charlie Ruffing won fifteen games—but he lost twelve. Gomez, a great pitcher for the Yankees for nine years, had slipped so badly that he was in only nine games all year and received credit for only three victories.

Off to a ragged start, the Yanks were in last place by the second week in May and stayed there for two weeks. Then they began to move up slowly. But by August 9 they were only in fifth place and had lost exactly as many games, fifty-one, as they had won. The Indians and the Tigers were making a two-club race of it.

Then the Yanks started to move. Through the last three weeks of August they won sixteen games and lost only three, and now they were crowding the leaders. On September 11, in Cleveland, they beat the Indians in the first game of a double-header and went into first place. But that was their peak. They lost the second game, fell back to second place, were driven back to third by defeats in Detroit, St. Louis, and Chicago. Going home, they rallied again, but the best they could do was to make it close as the Indians curled and the Tigers drove on to win. This was the final standing:

	W.	L.	P.C.
Detroit	90	64	.584
Cleveland	89	65	.578
New York	88	66	.571

There were three major factors in the slashing comeback the Yankees made from the depths of August. One was the hitting of DiMaggio, another the pitching of Ernie Bonham, and the third the skill with which Joe McCarthy held his team together under the press of adversity.

DiMaggio, for the second time in succession, led the league in batting. In order to do so, he too had to come from behind. From July 4 to July 30 he had hit in twenty-three games in a row, the longest streak compiled by any hitter that year. Then came a sharp decline; but he came swinging out of it as he reached the latter part of August. His steady slamming drove runs over the plate, keeping the Yanks up there the rest of the way. It also provided a batting race as thrilling as the pennant race itself. Rip Radcliff of the Browns had led most of the time since the opening bell, with Luke Appling of the White Sox closest to him. But DiMaggio came roaring up, with Ted Williams of the Red Sox and Barney McCosky and Hank Greenberg of the Tigers at his heels. It was a photo finish, and the print showed this: DiMaggio .352; Appling .348; Williams .344; Radcliff .342; McCosky .340; Greenberg .340.

Bonham didn't join the club until August 12. Maybe if he had been held in the spring instead of being sent back to Kansas City—he had come up, step by step, through the farm system: Akron, Binghamton, Oakland, Newark, Kansas City —he might have meant the pennant. But McCarthy, Weiss, and Barrow thought another year on the farm wouldn't hurt him, so back he went. It wouldn't have hurt him, or the club, either, if Gomez had been able to win—or Sundra or Hadley. But they weren't, and Bonham was hauled back and tossed into the breach.

The figures show how well he filled it. He started twelve games and won nine. Two of his victories were shutouts. He had the lowest earned-run average—1.91—in the league. The games he lost were low-score games. He was unquestionably the best pitcher in the league at the end of the season.

McCarthy's job was a difficult one. To quote Huggins again, the first pennant is the easiest to win. After that, they get much tougher. And McCarthy had won four—and four world championships—in a row. Now his team was staggering. It was last in May. That was when it could have got out of his grip and cracked wide open. That's the way these great ball clubs usually go. All in a hurry, overnight. Here today and gone tomorrow.

But McCarthy, instead of losing his grip, tightened it. He never let the players forget for a moment that they had a chance to win. He really meant it—and he almost pulled out another pennant. Even though he missed, he was considered by baseball men who understood his problems to have done a better job of managing than he ever had done before.

Lou Gehrig was a fairly frequent visitor in the dugout that year. Mayor LaGuardia had appointed him to membership on the New York City Parole Commission in the fall of 1939, and the spring of 1940 was the first in sixteen years in which he had not gone South with the Yankees. He was busy now with the cases of wayward youths that came before him, and his strength was seeping from his wasting frame. But every once in a while his halting step would be heard on the stairs leading to the dugout, and he would sit with the players and talk to them of the things they were doing or of the days that used to be.

2

The Yankees had finished in good order in 1940, but Mc-Carthy had a lot of doubts about them by the time he reached St. Petersburg in the spring of 1941. He was faced with more problems then than at any time since that spring, ten years before, when he had been a stranger, just come over from the National League.

For one thing, he didn't know about Crosetti, who had been almost pitifully weak at the plate the year before. He didn't know about Gerald Priddy and Phil Rizzuto, the second-base combination brought up from Kansas City. They were highly rated by everyone who had seen them, but Joe would have to see them for himself. Rizzuto might be good enough to take over the short field—but what was he going to do about Priddy, when he had Gordon for second base? And what of Dickey, whose batting average had dropped to .247? And of Gomez, who couldn't win more than three games?

The only point on which he seemed clear from the moment he reached St. Petersburg—and this came as a surprise to almost everyone else—was that he didn't want Dahlgren on his ball club any more. On February 25, as the squad still was assembling, he announced that Babe had been sold to the Braves at the waiver price.

"But why?" a puzzled correspondent asked.

"His arms are too short," McCarthy said.

It didn't seem to make sense, but there it was. Admittedly, Dahlgren was no great shakes as a hitter. He had hit .235 in 1939 and .264 in 1940. But he drove in a lot of runs for one with an anemic average and played every day—he hadn't missed a day since he had taken Gehrig's place. And, as far as the writers and the fans were concerned, he was a remarkably clever fielder.

"His arms are too short," McCarthy said again. "He makes easy plays look hard."

Somebody hinted that Joe felt that Dahlgren had cost the Yankees the pennant in 1940 by blowing a couple of easy chances in critical games near the end of the race, but he wouldn't comment on that.

"What's all the fuss about Dahlgren?" he demanded. "I've got at least two men to take his place."

"Sturm and who else?"

"Gordon," he said.

Johnny Sturm had been the Kansas City first baseman. Gordon never had played first base.

"What difference does that make?" McCarthy countered. "A good ball player can play anywhere."

Crosetti had been slow in reporting, apparently feeling that Rizzuto was going to play short stop and there was no reason for him to hurry. Red Rolfe was in camp but bothered by a leg injury.

"How about him, Joe?"

"He'll be all right."

That was the way they lined up: Gordon on first base, Priddy on second, Rizzuto at short stop, and Rolfe on third. The outfield was all right, of course. DiMaggio, Keller, and Henrich, with Selkirk to fill in. There was Buddy Rosar, only a fair catcher but a pretty good hitter, to work behind Dickey, and Ken Silvestri, a kid catcher from the White Sox, who might beat Rosar out. Add Steve Peek and Charlie Stanceu from the farms that spring, and the pitching staff was the same.

Gordon looked strange and felt stranger at first base. He got a bone bruise on his left hand because he didn't know how to use his mitt. He frequently got tangled up trying to get back to first base to complete a double-header he had started.

"Don't worry," McCarthy said. "He'll be all right."

"Sure," Gordon said. "I'll be all right."

Just before the season opened, Gordon got a break: Priddy suffered a wrenched ankle and couldn't play. McCarthy sent Gordon back to second base, where he belonged, and posted Sturm on first. Priddy wasn't altogether lost. He played a few games at first base and a few more at third when Rolfe wasn't feeling well—Red having occasional bouts with colitis that kept him out of action. But the regular alignment was Sturm, Gordon, Rizzuto, and Rolfe. Rizzuto made good very quickly. Now and then he needed a rest, being a young fellow and under high pressure. When he did, Crosetti took over.

The team lagged in the beginning, and then DiMaggio got into a hitting streak. It started on May 15 and, naturally, nobody paid much attention to it for a while. But when it was still going by June 1, they paid attention. Particularly as Joe was pulling the rest of the team along with him.

3

On the night of June 2, Gehrig died. He had been bed-ridden for some time, and it was certain that the end was near. Yet when it came, it was sudden, as though he had just dropped off to sleep after a day on which, propped against his pillows, he had read until twilight dimmed the pages of his book.

The Yankees were in Detroit. McCarthy, Dickey, who had been Lou's roommate, and some of the other players went to New York for the funeral, which was held from Christ Episcopal Church in Riverdale.

Lou's Number 4, which no one but he had ever worn, had been retired with him. His locker in the clubhouse, kept open and ready for his use at any time by Fred Logan, the attendant who has been with the Yankees since the old days on the hilltop, now was sealed. He has his niche in the Hall of Fame at Cooperstown, N. Y., and there is a plaque to his memory on the wall at the Stadium.

These are but the tangible reminders that once he passed this way. There are so many others in the hearts of his . friends.

4

DiMaggio went on hitting, smashing one record after another, the most notable of which was Willie Keeler's mark of forty-four games, made in 1897. Joe tied that one in a double-header with the Red Sox before a packed house at the Stadium on July 1, and broke it on July 2. The streak ran through fifty-six games and was broken in the Municipal Stadium in Cleveland in a night combat on July 17, with a crowd of 67,468 looking on. Officially, he was stopped by two pitchers, Al Smith and Jim Bagby. Actually, Ken Keltner, the third baseman, halted him with spectacular plays that took two doubles away from him.

"Smith and I just happened to be in the ball game," Bagby said later. "We didn't have anything to do with it. They ought to put Keltner's name in there as the one who did the dirty work."

Dan Daniel of the New York *World-Telegram,* writing in the *Sporting News Record Book,* offered this breakdown on the string:

Consecutive games, 56. At bats, 223. Hits, 91. Average for streak, .408. Total bases, 160. Runs scored, 56. Runs driven in.

55. Home runs, 15. Triples, 4. Doubles, 16. Struck out, 7 times. Bases on balls, 21. Hit by pitcher—twice.

As DiMaggio approached the records, the eyes of the fans of the nation were turned on the Yankee Clipper. As the pitiless spotlight was trained on Joe, official scorers, too, found themselves in the limelight. Scoring standards became the most stringent, the most exacting, under which a big league hitter has performed over a long stretch of games.

Before the month of July was out, the Yanks were in front by seven games. On September 4 they clinched the pennant. New York fans yawned at the news, then looked to see what the Dodgers had done that day. The Dodgers were fighting it out with the Cardinals for the National League pennant, and if they could win.--

They won, all right. When they came back to town the crowd that greeted them swamped the Grand Central. Frenchy Bordagaray, who had been a Dodger himself once upon a time but now was being carried by the Yankees as a spare outfielder, heard about the mob that greeted the Brooklyn players.

"It ain't fair," he said. "There wasn't anybody there to meet us when we came back with the pennant. I couldn't even find a redcap to carry my bag."

It was natural, of course, that the Dodgers should create excitement. They were an exciting ball club, and the Yankees were not—not in the sense the Dodgers were. And this was the first pennant the Dodgers had won in twenty-one years. Still, the Yankees had done pretty well, too. They had won 101 games and lost only 53. Their margin over the second-place Red Sox was seventeen games. And this had been a triumph for team play. DiMaggio had shown the way, but he hadn't done it all. Everybody on the ball club had helped. One interesting detail was that only three players—DiMaggio. Ruffing, and Rizzuto—had hit over .300 and that only two pitchers—Ruffing and Gomez—had won as many as fifteen games.

5

When they were dusting off the seats at the Stadium the day before the series opened, Sid Mercer said:

"Well, the secret is about to come out. The public will learn, any minute now, the identity of the team that is to meet the Dodgers in the World Series."

It was almost as bad as that. The Dodgers had made a red-hot finish, and Brooklyn was a red-hot town. And as it was nearly a month since the Yankees had clinched their pennant, they practically had dropped out of sight. In the papers and on the air the stories, the poems, the word pictures, were about the Dodgers. Wyatt and Higbe and Camilli, Owen and Walker and Reese, Reiser and Medwick and Herman. And, of course, over all, Leo Durocher and Larry MacPhail.

The only effect this seemed to have on the Yankees was to bore them. Maybe, in the final analysis, that was what was the matter with the Yankees all through the series. They won, as they figured to win. But with the exception of Gordon and Keller and Dickey, there was nothing very sharp about them, and two of their victories followed totally un-expected breaks in their favor.

In the first game, which drew a record crowd of 68,540 and a record gate of $265,396, Ruffing outpointed Curt Davis as the Yankees won, 3 to 2. Each team made only six hits, but the Yankees were better at placing theirs. Or, rather, Gordon was. He made a home run in the second inning and then drove in the winning run with a single in the sixth.

The Dodgers won the second game, 3 to 2, with Whitlow Wyatt pitching remarkably well to overcome Chandler and Murphy. This was the first defeat suffered by the Yankees in a World Series game since 1937, and they had won ten in a row.

An injury to Fred Fitzsimmons may not have won the third game—the first at Ebbets Field—for the Yankees. But, as the Yankees admitted, getting Fitz out of the game was a big help. For six innings he and Marius Russo pitched flawlessly, but it seemed to be his destiny not to have any luck against the Yankees—remember the way they beat him when he was pitching for the Giants? In the seventh inning, then, after two were out, Russo hit a ball back at him so sharply it struck him on the left leg, crippling him. He was helped from the field, and in the eighth inning the Yanks fell on Hugh Casey, his successor, for two runs, ultimately winning the game, 2 to 1.

The fourth game was the one that will not be forgotten in Brooklyn, ever. That was the game the Dodgers lost after —well, it seemed that way, anyhow—three Yankees had been retired in the ninth. Atley Donald started against Higbe, but by the time the teams reached the ninth with the score 4 to 3 in the Dodgers' favor, Casey was pitching for the home club. Sturm led off, and Coscarart threw him out; and then Casey threw out Rolfe. Casey got two strikes on Henrich and then a third—but Owen failed to hold the third strike, and Henrich romped to first. Then the Yankees broke loose. DiMaggio singled to left and Keller doubled to right, scoring Henrich and DiMaggio. Dickey walked and Gordon doubled to left, scoring Keller and Dickey. This was the lone flash of concentrated Yankee power in the series—and Owen had to muff a third strike to bring it out.

That game really finished the Dodgers. There was very little excitement the following day as Bonham pitched a four-hit game and the Yankees beat Wyatt, 3 to 1, Gordon once more driving in the winning run. Complete dullness was averted that day only by a brush between DiMaggio and Wyatt and the threat of a fist fight. The crowd, dispirited, filed out. Downtown, an eight-column line on the front page of the *Brooklyn Eagle* screamed:

"WAIT TILL NEXT YEAR!"

XXI · End of an Era

⊖

O
                        1

N January 16, 1942, roughly five weeks after Pearl
Harbor, President Roosevelt wrote a letter to Judge Landis
in reply to the Commissioner's plea for guidance. It was a
hearty endorsement of the sport.

The Yankees, in common with the other ball clubs, had
been wondering where they stood with the nation at war.
Barrow remembered very well the indecisions, the mistakes,
the hysteria, the confusion, into which baseball had been
hurled by the last war. Now he, and the others, knew. The
President wanted, not less baseball, but more—provided, of
course, it was so shaped as to fit snugly into the war effort.

Barrow never has been given much to the making of state-
ments or the issuing of announcements. If he had anything
to say of an official nature at the time of the President's
letter, it seems to have been lost. He simply has run the ball
club as well as possible under wartime conditions.

Two Yankees had gone off to the armed forces before the
rest of them showed up at the training camp. One was Silvestri, who, with Dickey catching well again and Rosar also
ahead of him, had little opportunity to show his wares in
1941 and had been called to the Army shortly after the end
of the season. The other was Sturm, who had to be replaced
at first base.

There were two candidates for Sturm's job. One was Ed
Levy, called up from Kansas City. The other was Buddy

Hassett, who, in his wanderings about the baseball trails, had returned to the Yankees—the point at which he had started away back in 1933.

Hassett's case is one of the prize examples of the shrewd trading of George Weiss. He was signed upon graduation from Manhattan College, farmed out for two years, and then, since Gehrig was in his prime and there was no room for him at the Stadium, he was sold to Brooklyn in 1936 for $40,000 and two players, Buzz Boyle and Johnny McCarthy. Weiss then sold McCarthy to the Giants for $40,000, sent Boyle to Kansas City as a replacement for Jimmy Gleeson, and sold Gleeson to the Cubs for $25,000—thus netting $105,000 for a player the Yankees couldn't use. Hassett spent three years in Brooklyn and three more in Boston. In February of 1942 the Braves wanted Tommy Holmes, a player the Yankees had in Newark, so Weiss sold him to them for (believe it or not) Hassett, Gene Moore—who promptly was sold to Montreal—and cash!

Now Hassett was back, and McCarthy knew about what he could do. But first he wanted to see what Levy could do, so he gave him the call at St. Petersburg. Levy managed to hang on until the season got under way, but he wasn't quite a major-league first baseman, and McCarthy farmed him out again and turned the job over to Hassett. Gordon, of course, was at second base and Rizzuto at short stop. Rolfe's health was poor through the first part of the season, and Crosetti and Priddy did most of the work at third base, but Rolfe came back to take over his old position.

The winning of the pennant was the, by now, familiar story: hopes flaring in the other towns for a while—and then the Yankees taking command. The war afforded an opportunity for young men from all over the country to see them play at home. Thousands of soldiers, sailors, Marines, and Coast Guardsmen were admitted free every day. Meanwhile, two of the younger pitchers, Charlie Stanceu and Steve Peek, had joined Silvestri and Sturm in the Army.

The Giants and Dodgers having played each other in regularly scheduled games at Ebbets Field and the Polo Grounds, first for the Navy and then for the Army funds, Barrow rigged up an unusual show for the Yankees. Between games of a double-header with the Senators on Sunday, August 23, Babe Ruth went to bat against Walter Johnson, with Billy Evans umpiring. That was tearing a leaf out of the book of memories, and the crowd loved it. So did the ball players, who piled out of their dugouts for a close look at the Babe swinging against Walter again—and hitting a couple into the right-field stands. This exhibition, plus a field day, with the players on the two clubs competing in fungo hitting, base running, throwing for accuracy, etc., drew a big crowd in spite of threatening weather. The entire receipts were donated to the Army Emergency Relief.

On August 30 Tommy Henrich left the team to enlist in the Coast Guard. The crowd at the Stadium that day—a Sunday—was unaware that he was leaving until he went to bat for the last time. Then, much to his embarrassment, it was announced over the public address system, whereupon the crowd stood up and cheered.

The Yanks bought Roy Cullenbine from Washington to take Henrich's place and brought the veteran Jim Turner up from Newark to help out with the pitching, most of which, as usual, was being done by Ruffing, Bonham, Chandler, Donald, and Murphy. Russo had a lame shoulder and, as the season waned, did very little.

Technically, the pennant was clinched in Cleveland on September 14. There was little comment about it, in New York or elsewhere. Some of the critics did point out that this was by no means a great—or even a typical—Yankee team. However, it admittedly was the best in the league and would wallop the Dodgers again in the World Series—or the Cardinals, should the Cardinals prove to be the better club.

2

The Cardinals had won the pennant in a great stretch run, and the Yankees were on their way to St. Louis to open the World Series.

"Somehow," Bill Dickey said, "I can't seem to get it through my head that we are going out there to play the series. It seems just like any other trip to St. Louis."

"But you really are going to play a World Series, you know," a baseball writer said.

Bill grinned. "Yes," he said. "I know. I see fellows like Grant Rice and some other writers on the train that are with us only during a World Series, so I know something is up."

If there had been no excitement in New York, there was plenty of it in St. Louis. This was the town's first pennant since the Gas House Gang had won in 1934, and Billy Southworth and his crew had captured the public affections, just as the Dean brothers and Pepper Martin had, eight years before. The Yankees were favored, of course. Even in St. Louis, Cardinal fans wanted odds. And yet there was a strong feeling in St. Louis that the Cards would give the Yankees a tussle—that they wouldn't fade and fold, as some of the Yankees' other World Series foes had done.

The first game followed, for seven innings, a familiar pattern. Ruffing, for the Yankees, was pitching hitless ball. Mort Cooper, starting for the Cardinals, was being shelled. And then, suddenly, the Cardinals were storming at the Yankees. Ruffing's hitless string had been broken in the eighth. The ninth was a nightmare for the Yankees as Ruffing was driven to cover and Chandler was rushed in to preserve their crumbling lead. The final score was 7 to 4—but the bases were filled and the last out was made by Stan Musial—who might have hit one into the stands.

No club, winning a game, ever was shaken as the Yankees were shaken by that one. One minute they had been far in front and the Cardinals had looked so bad the crowd was hooting. The next minute black disaster was staring them in the face. In the clubhouse it was some time before they could pull themselves together. First they had to stop thinking how awful it would have been if Musial had hit a home run.

It is doubtful if they ever recovered from that ninth-inning jam. Certainly, they never looked the same again and, as the series wore on, they became angry and jittery and snarled at the umpires and, because their nerves were frayed, made stupid plays.

Had they been on their way to recovery when they moved into the second game, the events of that afternoon probably would have brought about a relapse. Johnny Beazley, a youngster who wasn't supposed to beat them, outpitched Bonham. Whitey Kurowski, a kid third baseman whom the Yankees scarcely knew by sight, made a triple—which the Yankees claimed was foul, by the way—that hurt them badly; and then, when they had come from behind to tie the score at 3-3 in the eighth inning, the Cardinals, instead of being dismayed, simply lashed back at them and won the game in their half of the inning.

An eccentric piece of base running by Cullenbine gave the Yankees the opening through which they scored the tying runs. With the score 3 to 0 and two out, Cullenbine singled and—no one knows why—stole second. DiMaggio followed with a single to center, scoring Cullenbine, and Keller hit a home run over the right-field stand; and there they were, all tied up. Another young pitcher in a spot like that

might have folded. But not Beazley. He fanned Gordon—
who had a wretched series—for the third out. Then, in the
home half, a double by Slaughter, an error by Rizzuto, and
a single by Stan Musial finished the Yankees off—that and
some reckless base running by Tuck Stainback that ruined
whatever chance the Yanks had to win in the ninth.

On the train that carried the teams to New York, Judge
Landis looked up quizzically from his table in a dining car
at a sports writer who stopped to talk to him.

"Am I right in believing that this is the kind of World
Series we used to see?" he asked.

"You are."

"What's the reason for it?"

"The Yankees finally have found a team they can't
frighten half to death just by walking out on the field and
taking a few swings in batting practice."

The Judge smiled.

"What's the matter with these fellows—I mean the Cardinals?" he asked.

"Why," the sports writer said, "they're just a lot of
ignorant country boys, Judge. They haven't been around
and they don't read the papers, so the chances are they don't
even know these are the Yankees they are playing."

For the third game, played at the Stadium, McCarthy
picked Chandler. Southworth countered with the left-
hander, Ernie White. This was the tightest, toughest ball
game of the series, with the Cardinals winning, 2 to 0. Their
outfielders—Slaughter, Terry Moore, and Musial—really won
that one for them. There had been something clownish
about Slaughter and Musial in the opening game in St.
Louis—Moore, of course, always is the artist—and some of
the boys, talking on the train on the way East, were wondering how they would show up in the strange confines of
the Stadium when they looked so bad on their own grounds.

They showed up magnificently. Keller, Gordon, and DiMaggio were the chief sufferers.

The fourth game saw the Yankees at their worst. In this game they were outhit, outfielded, outrun, and outwitted; and they wound up fighting furiously with the umpires as the Cardinals won, 9 to 6. Hank Borowy, who started for the Yanks, was hacked, slashed, and mauled. The Yanks knocked Cooper out again, but it didn't make any difference. The tip-off on this game was that Bill Dickey not only made an unnecessary throw to second base, but threw the ball over Rizzuto's head into center field. Nobody ever had seen anything like that before.

Beazley beat the Yanks again in the fifth and final game, getting the nod over Ruffing, who was tired—but who was the only one McCarthy could call on with any degree of confidence at that stage. The score was 4 to 2, and the Cardinals were the champions of the world. With the final put-out—George Selkirk slapped to Jimmy Brown, who threw to Johnny Hopp at first base—an era ended—the era in which the Yankees were invincible in a World Series. It dated back to 1927.

XXII · Spring, 1943

⊖

T HE PUBLIC REACTION to the outcome of the World Series
was a natural one, but it exasperated McCarthy. He didn't
take it as a compliment that fans should exult over the
triumph of the Cardinals or wag their heads in chagrin over
the toppling of the Yankees.

"What's the matter?" he asked, petulantly. "Have they forgotten that this ball club had won eight World Series in a
row? What do you have to do—win all the time?"

And then, bitterly:

"Well, I got my name in the papers this time, anyway."

His reference was to press-box comment on the tactical
errors he had made.

Yet, when the elation in some quarters and the disappointment in others had worn off, the critics were in general agreement that the Yankees, although they had won the pennant
so easily, were not up to their usual standard. They said—as
someone had said back in 1930—that there were too many
players on the team who were not Yankees. They took it for
granted that Barrow and McCarthy would rebuild for the
1943 campaign.

Articles pointing this out still were being written when
Barrow announced that McCarthy had released the trainer,
Earle Painter, and engaged Eddie Froelich, trainer of the
White Sox, to take his place. It was an ill-timed move on the
part of one who is famous for his timing. Some of the critics

ascribed it to McCarthy's anger at losing the Series and intimated he was venting his spleen on the hapless Painter.
Doc, in New York when the news broke, and taken completely by surprise, rushed to Barrow to ask why he had been
dismissed.

Barrow shrugged.

"I don't know," he said. "You'll have to ask McCarthy."

Painter went at once to McCarthy's home in Buffalo. He
returned with nothing but a promise of a recommendation.

"Joe wouldn't tell me why he had let me go," he said. "I
pressed him for a reason, but he evaded me. All he said was
that if I wanted a job with another ball club he would be
glad to recommend me."

Since McCarthy would not tell anyone else why he had
made the change, it is reasonable to surmise that he simply
had been waiting patiently for an opportunity to obtain an
adequate replacement for a man he never had liked. He had
inherited Painter who, before his arrival in New York, had
made a favorable impression on Ruppert. He didn't want
Painter then nor at any time, refusing to weaken in his attitude no matter how hard the trainer tried to please him.

Meanwhile, he was interested in the development of Froelich, who was the Cubs' bat boy when he was in Chicago
and, having made a study of the care and conditioning of
athletes at his suggestion, had trained the Chicago Black
Hawk hockey team and the Dodgers before going to the
White Sox. McCarthy, steadily observing his progress, undoubtedly concluded last year that he was ready for the job
at the Stadium. The moment he reached that conclusion,
Painter's number was up.

With that off his mind, Joe proceeded to confer with Barrow on player changes. In normal times, few would have been
needed and those few could have been made easily. But, as
the season had waned, Rizzuto and Selkirk had enlisted in

the Navy and they reported shortly after the Series, while Hassett was commissioned in the Navy, and Norman Branch, a young pitcher of promise, was inducted into the Army. The last game of the Series also was Rolf's last with the Yankees, as he had accepted the post as baseball and basketball coach at Yale. Gomez went to work in a defense plant in Massachusetts and Ruffing entered one in California. (Gomez, asked how he liked his new job, said: "It's all very strange. I work eight hours a day—and no Murphy to relieve me.")

A little later, two players who had been called up from the farms were called up by the Army. One was Herbert Karpel, a left-handed pitcher who won eleven games for Kansas City last year while losing only one. The other was Steve Souchock, a first baseman with the Binghamton club and the leading hitter in the Eastern League. Scanning the list of other candidates for berths at the Stadium, Barrow and McCarthy could not be sure who among them, save one, would be available when another spring rolled around.

That one was George Stirnweiss, the only rookie in whom the Army had expressed no interest, at least for the time being. Stirnweiss, whose father was a New York City policeman, learned to play games on the sandlots of the Bronx, attended Fordham Prep and then matriculated at the University of North Carolina, where he distinguished himself as a baseball and football player. Paul Krichell, who had known him as a kid in the Bronx, signed him as an infielder out of Chapel Hill, and he spent a half a year at Norfolk and two years in Newark. In 1942 he hit .270 and led the International League in stolen bases with seventy-three, gathered in eighty-three attempts. He is an old-fashioned, tobacco-chewing, head-first-sliding ball player, rugged in appearance and terrifically fast. But the Army couldn't use him. Because of a condition brought on by stomach ulcers, he must stick to a rigid diet and Army doctors, having examined him carefully over an extended period, were of the opinion that he could not live on Army chow.

A trade then was made with the Cleveland club in which the Yankees gave up Buddy Rosar and Roy Cullenbine and, in return, got Roy Weatherly, outfielder, and Oscar Grimes, infielder. Rosar had been marked for shipment one night in 1942 when, in defiance of McCarthy's orders to remain with the team, he went to his home in Buffalo to take an examination for the Police Department. Dickey had been hurt, Rosar was doing most of the catching and the Yankees needed him badly but he said that, with the future of baseball doubtful because of the war, he wasn't going to pass up a chance to obtain steady employment with a pension at the end of it. When he left, McCarthy summoned the veteran Rollie Hemsley, a free agent at the time, and pressed him into service—the day Rollie arrived he caught a double header in sweltering heat and was in a state of near collapse when the second game was over. Rosar returned a day or two later but he must have known, as everyone else did, that his stay with the Yankees would end with the season.

So he was through and Cullenbine, in his short shift with the Yankees, had failed to impress McCarthy, who needed help in the outfield with Henrich gone and DiMaggio on his way. Weatherly, a product of the Cleveland farm system —out of Opelousas in the Evangeline League via New Orleans—was a good ball player with the Indians. Grimes, a son of Roy Grimes, first baseman with the Cubs and the Phillies twenty years ago, had played all over the Cleveland infield. McCarthy wanted him for protection.

In late December, Joseph B. Eastman, head of the Office of Defense Transportation, asked the major leagues what they proposed to do about shaping their plans to the end that man-miles would be saved for the duration. He gave no orders and hinted at none, saying that he knew nothing of the baseball business and simply was curious as to what they had in mind.

The clubs already had arranged to train in the South as usual and to play exhibition games on the way back. Some of the owners, rattled by the gently phrased request from Washington, promptly offered to train nearer home—in Virginia or the Carolinas, for instance. There was a lot of talk, some of it senseless. Barrow cut sharply into the rapidly growing confusion.

"I don't know what the Government wants," he said, "but, whatever it is, I am for it. I don't think we can solve anything by going halfway into the South. If it will help, we will train in the Stadium."

It is unlikely that he had any intention of doing anything of the sort, unless that was precisely what Eastman wanted. But he sought to get the minds of his colleagues working on an orderly and practical plan and in that he succeeded. Commissioner Landis went to Washington to see Eastman, then returned, close-mouthed, to Chicago and called a meeting of both leagues. At that meeting, the club owners voted to train at home or close to it, to shorten the training season, to start the regular season a week late and to continue it a week beyond the original closing date, thereby getting in a 154-game schedule. Some of them, Barrow included, wanted to cut the season to 140 games but were overruled. Apprised of their plans, Eastman expressed his approval.

In January there was another flurry when Paul V. McNutt, co-ordinator of man power, was nudged by a reporter into saying that he did not regard baseball as being essential to the war effort. There were scare heads in some of the newspapers and apprehension in some of the club offices, where the owners fidgeted, visions of a repetition of 1918's "Work or Fight" order dancing in their heads.

"Did you hear," an excited reporter asked Barrow, "that McNutt says baseball isn't essential?"

Barrow grunted.

"Who ever said it was?" he demanded.

The flurry subsided. McNutt merely had said what everyone else had been thinking.

The quest for a training site was conducted by McCarthy and Krichell. They rejected, unseen, many of the spots offered to them, looked over some others, and finally selected Asbury Park, New Jersey. This drew a satisfied nod from Barrow. In the old days he had trained the Toronto club on the Jersey coast with excellent results. He said he could see no reason why the Yankees couldn't get in shape there, too. And yet, for most of the Yankees, the abandonment of St. Petersburg was not accomplished without a wrench. To some of them it had become a winter home, where they played golf at the Jungle Club or fished in the waters of the Gulf. There had been laughs there . . . and heartaches . . . and pennant drives had been launched from the soil of Huggins Field.

There had been speculation as to whether Ruffing and Gomez would remain in their jobs as defense workers. The Army furnished the answer in Ruffing's case by inducting him. Rising thirty-eight and minus four toes that he lost in a coal mine blast when he was sixteen, he was accepted for noncombat duty. In the case of Gomez, the answer, so far as the Yankees were concerned, was given by McCarthy who sold him to the Braves. A day or so before the Yankees had bought Nick Etten, first baseman, from the Phillies.

This was followed by another deal, in which Gerald Priddy and Milo Candini, a young pitcher with Newark last year, were sent to Washington for Bill Zuber, a pitcher, who, having bounced up and down in the Cleveland farm system for a few years, and was purchased by the Senators in 1941. Thus the second base combination of Priddy and Rizzuto, which was a wow in Kansas City but a flop in the Stadium, was broken up.

There had been, too, the expected announcement from DiMaggio that he had enlisted. They asked Barrow what he thought about that and he said:

"I am glad to hear it. It is my belief that every ball player who is in a position to do so should enter the armed forces with as little delay as possible."

XXIII · Heights Recaptured and Lost Again

⊜

I T WAS A drab and uncomfortable spring training season the Yankees spent at Asbury Park in 1943. The weather was disagreeable, even for March, all over the East that spring but—or maybe it only seemed that way to McCarthy and his ball players and the newspapermen who huddled in the stands of a high-school field to watch them work—it was most disagreeable at Asbury Park. The wind howled off the ocean much of the time and the skies were gray. There were many days on which playing ball was a hardship, few on which it was a pleasure.

There were many things on McCarthy's mind besides the weather. One was his infield. Joe Gordon was late in signing and even later in reporting. Crosetti, having been suspended by Judge Landis for the first thirty days of the 1943 season as a penalty for a flare-up against umpire Bill Summers in the 1942 World Series, was working in a war plant in California and wasn't sure whether he would return to baseball. With those two absent temporarily and Hassett gone for the duration and Rolfe for good, McCarthy labored with four new infielders through most of the stay at the camp: Etten at first base, Grimes at second, Stirnweiss at shortstop and Bill Johnson, a kid up from Newark, at third. To add to Joe's uncertainties, William Cox, who had bought the Phillies after the Etten deal had been made, tried to have the deal called off and went all the way up to Judge Landis to get the first baseman back. Landis refused to entertain his complaint, so Etten was safe with the Yanks and then Gordon showed up and McCarthy began to feel better.

Only Keller had survived among the regular outfielders who had started the 1942 season. The others at Asbury Park were Weatherly, Stainback, Bud Metheny, called up from Newark, and Lindell, who, because of his hitting, had been converted from a pitcher into a fifth outfielder and an understudy for Etten at first base. Bill Dickey, who had looked bad in the World Series the fall before, looked no better in the spring. To help him bear the catching burden were Hemsley, Ken Sears, up from Kansas City, and Aaron Robinson, up from Newark. The pitchers on hand were Chandler, Borowy, Breuer, Donald, Bonham, Murphy, Russo, Zuber, Turner, and a couple of youngsters, Charley Wensloff and Tommy Byrne.

These, the baseball writers agreed, not only were not the Yankees but were much less like the Yankees than even the 1942 team. They scoffed, privately and openly, at the young men and in time this got on McCarthy's nerves and relations between him and the writers were not as pleasant as they had been, and when they met for the daily interviews there frequently was churliness on both sides. McCarthy, cautious in his comments when he had great teams, was, curiously enough, suddenly optimistic in his discussions of this one, although his manner during the interviews, on the field, or when he was sitting alone in a corner of the Hotel Albion lobby, smoking a cigar and mulling over his problems, was such as to seem to belie his words. When the Yanks couldn't beat the Giants, the Braves, or the Dodgers in exhibition games, the writers shrugged.

"Well," they said, "we expected it."

But McCarthy continued to be silently scornful of their opinion or to challenge it, once in a while, with sharp replies to their questions. The day the season opened, Joe had got over his uneasiness and dismissed most of his worries.

"Like all the other clubs in our league," he said, "we'll have to play ourselves into shape. But right now we're as ready as anybody else and we have as good a chance as anybody to win the pennant."

"How do you rate the other clubs?" they asked him. "How about the Red Sox? The Indians?"

He shook his head.

"The Senators are the ones we have to beat," he said.

The Senators had finished seventh in 1942, somebody said.

"Yes," Joe said, "but this time they have Ossie Bluege to manage them. I say that's the club we have to beat."

The Yanks beat the Senators in the opening game and, having leaped to the front, stayed there. Stirnweiss faltered at shortstop and, Crosetti having rejoined the team, George was benched and Frank took over. Johnson proved to be the rookie of the year. Gordon, coming out of an early season slump, was himself once more. Etten finished second to Rudy York in runs batted in and Keller battled York right down to the wire for the home-run-hitting championship, finishing with 31 to Rudy's 34. Lindell developed into a better than fair outfielder. Chandler was the league's leading pitcher— and was voted its most valuable player—winning 20 games and losing only 4. Bonham won 15 games, Borowy 14, Wensloff 13, and Murphy 12. The Yanks won the pennant by eleven games. Washington was second.

The Cardinals won again in the National League and now the teams were squaring off for another meeting in the World Series.

"I'll take the Yanks," a baseball writer said. "McCarthy is laying for Southworth and any time he is laying for anybody I will take a ticket on him."

The series opened in New York and the Yankees won,

4 to 2, with Chandler pitching against Max Lanier. Or perhaps it should be said that the game practically was handed to the Yanks by Lanier, for it was an error by the Cardinal pitcher that gave them their first scoring opportunity and his wild pitch in the sixth inning that sent Crosetti scampering across the plate with the decisive run.

The count was evened in the second game, when Mort Cooper outpitched Bonham, winning 4 to 3, on home runs by Martin Marion and Ray Sanders, but in the third game the Yanks went to the front once more, winning 6 to 2. It was on this game that the series turned and whether or not the Yanks would have won it anyway, it is indisputable that a crash at third base in the eighth inning precipitated the fall of the Cardinals.

Alpha Brazle, pitching for the Cardinals, had an edge on Borowy and was leading, 2 to 1, when the teams reached the eighth. Then Lindell, leading off, singled to center and raced to third when Harry Walker fumbled the ball. Stirnweiss, batting for Borowy, bunted to Sanders and Ray threw to Kurowski to head Lindell off at third. The ball had Lindell beaten but big John hurled himself at the bag, smashing into Kurowski and knocking the ball out of his hands. That was the break, for instead of having one out and a man on first base, the Yanks had none out and men on first and third. Stainback flied out but Stirnweiss hustled to second after the catch. Crosetti was intentionally passed to set the stage for a possible double play but Johnson cleared the bases with a triple. The jig was up now and the Yanks got two more runs before the inning ended, clinching their victory at 6 to 2.

The teams moved to St. Louis and the Yanks, rolling now, closed out the series by winning the next two games. Russo was almost the whole show in the fourth game, holding the Cards to seven scattered hits, earning a shutout that he missed only because of errors by Crosetti and Johnson in the seventh inning, making two doubles, scoring one run, and winning 2 to 1. Lanier started this game for the Cards and Brecheen finished it.

In the final game Cooper tried to beat the Yanks again but failed, a single by Keller and a home run by Dickey in the sixth inning deciding a fine pitching tussle between Cooper and Chandler, 2 to 0.

McCarthy was content once more. He had won his eighth pennant for the Yankees and his seventh World Series. He had evened his score with Southworth and the Yanks were supreme again.

Shortly after the World Series, Ed Barrow became ill and was taken to the New Rochelle Hospital. Bulletins on his illness were tempered so that few knew how grave his condition was. Actually, there was a period during which he was not expected to live and even when he had passed the crisis it was clear that his recovery would be slow. It was not until the spring of 1944 that he was able to return to his desk.

Meanwhile, the team was disintegrating under pressure of the war. The only player to depart in 1943 was Robinson, who joined the Navy early in the season, but now they were going fast. Russo went to the Army and Dickey, Sears, and Byrne to the Navy. Gordon joined the Army Air Corps and Keller and Johnson the Maritime Service. Murphy, Breuer, and Wensloff remained in war plant jobs.

The training camp site was switched from Asbury Park to Atlantic City and McCarthy started, all over again, to put a team together. Crosetti having decided to remain in his war job at Stockton, California, Etten was the only one left of the infield that had finished the 1943 season. McCarthy posted Stirnweiss at second, a youngster named Mike Milosivich at short, and alternated Grimes and Don Savage at third. He picked up Herschel Martin as a replacement for Weatherly in the outfield and divided the catching between Hemsley and Mike Garback, a youngster up from Newark. Chandler, whose induction into the Army had been deferred, headed the pitching staff.

As the team broke camp and moved up to New York, McCarthy became ill and for the next month Arthur Fletcher was acting in charge. Chandler pitched one game and was ordered to report to the Army. The team struggled on its way, spurting, reeling, spurting again. Stirnweiss soon proved that he had become a major league ball player and his second base play, his timely hitting, and sensational base running made him a hero at the Stadium. In July Crosetti changed his mind and joined the team in St. Louis, although it was not until Aug. 4 that he started his first game. In August, too, Al Lyons, young relief pitcher, and Hemsley were inducted into the Navy.

The Yanks smashed on, joining the Tigers in pursuit of the league-leading Browns and, as the season neared its end, appeared likely to win the pennant. That, however, was too much to expect and the illusion passed. They finished third as, on the final day of the season, the Browns beat them in St. Louis to nose out the Tigers for the title. In New York, Barrow issued a statement praising McCarthy and the players and adding that, in his opinion, this was the best job McCarthy had done in his fourteen seasons in New York. Joe had refuted Jimmy Dykes's crack, made just before the season opened, that he was a "push-button" manager who, always having had the best players at his disposal, had only to push a button now and then to get results, and would be lost now that he had to struggle with second raters.

Well, there they are, these Yankees. They have come a long way from the days of Farrell and Devery and Griffith, of Chesbro and Keeler and Chase and a wooden bandbox of a ball park on the hilltop. They have survived bumps, bruises, and brawls and though at times the road they have followed has had its detours, they have reached a higher peak than any other ball club ever has known.

Great players have worn their uniform and great managers have led them. In the last twenty-three years they have won fourteen pennants and ten World Series and left behind them a trail of shattered records. The Stadium, considerably enlarged and improved in recent years, has been the goal of ambitious kids all over this broad country. For there Huggins crouched on the dugout steps, Ruth and Gehrig and Dickey and DiMaggio have smashed enemy pitchers, Pennock and Hoyt and Ruffing and Gomez have made the crowds roar with their pitching artistry. There heroes have risen and performed their astonishing feats . . . and have passed on . . . and other heroes have moved up to take their places.

The time of the Yankees' greatness dates from that day on which Barrow first walked into Ruppert's office and agreed to become the general manager of the club. Barrow has made mistakes, of course. But in the main his decisions not only have been sound but have guided the officials of other clubs on their way. There is no touch of magic in his formula. It simply is based on long years of experience that have endowed him with keen discernment of what the customers want. There was, for instance, night baseball. It was his judgment that, while it was popular in Brooklyn and elsewhere on both major league circuits, it would not be popular in New York—Brooklyn and New York being separate and apart, so far as baseball is concerned—wherefore he declined to adopt it. For this he was howled at as a reactionary by the proponents of baseball after dark, yet there is no reason to believe, in view of the Giants' experience under the lights, that he was wrong.

Sure of himself, indifferent to adverse criticism as he is to applause, he has moved steadily on his way in his twenty-four years in New York. Sometimes he has moved ponderously, sometimes arrogantly. But he always has known in which direction he was headed and so, under his guidance, have the Yankees.

These are troubled times and baseball will have to wait until they are over to recapture the importance it once knew in our national life. When that time comes the Yankees will be ready for it. They have wrought, in their own time, a tradition founded on alertness and progress that will be perpetuated when the skies are clear again.

Index

Robert McConnell of the Society for American Baseball Research prepared this index. Corrections of spelling errors in the original text are from John Thorn and Pete Palmer, eds., *Total Baseball: The Ultimate Encyclopedia of Baseball*, 3rd ed. (n.p.: Harper Perennial, 1993).